No Small Lives

Handbook of North American Early Women Adult Educators, 1925–1950

No Small Lives

Handbook of North American Early Women Adult Educators, 1925–1950

Edited by

Susan Imel
The Ohio State University

and

Gretchen T. Bersch
University of Alaska Anchorage

Information Age Publishing, Inc.
Charlotte, North Carolina • www.infoagepub.com

Library of Congress Cataloging-in-Publication Data

CIP data for this book can be found on the Library of Congress website:
http://www.loc.gov/index.html

Paperback: 978-1-62396-883-0
Hardcover: 978-1-62396-884-7
E-Book: 978-1-62396-885-4

Printed in the United States of America

CONTENTS

PART III: CONCLUSION

FOREWORD

M. Carolyn Clark
Texas A&M University

I was somewhere in my late 20s, I think, when I first heard of the Chinese proverb, "Women hold up half the sky," and it captured my imagination. I was drawn to the affirmation of the importance of women's lives and women's work, and it inspired me to create a silkscreened print. It's a simple image: a swatch of blue across the top and a cluster of sapling-like shapes on the right half of the print with limbs spread wide at the top as if supporting that blue sky. The words of the proverb are written down the length of the furthest sapling, suggesting that those figures represent women. Well, that was my initial interpretation. As my identity as a feminist deepened over time, a function of more life experience as well as exposure to the rich work in feminist theory, I began to see the print differently. My focus shifted to the other half of the sky, very much in place, although apparently unsupported. It became a kind of figure-to-ground shift in perspective for me, where the empty space came forward and the rest became background. *That's* where the women are—it's the empty space that they inhabit and within which they leave their imprint on the world. The sapling-like figures—the men—draw our attention away and suggest that through some masterful leverage they support the whole sky. The central message of the image becomes the invisibility of women and the taken-for-grantedness of their work.

I hadn't thought about this old print for years, but as I read chapter after chapter of this book, that image came to mind again, and I couldn't erase it. It is hardly a surprise that we know very little about the women

No Small Lives: Handbook of North American Early Women Adult Educators, 1925-1950,
pp. ix–xi

who helped shape the field of adult education in its early days, and even less about the work they did. Patriarchy is a powerful force, as we know too well. This book pushes back, making a significant contribution to the important task of making these women visible once again. It is a labor of love—on the part of the editors, to be sure, who for years have worked steadily and even relentlessly to identify and learn about the women who were the early adult educators—and also by the chapter authors, who carefully pieced together the stories of the lives and the work of these women. That was no easy task. These women don't appear in the histories of the field; they are not only outside the canon, they exist in some kind of netherworld, where there are few traces of their lives or of their life works. Their colorful portraits in this book are the result of diligent scholarly research, bordering on detective work, by all the chapter authors, and we are in their debt. What you have in your hands is history reclaimed and absence made present. No small gift.

What to say about these early women adult educators? I think the first thing that struck me was their diversity. The broad outlines reflect the intentions of the editors; included are a mix of nationalities (Canadian and American) and ethnicities (Native Peoples, Hispanic American, Anglo American). But when you examine their lives, there is more richness of difference. They come from different classes, have different levels of education, and make different contributions to the field. Some wrote extensively, others were in administration at the state/provincial and national levels, and a few worked internationally. Some were in leadership roles in adult education organizations or university programs, many were designing and implementing various adult education programs, while a few had only an implicit connection to the field. Some were social activists. The work of many was addressed to the development of an enlightened citizenry; others focused on the domestic sphere. They were, quite literally, all over the place.

But there are also some striking commonalities among these women. An early impression they made on me was their high energy level—each one of them was a Force! The major obstacles they faced were matched by even greater persistence, resilience, and resourcefulness. Furthermore, most had more than one area in which they made significant contributions. And they were a Force with staying power: of the 26 women, 19 lived into their 70s and beyond, with the largest group living well into their 90s (four of the nine in that group lived to 95 or older, with one, Dorothy Rowden, living to 99). Those statistics look like they belong in our own era, and not from an historical period with a less advanced medical system than we have now.

The second thing about these women that struck me is that they didn't follow established paths. Certainly they were not limited by the gender expectations of their times, which is no small achievement, but I see even more at work here. Established paths didn't exist for them. They had to carve out new paths in order to achieve their goals, and that required a remarkable combination of creativity and resolve. Their ability to create those new paths is itself an accomplishment that stands alongside their specific contributions to the field of adult education. The women who followed them have learned to be equally innovative and resourceful.

And speaking of innovative and resourceful women, we have the editors and the chapter writers of this book to thank for this wonderful contribution to the field we all love. But the editors especially: Susan Imel and Gretchen Bersch, mirror the women whom they make visible—in their gentle way they too are a Force! This book would never have come to life without their constancy of vision, their relentless commitment to purpose, and their pure-hearted determination to make the lives of these early women adult educators available to us. Gretchen and Susan, we are in your debt! And a final word, this one to readers holding the book in your hands for the first time: what you hold is no small gift of no small lives. Receive it with joy!

PREFACE

Susan Imel and Gretchen Bersch

No Small Lives contains the stories of 26 North American women who were active in the field of adult education sometime between the years of 1925 and 1950. According to Hilton (1982), in the 1930s, "Women were an integral part of the adult education fabric: as planners and innovators, as thinkers, and especially as writers and editors of the scores of articles, books, and handbooks that characterized the period" (p. 12). Although the names of several of these women are known in the field, details about their lives have remained largely hidden, and they have been left out of the field's histories. No extended analysis of the early women, their contributions, and any of their writing has been conducted. Furthermore, the women whose names are usually associated with the field's early development are white, so a need exists to learn about women from other racial or ethnic groups who were active in the field during its early years.

Welton (2010) sums up the situation regarding the status of women in the field when he succinctly states, "Adult education history in Canada and the U.S. has been (and still is) White, male, and middle class in sensibility" (p. 85). Women's contributions need to be acknowledged and included in the field's histories. But these efforts should do more than just restore women to their rightful place; they should include a critical examination of previous assumptions based on gender (Hugo, 1990) as well as begin to celebrate more than so-called scholarly writing. The book is designed to address this gap and restore women to their rightful place in the history of adult education in North America.

No Small Lives: Handbook of North American Early Women Adult Educators, 1925-1950,
pp. xiii–xv
Copyright © 2015 by Information Age Publishing

The book is divided into three sections. The first section, "Historical Background," contains two foundational chapters that set the stage for the context for the period covered by the book. The first of these, by Amy Rose, provides a historical overview and describes generally the roles women played in the founding of the American Association for Adult Education and in its publication program. The second chapter by Jane Hugo discusses how histories of adult education have dealt with women's roles and participation in adult education, how perspectives about gender have shaped women's roles in adult education, and proposes ways of reframing how history could be rewritten to be more inclusive.

Section two presents the stories of 26 women active in some capacity in adult education—broadly defined—in the years between 1925 and 1950. The women selected for inclusion achieved a range of accomplishments. Some were primarily editors and writers, while others were practitioners who founded organizations, worked for justice and peace, and/or served in government agencies or professional associations. All contributed to the field's growth and development, although—in many cases—those contributions have never been fully acknowledged.

A variety of methods was involved in identifying and selecting the women who are profiled. The research that led to the book started with a descriptive analysis of the American Association for Adult Education's *Journal of Adult Education* to identify those women who contributed articles. Research conference presentations profiling some of these women generated interest from Canadian colleagues who were also working to uncover the contributions of women in their country. Because the women identified through these methods were white, an effort was made to find nonwhite women to include.

Section three, "Conclusion," includes two chapters. The first, by Juanita Johnson-Bailey and Elizabeth (Libby) Tisdell, examines the question "Have things changed?" and looks at the current context for women in the field. The second chapter, written by the editors, draws together some common themes across the women's stories. An appendix of short biographies of women who were active during the period but were not included in the book follows the last chapter.

The primary audience for this book is adult education professors and their graduate students. This book can be used in a number of courses, including history and sociology of adult education, the adult learner, courses specific to exploring women's contributions and activities. With this addition of the women who played key roles and the social milieu at the time, the book corrects the field's history to more accurately portray adult education in the early to mid-1900s. It can be a useful source for faculty and graduate student research that focuses on historical roles and involvement of women as the field of adult education was established and began to flourish; it would broaden the available source material for those examining social movements and early adult education movements such as forums and democratic movements in the United States and Canada.

The secondary audience is the broader fields of women's studies, feminist history, sociology, and psychology or those fields that include an examination of women in the early 20th century. It would also be useful to those focusing on more specific topics such as gender and race studies, prejudice, marginalization, power, how women were sometimes portrayed as invisible or as central figures, and women in leadership and policymaking.

REFERENCES

Hilton, R. J. (1982). *Humanizing adult education research: Five stories from the 1930s.* Syracuse, NY: Syracuse University Publications in Continuing Education.

Hugo, J. M. (1990). Adult education history and the issue of gender: Toward a different history of adult education in America. *Adult Education Quarterly, 1,* 1–16.

Welton, M. R. (2010). Histories of adult education: Constructing the past. In C. E. Kasworm, A. D. Rose, & J. M. Ross-Gordon (Eds.), *Handbook of adult and continuing education* (pp. 83–92). Thousand Oaks, CA: Sage.

PART I

HISTORICAL BACKGROUND

CHAPTER 1

SEARCHING FOR THE WOMEN IN A DEFEMINIZED PAST

American Adult Education Between the Wars

Amy D. Rose

The history of adult education is an understudied area, and the role of women within this history is also understudied. This is not to say that it has been ignored. There have been interesting studies of women's importance in labor education (e.g., Heller [1986] on the women workers summer school and Kornbluh [1988] on the "she-she" camps) and of course in community work (e.g., Jane Addams and others involved in the settlement house movement). There have been interesting studies of specific women such as Dorothy Canfield Fisher (Sexton, 1993) and Septima Clark (Easter, 1996) among others. However, so far there has been little effort made to understand the totality of women's contributions to the history of professional adult education. While Hugo (1990) highlights the ways that women had been left out, the real question is what were their contributions? In a way, this very question is somewhat gendered. We can either pick out prominent women who may or may not have been overlooked or we can try to recast the entire history in a

No Small Lives: Handbook of North American Early Women Adult Educators, 1925-1950,
pp. 3–16
Copyright © 2015 by Information Age Publishing
3

different way, with different questions. In this chapter, I think I am trying to do a little of both.

So for example, the few early histories that we have dealt with were
perceived to be the pivotal figures within adult education. Adams (1944)
traced the history of adult education, looking at it as a source of democracy. Grattan (1955) followed suit. Knowles (1977) and Stubblefield and
Keane (1994) both attempted to trace the profession of adult education
within an historical context. Kett (1994) attempted to place adult education history within a broader context. In all of these, women have been
virtually ignored and their roles bypassed entirely. Even Stubblefield
(1988) who provides an overview of the Carnegie Corporation activities
does not even mention women.

The point here is not that women played a role, but that they were integral to the development of adult education in the 20th century. However,
part of the problem is that it is hard to distinguish the parameters of adult
education and so the history itself is unclear. Is the history of adult education that of all educative efforts for adults or is it the history of a profession? This chapter takes a middle ground. It will examine the founding of
the profession in the 1920s, discussing the role of key women, but also
truthfully indicating their limited role. This is not a story that has been
overlooked, it is the story of a group that was substantially sidelined. This
in itself is of interest. It is simplistic to think that women were there as the
heads of organizations and they have not been recognized. This is tempting, but not true. They were the workhorses. They did the grunt work.
Were they the conceptualizers? It is hard to say. The rest of this chapter
will examine this issue.

In particular, this chapter will explore the early days of professional
adult education. One way into this examination is through the lens of the
founding and early years of the American Association for Adult Education
(AAAE or A^{3}E). The A^{3}E was founded through a convergence of interests.
In the 1920s, there was a renewed interest in the education of adults at all
levels. Hence, the National Education Association (NEA) founded a
Department of Immigrant Education in 1921, which became the Department of Adult Education in 1924. Interestingly, this department's precursor was the Department of the Wider Use of School Houses founded in
1915 (Stubblefield & Keane, 1994). Additionally, the National University
Extension was founded in 1915 (Knowles, 1977; Stubblefield & Keane,
1994). The A^{3}E has been seen as the precursor of modern adult education. I am not sure that this is a correct picture, but for the moment we
will accept this at face value. This chapter will look at the founding of
A^{3}E, the connection between the Association and the Carnegie Corporation, and the role of women in this endeavor.

BEGINNINGS

The A^{3}E was founded in 1926. The primary impetus behind this founding was the Carnegie Corporation of New York. This foundation decided in the early 1920s that adult education was an appropriate area of endeavor. Primarily through the sponsorship of the foundation's president, Frederick P. Keppel, the Association explored several avenues for funding before deciding that an association, modeled on the American Library Association, would be an appropriate conduit for Carnegie Corporation grants.

Lagemann (1989) indicates that Keppel was looking for a way to make his mark on the Corporation. He was interested in a recent book, *The Way Out* (Stanley, 1923), put together by the British Workers' Education Association. This book intrigued Keppel because it saw adult education as a source of social stability (p. 105). Keppel called together a group of men to discuss the issues. These men were Carl Milam of the American Library Association, John Cotton Dana of the Newark Library, Eduard C. Lindeman of the American Country Life Association, Everett Dean Martin of the People's Institute, Spencer Miller Jr. of the Workers' Education Bureau, C. R. Dooley from Standard Oil of New Jersey, Charles Beard who had help found the new School for Social Research, Alfred E. Cohn of the Rockefeller Institute, and James Earl Russell of Teachers College, Columbia University (Lagemann, 1989; Rose, 1979, 1989). A small subgroup of these men also became the planning group. The A^{3}E differed from the NEA's Department of Adult Education in two ways. In the first place, the A^{3}E eschewed the NEA's focus that was on public school adult education, primarily immigrant education and literacy education. The second distinction between the Department of Adult Education and A^{3}E was in fact gendered (Lagemann, 1989). The Department of Adult Education was concerned with instructional issues and was overwhelmingly female. The A^{3}E, at least in the planning stages, had no interest in public education and had virtually no women leaders involved. Keppel had a vision of what adult education could be and he was trying to evangelize. He was not seeking to help those who were already educators. While Keppel preferred not to work with the NEA, he worked closely with the American Library Association (ALA) and envisioned a close relationship between the two associations. Unlike the NEA, the ALA was administered by a group of men, although the state and local library associations were represented by women. Lagemann (1989) states that, "Keppel's preference for alliances with groups dominated and controlled by men was evidence of this transition. Men were more likely to hold professional status than women" (p. 108).

Not only did the A^3E ignore literacy education, the Carnegie Corporation was also not interested in any kind of education connected with what was called "vocationalism" (Kett, 1994, p. 336). Keppel was not averse to extension or vocational programs, but he was searching for a unique area for the new organization, one that would organize all of those activities which did not already fall under the purview of another type of association or entity.

Kett (1994) maintains that while the early years of the A^3E were focused on elevation, the 1930s focus was on what he calls "mediocrity" (p. 371). He quotes Lyman Bryson, an early adult educator, as stating his view of the purpose or direction of adult education.

> Having begun in America with the frankly remedial effort to give the immigrant a few words of English and a muddled but highly emotionalized "Americanism," and leaping thence to the opposite pole and trying to dissolve the mental stasis of the privileged, we are now coming to realize that the greater problem lies in between. (p. 371)

Kett goes on to discuss what he calls "the discovery of mediocrity" (p. 371). Because the association had deliberately stayed away from vocationalism, literacy, and immigrants, the search for a center was fraught with difficulty. While the early A^3E focused on organizations for diffusion, it soon became clear that this was not sufficient. For starters, new reading research was clarifying that individuals who could read often did not make sense of what they were reading. Hence, there was a new interest in looking at what adults read and how they interpreted it. This also related to the earlier interest in understanding and interpreting modern life. Kett adds that although by the 1940s, adult education as a field had been completely marginalized, it had a long lasting impact, particularly in terms of its emphasis on community education (p. 402).

Thus, while Lagemann (1989) portrays the Carnegie interest as one of cultural interest, Kett (1994) goes beyond Carnegie to the writers in the field and sees something at once broader and narrower. While the initial impetus for the A^3E was in Lagemann's view "cultural leadership" or stewardship, Kett sees the later period as one of discovering "mediocrity." In summary, we can see these early years as an attempt to organize culture that ended instead in mediocrity or what Rubin (1992) calls "middle-brow culture."

So how did an association, explicitly founded to work against a more female-oriented association, function? And more importantly, did this association gain primacy because of this original function? Early grants focused on arts-related projects. Some, in fact, were quite innovative. This notion of cultural leadership was expanded through Carnegie Corporation funding of the ALA and of specific museums. The main thrust was on liberal education, an education for all but a particular form of education which emphasized the "Great Books" and democratic principles. Yet, despite this bleak assessment, it is also clear that while women never attained leadership within the inner core of the association, several were active.

As indicated earlier, Lagemann (1989) indicates that the Carnegie Corporation particularly sought to change public opinion through the courting of influential men. They particularly wanted to stay away from the female-centered NEA and the twin considerations of vocationalism and immigrant education. However, if we adopt Kett's interest in "mediocrity" or what Rubin (1992) calls "middle-brow culture," we introduce some interesting theoretical issues. This notion of culture was complex. Ever sensitive to the charge of elitism, Morse Cartwright, the Executive Director of the A³E, tried to lay out his vision as he responded to a critique by Robert Staughton Lynd. Yet, to the modern reader, Cartwright still appears condescending as he discusses his view that the aim of adult education is not elitist but rather to lift the level of discourse:

> Naturally enough Dean [James Earl] Russell, Martin and the rest of the members of our Board as well as myself have been keenly sensitive to the charge of running a high-hat association. There is some basis for the charge, in that we are aiming more directly at the constantly growing minority who appreciate the best or cultural values in adult education, and less directly (perhaps it would be better to say it affirmatively, "aiming directly") at the tabloid-readers—movie fans.... If we should propagandize and over-popularize we'd lose immediately the support of the kind of people who make up our governing board and the Council. On the other hand, if we don't keep in touch with the people, we shan't make a dent in our problem. (Cartwright, 1927b)

Part of the problem was the confusion about the source of Carnegie (and A³E) support. So for example, while a focus was the development of community, the role of the university was seen as pivotal. Cartwright rejected outright calls to diversify the Board and shift emphasis. Rejecting John Cotton Dana's call for greater diversity and less reliance on university extension, he offers the same casual dismissal that he accuses Dana of:

> He dismisses the universities from this field with a wave of the hand; I am convinced that they must lead in this work, just as Oxford University and Cambridge have in England. Evidently Mr. Dana has not read the Hall-Quest book and is judging university from the activities of Columbia and from other viewpoints which I think are largely misconceptions. (Cartwright, 1927a)

ORGANIZATIONAL ISSUES

Within the time period under discussion, roughly the 1920s and the 1930s, the aim of the A^3E was to encourage an awareness of culture and the arts, to think about different issues related to the dissemination of these, and to encourage the skills necessary to do this dissemination. In addition, the Association, and by extension the Carnegie Corporation, was very concerned with stabilizing communities. Internally, the decisions about the Association were all clearly linked to the Carnegie Corporation. Keppel kept close watch on the direction of the Association, all of the main characters of which were men. As stated earlier, Dean James Earl Russell from Teachers College played a key leadership role in the early years and certainly in consulting with Keppel. However, E. L. Thorndike, who wrote one of the key early studies on adult learning, had concerns about Russell's interest. He suggested to Keppel, "It might be worth while for us to interest some of the TC Trustees." He went on to specifically name some of the Trustees, including Mrs. Swan and Mrs. Fosdick (Keppel, 1927).

From the time of the first exploratory conferences, women were included in the list of participants and even among the organizers. Early women members of the Adult Education Group included Mrs. John C. Campbell (Secretary of the Conference of Southern Mountain Workers); Linda A. Eastman (Librarian, Cleveland Public Library); and Mrs. V. C. Simkhovitch (Director, Greenwich House in NYC) (Carnegie Corporation, 1925). After the first national conference in October 1925, a series of regional conferences were held around the country. Local committees had the task of organizing these. Women were to be found on these, although their presence was not overwhelming and there is no way to really know their input[1] (Carnegie Corporation, 1926). From the beginning, women served on the Board and even the Executive Board of the Association. So for example, the minutes of the first meeting of the Executive Board on March 27, 1926, indicate that four women were on the Executive Board: Olive Campbell, Linda Eastman, Agnes Nestor, and Margaret Burton, who also served as secretary (Executive Board, 1926). In 1929, the Association's delegates to the World Conference on Adult Education included Linda Eastman, who was the President of the American Library Association at the time; Mary Ely, the editor of the *Journal of Adult Education;* and Hilda Smith of the Bryn Mawr Summer School for Women Workers in Industry (Cartwright, 1929). By 1941, several women had made their way onto the Executive Board of the A^3E. These were Beulah Amidon, Jennie M. Flexner (the Association Secretary), Caroline A. Whipple, Edith J. R. Isaacs, Agnes Seasongood, and Hilda W. Smith (American Association for Adult Education, 1941). However, during this time, when decisions about the future of the Association were being made, the key decision makers met in executive and special committee sessions where no women were present (e.g., Carnegie Corporation, 1941).

While women were not part of the inner circle, they were becoming recognized as experts. So for example, in contemplating several representatives to the meeting of the Council of the World Association for Adult Education in 1928, Cartwright considered inviting Linda A. Eastman, a librarian from Cleveland, along with other academic luminaries such as John Dewey (or Kilpatrick or Morrison or Meiklejohn, E. L. Thorndike, James A. Russell, Spencer Miller and Leon J. Richardson) (Cartwright, 1928).

However, by September of 1930, there was concern about the ways that decisions were being made and who was being consulted. Dean Russell of Teachers College, voiced his concern about "whether AE is really getting just a little routine and whether we shouldn't have a meeting of a new crowd to see what, with the present economic conditions, should be done" (Keppel, 1930). But this is a reference to the issues related to ever-increasing depression and not to an expansion of the base of decision making.

By 1930, there was some concern about the paucity of women involved with the A^{3}E. Cartwright first approached Dorothy Canfield Fisher with an offer of the presidency. She turned him down (Fisher, 1931). He then tried to think of other women who could be approached. In early 1931 he wrote,

> I have been trying to think of some woman who might be groomed for the Presidency of A^{3}E. How about old Jane Addams? It would please her tremendously and please the library group among our constituency. I think the super-patriots have forgotten how much they hated her 13 years ago. If she's in form next year, she'd make a good address (Keppel, 1931).

However, Canfield Fisher must have acquiesced because she was indeed the fourth president of the Association, serving from 1932 until 1934 (Cartwright, 1936a). This was primarily an honorary position.

For the purposes of this chapter, I am most interested in those women who played some role (any role?) in the policy formation of the Association. For example, Mary Ely wrote the foreword to the volume celebrating the association's 10th anniversary (Ely, 1936a). Ely was the first editor of the *Journal of Adult Education*. Her feedback on the Journal was valued. In 1931 she provided a critique of the journal that echoed the critique coming from other quarters when she updated Keppel on her informal survey of associates and noted that the journal is not reachable to a general audience. She went on to add that responses were positive but that some were also critical. She summed up some of the responses:

But it is academic, and solemn and pedantic and formal and high brow and over serious and, well I think what they mean—some of them kindly and some not so kindly—is that it is dry-as-dust and uninteresting to ordinarily intelligent and wide-awake person. Is it? *Must* it be? Why *should* it be? (emphasis in original) (Ely, 1931)

Thus, while Lagemann is undoubtedly correct about the biases of the Carnegie Corporation, in actuality women were not exactly overlooked in the leadership of the A^{3}E. They were called on as writers, editors, and researchers. They served on the committees (even the Executive Committee) and received funding.

Funding Imperatives

Women and certain women's issues did receive funding. Of course, it also seems clear that some of the rigid positions held by Cartwright limited broader appeal. For example, in his 10-year report, he notes the consistent concern with democracy that had been a theme within the history of the association. He also eschews the view that the "school is and should be an agency for social action" (1936a, p. 41). In delineating the areas of association interest as of 1936, Cartwright makes no mention of women's education as an area of funding. However, women were certainly in receipt of A^{3}E funding. Areas where women were deeply involved included rural education, libraries, and workers' education (Cartwright, 1936a).

Looking more closely at funded projects, the two related areas of alumni education and parent education were also of interest. In fact, both were listed as areas of potential Carnegie interest (Cartwright, 1936b). In 1930, the American Women's Association received funding from the Carnegie Corporation to inaugurate a program of adult education. In addition, Dr. Jessie Charters, who had been appointed as a faculty member in parent education at Ohio State University in 1928, received funding to develop adult education materials in parent education for OSU alumnae and alumni groups (Carnegie Corporation, 1930). In addition, funding was also given to programs offered by the YWCA.

In recognition of the exigencies of the depression era, coupled with a concern for broadening appeal, the projects funded in 1931–1932 included some expansion of population. These included funding of Welfare Councils (which had arts for the aged programming); Negro Education Experiments (based in libraries so not far from the original Carnegie concept); funding for Hilda Smith's Art Workshop for working girls; and funding for the Association for Personality Training headed by a Mrs.

Sidonie Gruenberg (Carnegie Corporation, 1932). Mrs. Gruenberg appears to have been well-thought-of within the philanthropic world. Her opinion was sought in a variety of circumstances. Her work was primarily connected to the different facets of parent education. Again, this was closely related to the area of parenting, which was one of the key areas identified by the Carnegie Corporation as a funding imperative.

The Negro Adult Education projects are also of interest, because while Alain Locke has been at the center of most discussions of these projects, in fact they were run almost entirely by women. The Executive of the Programs (and a librarian) in Harlem was Ernestine Rose (Rose, 1932; Sandford, 2011). Mae C. Hawes directed the Atlanta project and Miss Jessie Hopkins, a librarian at the Carnegie Library in Atlanta, served as chair of the Atlanta project. In addition, women were the ones who primarily worked in the field (Cartwright, 1933).

The leadership of the A³E voiced different approaches for responding to the crisis of the Depression. Describing a meeting on exactly this topic held at the end of 1932, Mary Ely noted with interest the possibility of cooperative efforts on a community level that could lead to greater cooperation among different local entities. She attended the meeting as a representative of A³E and submitted a report about how community groups could be encouraged to affiliate with A³E (Ely, 1932).

Publications

It is interesting that while women were not a strong part of the operation of the Association, they did play a major role in the publications. The best-known names were Mary Ely, Dorothy Rowden (Loemker), Dorothy Canfield Fisher, and Ruth Kotinsky. By 1941, for example, women ran every aspect of the publications program. Mary Ely was the editor of the *Journal of Adult Education* and Dorothy Rowden Loemker was the editor of the Special Publications sections. Unlike the men, who had academic positions elsewhere (except of course for Cartwright, who had a paid position and when funding ceased he continued in a paid position at Teachers College where the funding moved, although his official connection with the Association was as unpaid Director), these women were actually paid by the Association and lost their jobs in 1941 when funding from the Carnegie Corporation was ended (American Association for Adult Education, 1941). In fact, while the Association continued, the Journal itself was officially ended with the cessation of funding.

Ruth Kotinsky worked on several Carnegie-sponsored projects and wrote three books on adult education that were sponsored by the A³E.

Perhaps the best known of the women writers was Dorothy Canfield Fisher, whose interest was primarily in the uses of leisure. Fisher was the author of one of the earliest adult education texts commissioned by the Carnegie Corporation, *Why Stop Learning*, published in 1927. This was followed by *Learn or Perish* in 1930.

Handbooks

Starting in 1934, the Association published Handbooks of Adult Education. The first two were edited by Dorothy Rowden (1934, 1936). These books were primarily listings of programs with no analysis or real content. Chapters dealt with the range of adult education organizations and institutions. However some chapters did focus almost entirely on women's organizations. Thus, in 1934, Hilda Smith wrote a chapter on "Schools for Women Workers in Industry" and another chapter (with no author listed) focused on Men's and Women's Clubs. Another publication, *Adult Education in Action* (Ely, 1936b) is sometimes classified as a Handbook, although, as Wilson (1991) points out, it is really a collection of articles published in the *Journal of Adult Education*. It is of interest because the very act of selection may say something about the ideology of the field at the time. This book was edited by Mary L. Ely and included broader statements about the purpose and organization of adult education. While numerous women contributed, few of the chapters themselves focused on women or women's issues (Ely, 1936b). Another Handbook did not appear until 1948, again edited by Mary Ely. This was more developed than the 1936 book and again numerous women contributed chapters.

The earlier Handbooks are simply recitations or listings of programs with little to no analysis. Certainly, for example, the inclusion of a chapter on "Negro Adult Education" is of interest, but since there is no analysis, it is difficult to make a statement about it. As Wilson (1991) points out, these handbooks are full of what we now consider to be racist and sexist comments and word usage that are indicative of the orientation of the writers. They also corroborate Lagemann's view that Carnegie Corporation, through its funding of the A^3E, was endeavoring to define culture and identify the powerful men who could promulgate it.

But it is also noteworthy (although outside of the scope of this chapter) to indicate that presence of women was sharply reduced as the handbooks became more analytic and professional. The number of women participating in the 1960 Handbook (Knowles, 1960) was sharply down from even the transition 1948 edition (Ely, 1948).

CONCLUSIONS

Women were certainly involved with adult education; however the A^3E was not formed with women's interests in mind. It was explicitly designed to bypass the feminine bastion of the National Education Association and its emphasis on immigrant education. Working with foundations was becoming a specialization, although nowhere near the situation that we find today. So we can see that the women involved fell into the same categories as the men. They were committed to a vision of adult education (i.e., Dorothy Canfield Fisher and Mary Ely); they fell into adult education through their foundation work (i.e., Dorothy Rowden Loemker, who went on to work for another foundation following her Carnegie Corporation colleague John Russell); or they had particular interests in areas such as immigrant education or labor education or communities, and they passed through the A^3E. It is difficult to state their importance because the importance of the organization itself is unclear. It set the stage for organized adult education but really had no interest in the professionalization of the field. In fact, it could be argued that professionalization increasingly sidelined these women, at least until the 1970s when more women participated in advanced graduate study.

NOTE

1. The Eastern Regional Conference had Clara Taylor from Bryn Mawr, Pennsylvania, and Bertha Wallerstein from New York: the Western Regional Conference Committee included Ethel Richardson from Los Angeles; and the Southern Regional Conference Committee included Olive D. Campbell from Brasstown, North Carolina, and Jennie M. Flexner from Louisville, Kentucky.

REFERENCES

Adams, J. T. (1944). *Frontiers of American culture: A study of adult education in a democracy.* New York, NY: Charles Scribner's & Sons.

American Association for Adult Education. (1941, May 20). Minutes of the special meeting of the Executive Board. Carnegie Corporation Files (Folder AAAE, 1941).

Carnegie Corporation. (1925, January). Member of Adult Education Group. Carnegie Corporation of New York Files. Adult Education, 1925.

Carnegie Corporation. (1926, February 27). Invitation. Carnegie Corporation of New York Files. American Association for Adult Education, 1926.

Carnegie Corporation. (1930, January 28). Memorandum for Mr. Keppel. Carnegie Corporation of New York Records, 1900–2004 (Series IIIA, Box 10, Folder 7). American Association for Adult Education, 1930. Columbia University.

Carnegie Corporation. (1932). Memorandum on projects, 1931–1932. Carnegie Corporation of New York Files. American Association for Adult Education, 1932.

Carnegie Corporation. (1941, May 6). *Summary of discussion at meeting of committee to study future relations of the corporation to the American Association for Adult Education.* Carnegie Corporation of New York Records, 1900–2004. (Series IIIA, Box 12, Folder 3). American Association for Adult Education—Committee to Study Future. Columbia University.

Cartwright, M. A. (1927a, February 19). [Letter to F. P. Keppel]. Carnegie Corporation of New York Records, 1900–2004 (Series IIIA, Box 10, Folder 5). American Association for Adult Education, 1926–1928. Columbia University.

Cartwright, M. A. (1927b, April 11). [Letter to F. P. Keppel]. Carnegie Corporation Files, American Association for Adult Education, 1927. Carnegie Corporation of NY. Carnegie Corporation of New York Records, 1900–2004 (Series IIIA, Box 10, Folder 5). American Association for Adult Education, 1926–1928. Columbia University.

Cartwright, M. A. (1928, September 29). [Letter to F. P. Keppel]. Carnegie Corporation of New York Records, 1900–2004 (Series IIIA, Box 10, Folder 5). American Association for Adult Education, 1926–1928. Columbia University.

Cartwright, M. A. (1929, May 8). [Letter to F. P. Keppel]. Carnegie Corporation of New York Records, 1900–2004 (Series IIIA, Box 10, Folder 6). American Association for Adult Education, 1929. Columbia University.

Cartwright, M. A. (1933, October 25). [Letter to Robert M. Lester]. Carnegie Corporation of NY Records, 1900–2004 (Series IIIA, Box 11, Folder 1). American Association for Adult Education, (General correspondence) 1933. Columbia University.

Cartwright, M. A. (1936a). A decade of adult education. In *Adult education and democracy: Issued in observance of the tenth anniversary of the founding of the American Association for Adult Education 1926–1936* (pp. 39–85). New York, NY: American Association for Adult Education.

Cartwright, M. A. (1936b, July 28). *Suggestions for a five year program of the A^3E, 1936–1941.* Carnegie Corporation of New York Records, 1900–2004 (Series IIIA, Box 11, Folder 2). American Association for Adult Education, 1935–1936 (II). Columbia University.

Easter, O. V. (1996). Septima Poinsette Clark: Unsung heroine of the civil rights movement. In E. Peterson (Ed.), *Freedom road: Adult education of African Americans* (pp.109–122). Malabar, FL: Krieger.

Ely, M. (1931, July 18). [Memorandum to Frederick P. Keppel]. Carnegie Corporation of New York Records, 1900–2004 (Series IIIA, Box 10, Folder 8). American Association for Adult Education, 1931. Columbia University.

Ely, M. (1932, December 21). [Memorandum of Interview]. Town Hall meeting called by Dr. Kilpatrick, Dr. Rugg and Mr. Bowman. Files of the Carnegie Corporation of New York, American Association for Adult Education.

Ely, M. (1936a). Foreword. In *Adult education and democracy: Issued in observance of the tenth anniversary of the founding of the American Association for Adult Education 1926–1936* (np). New York, NY: American Association for Adult Education.

Ely, M. (Ed.). (1936b). *Adult education in action.* New York, NY: American Association for Adult Education.

Ely, M. (Ed.). (1948). *Handbook of adult education in the United States.* New York, NY: Bureau of Publications, Teachers College, Columbia University.

Executive Board, AAAE. (1926, March 27). Minutes of meeting (Series I: No. 1).

Fisher, D. C. (1927). *Why stop learning?* New York, NY: Harcourt, Brace.

Fisher, D. C. (1930). *Learn or perish.* New York, NY: H. Liveright.

Fisher, D. C. (1931, March 23). [Letter to Mr. Cartwright]. Carnegie Corporation of New York Records, 1900-2004. (Series IIIA, Box 10, Folder 8). American Association for Adult Education, 1931. Columbia University.

Grattan, C. H. (1955). *In quest of knowledge: A historical perspective on adult education.* New York, NY: Association.

Heller, R. R. (1986). *The women of summer: The Bryn Mawr summer school for women workers: 1921–1938* (Doctoral dissertation). Rutgers University, New Brunswick, NJ.

Hugo, J. M. (1990). Adult education history and the issue of gender: Toward a different history of adult education in America. *Adult Education Quarterly, 41*(1), 1–16. doi:10.1177/0001848190041001001

Keppel, F. P. (1927, February 12). [Memo of interview with Prof. Thorndike Carnegie]. Corporation of New York Records, 1900–2004 (Series IIIA, Box 10, Folder 5). American Association for Adult Education, 1926–1928. Columbia University.

Keppel, F. P. (1930, September 16). [Memorandum of FPK and Dean J. E. Russell]. Carnegie Corporation of New York Records, 1900–2004 (Series IIIA, Box 10, Folder 7). American Association for Adult Education, 1930. Columbia University.

Keppel, F. P. (1931, March 27). [Memorandum for Mr. Cartwright]. Carnegie Corporation of New York Records, 1900–2004 (Series IIIA, Box 10, Folder 8). American Association for Adult Education, 1931. Columbia University.

Kett, J. F. (1994). *The pursuit of knowledge under difficulties: From self-improvement to adult education in America, 1750–1990.* Stanford, CA: Stanford University Press.

Knowles, M. S. (Ed.). (1960). *Handbook of adult education in the United States.* Chicago, IL: Adult Education Association.

Knowles, M. S. (1977). *The adult education movement in the U.S.* Huntington, NY: Robert E. Krieger.

Kornbluh, J. (1988). *A new deal for workers' education: The workers' service program 1933–1942.* Champaign: University of Illinois Press.

Lagemann, E. C. (1989). *The politics of knowledge: The Carnegie Corporation, philanthropy, and public policy.* Middletown, CT: Wesleyan University Press.

Rose, A. D. (1979). Towards the organization of knowledge: Professional adult education in the 1920s. (Unpublished doctoral dissertation). Teachers College, Columbia University, New York, NY.

Rose, A. D. (1989). Beyond classroom walls: The Carnegie Corporation and the founding of the American Association for Adult Education. *Adult Education Quarterly, 39*(3), 140–151. doi: 10.1177/0001848189039003002

Rose, E. (1932, July 1). *Report of the adult education experiment, Harlem.* Carnegie Corporation of New York Files of the American Association of Adult Education, Projects 1931–1934.

Rowden, D. (Ed.). (1934). *Handbook of adult education in the United States 1934.* New York, NY: American Association for Adult Education.

Rowden, D. (Ed.). (1936). *Handbook of adult education in the United States 1936.* New York, NY: American Association for Adult Education.

Rubin, J. S. (1992). *The making of middle brow culture.* Chapel Hill, NC: University of North Carolina Press.

Sandford, A. (2011). Rescuing Ernestine Rose (1880–1961): Harlem librarian and social activist. *Long Island History Journal, 22*(1). Retrieved from https://lihj.cc.stonybrook.edu/2011/articles/rescuing-ernestine-rose-1880-1961-harlem-librarian-and-social-activist/

Sexton, C. (1993). *The influences of the turn-of-the century midwest on Dorothy Canfield Fisher's educational philosophy.* Paper presented at Syracuse University History of Adult Education Conference, Syracuse, NY.

Stanley, O. F. G. (Ed.). (1923). *The way out, essays on the meaning and purpose of adult education.* London, UK: Oxford University Press.

Stubblefield, H. W. (1988). *Towards a history of adult education in America: The search for a unifying principle.* London, UK: Croom Helm.

Stubblefield, H. W., & Keane, P. (1994). *Adult education in the American experience: From the colonial period to the present.* San Francisco, CA: Jossey-Bass.

Wilson, A. L. (1991). *Epistemological foundations of American adult education, 1934 to 1989: A study of knowledge and interests.* (Doctoral dissertation 9133550, University of Georgia). ProQuest Dissertations and Theses database. Retrieved from http://search.proquest.com/docview/303954074?accountid=12846

CHAPTER 2

ADULT EDUCATION HISTORY AND THE ISSUE OF GENDER

Stepping Back to Move Forward

Jane M. Hugo

In 1990, the *Adult Education Quarterly* published an article I had written on the invisibility of women in the histories published about U.S. adult education work up until that point. I began this way:

> "Adult educators will never know who they are or where they are going until they understand where they have come from," wrote David Stewart, Eduard Lindeman's biographer (1988, p. 27). Adult education in America is not, however, well-chronicled. Only a few voices and a few stories have found their way into the printed word that has become the historical literature of the field. In fact, researchers have yet to exhaust any aspect of adult education history in this country, especially in light of historiographic critiques offered in revisionist and feminist scholarship at large. (Hugo, 1990, p. 1)

Almost 25 years later, adult education historians agree that the development of an adult education profession, its purposes and practices, and participation in adult learning warrant much more historical analysis. Why is historical study important to all adult educators? The study and

No Small Lives: Handbook of North American Early Women Adult Educators, 1925-1950, pp. 17–33
Copyright © 2015 by Information Age Publishing

construction of our educational past can create open exchanges about the knowledge, theory, practice, and politics of teaching and learning in adulthood (Kasworm, Rose, & Ross-Gordon, 2010; Sheared & Sissel, 2001; Welton, 2010). Unfortunately, historical research is not a common pursuit in adult education academic preparation (Welton, 2010). A basic ProQuest database search of dissertations and theses done in August 2013 illustrates the relative position of historical research to other adult education research topics. A basic search with subject words "adult education history" and "women," returned 13 results related to the United States and/or Canada between 1991 and 2012. A search on "transformative learning" and "adult education" between 1976 and 2013 returned 392 results. A search using the terms "program development" and "adult education" returned 4,549 results.

History of the adult education field has not taken hold as a valued subfield in the United States, Canada, or Britain (Welton, 2010). "Historical studies," writes Michael Welton, "are not perceived as either sources for the generation of critical theorems or essential building blocks for foundational studies in adult education" (p. 84). "Our bevy of historical work is pretty slim," notes Canadian researcher Leona English (personal communication, January 22, 2013). "Women in adult education in Canada have not been well studied, save for a few passing references in just about all our history work." Writing about women's contributions is "emergent and slow to come" (L. English, personal communication, January 22, 2013). In this context, issues I raised 20 years ago about the invisibility of women's experience in comprehensive histories of adult education in the United States may not have changed dramatically because the necessary primary research has yet to be done.

There have been, however, additions to the set of comprehensive histories of the field (Kett, 1994; Stubblefield & Keane, 1994) as well as research that seeks to reexamine and/or shift the definitional and conceptual boundaries that circumscribe our understanding of women's role in adult education as well as the role of adult education in women's lives (English, 2011, 2012; Hugo, 1996; Imel, 2010; Ross-Gordon & Gyant, 1993; Sheared & Sissel, 2001). Furthermore, the awareness of the exclusion of voices and experiences within adult education has changed.

Since the *Adult Education Quarterly* published my article in 1990, more scholars incorporate the intersection of gender, race, class, and sexual orientation within adult education as they prepare adult educators for their practice in present-day contexts. These critical perspectives give us new lenses to see through and thus render visible the historical cartography of our field. That matters not just because it makes a more interesting narrative, but because "what's past is prologue" (Shakespeare, *The Tempest*, Act 2, Scene 1). "When one is invisible one does not take up space in our minds, our hearts, nor our economic, historical, political, or social concerns. Such invisibility is directly connected to material conditions and personal and programmatic resources" (Sheared & Sissel, 2001, p. 6).

In this chapter, I revisit that earlier descriptive analysis in light of the intervening years of scholarship. My purpose is threefold. First, to recap and update on how adult education historians have dealt with women's roles and participation in adult education endeavors in the United States between 1925 and 1950, touching on Canadian parallels. Second, to highlight the gendered mechanisms within the field that frame our understanding of women's contributions to the development of adult education in North America. And third, to highlight historiographic trends that would enable researchers to create an even more situated, inclusive, complex, and critical history of informal, nonformal, and formal learning in adulthood.

WOMEN IN ADULT EDUCATION HISTORY

My 1990 article is an artifact of its time. I had started an adult education doctoral program at Syracuse University in 1984 and had had the opportunity to learn from a pool of interdisciplinary women faculty who were engaged with the emerging field of women's studies as well as being engaged with developing and using conceptual frameworks from feminist and postmodern theories and applying them to history, sociology, and education. From my exposure to women's studies and women's history, I came to appreciate the politics of knowledge making and knowledge dissemination.

In the course of my graduate studies, I compared the representation of women in recognized histories written between the 1940s and the late 1980s and in field-sponsored published evidence such as journals, books, and articles from the 1920s through the 1940s. The materials published by the emerging U.S. adult education field from the 1920s through the 1940s revealed a more robust involvement of women than did the accepted histories.

I argued that, over time, adult education historians in the United States marginalized women's historical roles in American adult education. The historians' choices legitimated knowledge about people, events, and the times about which they wrote and delegitimated or ignored others. The only woman recognized across all of the histories by Adams (1944), Grattan (1955), Knowles (1977), and Stubblefield (1988) was Dorothy Canfield Fisher, a prominent fiction author and social figure in the first half of the 20th century. Fisher wrote two books on adult education (Fisher, 1927; 1930), served on the editorial board of the *Journal of Adult*

Education, and was the first and only woman president of the American Association for Adult Education (AAAE), serving between 1932 and 1934.

Beyond Fisher, the adult education histories published in the United States before 1990 place a handful of other women in the narrative beyond a mere citation or quotation. These were Jane Addams, Jane Cunningham Croly, Mary Ely, Ruth Kotinsky, Margaret Fuller Ossoli, Bonaro Overstreet, and Hilda Smith. Between his text and footnotes, Grattan (1955) mentioned a number of women beyond Hilda Smith who were active in workers' education, including Fannia Cohn, Eleanor Coit, Alice Henry, and Louise McLaren (Hugo, 1990).

These choices reflected social, political, and disciplinary mechanisms that subordinated women to men and/or drew the boundaries of the adult education field in ways that excluded female practitioners (and learners, I would now add) from the historical narrative. The border-setting nature of these histories eventually precluded the inclusion of many of the educational sites in which women were traditionally active, such as voluntary associations, literacy education, cultural education, libraries and museums, parent education, immigrant education, settlement houses, faith-based communities, and jails or hospitals.

While the standard historians often acknowledged women's active role in early adult education efforts such as women's clubs, settlement house work, suffrage, and library development, they also discounted it by positioning it as a weak alternative to the organized, consecutive, and widespread programming promoted by the American Association for Adult Education (AAAE), which was founded in 1926. Grattan (1955), for example, praised women's contributions to workers' education but concluded that women's voluntary associations "added tremendously to the range and bulk of adult education without satisfactorily increasing in depth and penetration." Adult educators could, in Grattan's view, turn voluntary organizations "into more solid adult education enterprises" (pp. 257–258). The scope and depth of women's intellectual contributions and their loci of perceived activity became less visible as the histories written between 1944 and 1988 became more modern (Hugo, 1990). With the exception of labor and workers' education, U.S. historians of the field failed to take seriously women's leadership, ideas and activities once their narratives moved beyond the early 1920s and once institution-building, professionalism, and professional preparation took center stage.

A small sampling of Canadian historical research and reflections on the origins of adult education in Canada reveals at least surface indicators of similar patterns of women's visibility and invisibility, contested boundaries around what constitutes the field of adult education, and a marginalization of historical study as an important source of insight to inform current and future practice (Butterwick, 1998; English, 2011, 2012; Kidd, 1963; Rouillard, 1952; Weir, 2007; Welton, 1987).

The founding of the Canadian Association for Adult Education (CAAE) in 1935 built on and shaped the rich legacy of education in voluntary associations, workers' education, and community education in Canada. The organization started in response to a perceived need to organize the "confusion and multiplicity of demands and the services endeavoring to meet the demands" throughout Canada and a desire for educators to communicate with one another (Corbett, 1950, pp. 7–8). It also took guidance from American associational leaders such as Morris Cartwright and had grant funds from the Carnegie Foundation to do work in several provinces (Dunlop, 1936a, 1936b; Kidd, 1950).

By 1950, change had taken place. The "amateurism" that Kidd believed brought vitality to Canadian adult education earlier on needed, even in his view, to give way to the well-trained professional. Kidd's (1950, 1963) texts on the state of adult education in Canada were compilations of invitational pieces and reproduced articles from adult education journals as well as the popular press. Kidd acknowledged they were not comprehensive and were far more descriptive than analytical or evaluative. He believed that they reflected "themes that are of present and continuing significance" (1963, p. xiv). Of the 41 authors represented in *Adult Education in Canada* (1950), eight were women (20%): Isabel Wilson, Sister Frances Dolores, Violet Anderson, Mary Baty, Elizabeth Hay, Ruth McKenzie, Ethel Chapman, and Byrne Hope Sanders. Of the 25 articles in the book, women wrote seven (28%) and co-authored two with men (8%); men wrote sixteen (64%). The women wrote about consumer education, the use of radio for adult education, the role of libraries in adult education, Canadian involvement in international adult education, the Women's Institutes, Frontier College, and social education.

By contrast, Kidd's 1963 anthology, *Learning and Society*, had 52 authors, 7 of whom were women (13%): Monica Mugan, Florence O'Neill, Jean H. Morrison, Alison Hunt, Violet Anderson, Barbara Moon, and Aileen D. Ross. Of the 69 articles in the anthology, 61 entries had individual authors. The remaining eight entries were written by committees or as conference statements. Women wrote seven entries (11%); men wrote 54 (89%). The women authors wrote about citizenship education in the late 1950s, the early history of the Canadian Chautauqua movement, a personal remembrance of establishing an adult education program in a small rural community, a personal experience of being a night-school student, illiteracy in Canada, a poem about intellectual freedom, and a critical review of group-discussion techniques. Unlike *Adult Education in Canada* (1950), this later anthology no longer included a selected bibliography of books, pamphlets, reports, organizations, articles, and journals concerned with adult education.

Adult education in the United States and Canada experienced a shift toward professionalization between 1925 and 1950 and the rise of more centralized experiments to use the education of adults to solve or manage social and economic concerns. Welton (1987) argues that within Canadian adult education, there is a tension between "a constrained and managed adult educational process and a learner-centered, legitimated, and emancipatory learning process" (p. 2). Wilson and Hayes (2000) argue in the 8th AAACE *Handbook of Adult and Continuing Education* the field's embrace of professionalization during the 30s, 40s, and 50s came with the privileging of scientific positivism over field-based practice and knowledge generation. The small sample of two books, which set out to describe the emergence of adult education in Canada, points to reduced visibility of women in the multifaceted field on either side of this tension.

Field-Sponsored Evidence of Women's Engagement 1925–1950

My 1990 analysis of field-sponsored publications in the United States, such as the American Association for Adult Education (AAAE) handbook series up through 1970, pre-1950 issues of the *Journal of Adult Education*, and other publications of AAAE from that same period, showed a gendered publication pattern similar to what I had seen in the accepted histories of the field: men were far more visible than women. At the same time, the field-sponsored publications offered a richer representation of women and their areas of engagement than the field's historians had done.

Women wrote and the field published material on topics such as public libraries and museums; family and parent education; cultural interests like music and theater; intercultural education; civic education, folk schools, and independent adult education; women's issues; workers' education; and special program settings like settlement houses, jails, and hospitals (Hugo, 1990).

Like their male colleagues, women such as Jane Addams, Ruth Kotinsky, and Mary Ely debated the purposes, goals, and strategies of adult education in the United States. Women also wrote or co-authored almost half of the 27 books in the Studies in the Social Significance of Adult Education, a series commissioned by the American Association for Adult Education (AAAE) in the late 1930s and early 1940s.

While a more in-depth analysis would need to be done, a review of a small sample of Canadian field-sponsored publications from the mid-

1930s to the early 1940s suggests that, as in the United States, women had their place in "Corbett's House" (Armstrong, 1968). They served on the CAAE board of directors; secretaries of national and regional organizations; edited national publications; developed public libraries; wrote pamphlet material; were provincial representatives on the CAAE Council; were directors of university extension units concerned with drama and community theater or homemaking; and were chroniclers, advocates, managers, promoters of and participants in adult education in the provinces.

Women in the Adult Education
Historical Research Literature Since 1990

How visible are women in the comprehensive histories or essays on the state of the field's history written since 1990? How has gender consciousness influenced the writing of adult education history?

In the 1990s, there was disquiet within the American Commission of Professors of Adult Education (CPAE), a unit of the American Association of Adult and Continuing Education (AAACE) with regard to issues of inclusion and exclusion. In the her forward to *Making Space: Merging Theory and Practice in Adult Education* (Sheared & Sissel, 2001), Phyllis Cunningham recounts how participants at the Adult Education Research Conference (AERC) in Saskatoon, Canada, in May 1992 strongly critiqued *Adult Education: Evolution and Achievement in a Developing Field of Study*, published in 1991(Peters et al., 1991). This book was the 25th anniversary follow-up publication of the "black book," *Adult Education: Outlines of an Emerging Field of University Study* (Jensen, Liveright, & Hallenbeck, 1964). Intended to summarize achievements in the field of study of adult education since the 1964 publication and to suggest new directions for research, theory, and practice, the book met with strong resistance. Cunningham says it was rejected as "Eurocentric, racist, gender insensitive, elitist, and exclusionary" (Sheared & Sissel, 2001, p. xi). A resolution put forth and approved overwhelmingly at the Saskatoon AERC business meeting declared that the 1991 publication "reproduces the status quo and silences the voices that would challenge that perspective" (p. xii). The resolution went on to recommend that the AAACE publish a book that represented the perspectives excluded from the 25th anniversary publication and that the AAACE do this in consultation with the leaders of the AERC's feminist caucus.

Between 1992 and 1996, despite CPAE agreeing to sponsor a proposal for a book, AAACE's publication committee backing the effort, and editors in place, the development of the book stalled. Seeing a lack of support within AAACE, the editors, Vanessa Sheared and Peggy Sissel, withdrew the book from AAACE in 1996. Working with an advisory committee, Sheared and Sissel solicited chapter proposals, secured a publisher, and published *Making Space* in 2001. The editors wanted the book to be the beginning of a dialogue and critique of the "social, political, economical, and historical forms of hegemony operating in the field" (p. 3).

In this tumultuous period, two comprehensive histories of adult education in America came out in 1994: *Adult Education in the American Experience: From the Colonial Period to the Present* (Stubblefield & Keene, 1994) and *The Pursuit of Knowledge Under Difficulties: From Self-improvement to Adult Education in America* (Kett, 1994).

Harold Stubblefield and Patrick Keene (1994) set out to "critically address the broad context of adult learning and its relationship to social, economic, and political movements" (p. xii). Stubblefield and Keene acknowledge the limitations of earlier descriptive histories and the demand from revisionist historians for a more critical and inclusive narrative that deals with race, gender, and class. *Adult Education in the American Experience* reflects a concerted effort to include more about the educational experiences of women, Native Americans, African Americans, immigrants, and industrial and agricultural workers than did earlier histories. The authors acknowledge that gender, race, ethnicity, class, and religion affect adult education in its diverse manifestations.

As with earlier histories, however, women's experience falls more in the historical periods up through the First World War. After 1920, Stubblefield and Keene (1994) mention or lightly touch on women in relation to labor education, the human potential movement, the New Deal, women's rights, the anti-lynching movement, and World War II. Notable mentions included Hallie Flanagan of the 1935 Federal Theater Project, feminist author Betty Friedan, voting rights educator Septima Clark, early 20th century labor activist Fannia Cohn, and Catholic Worker movement co-founder Dorothy Day.

In trying to write a more inclusive, comprehensive history of adult education in America, Stubblefield and Keene add greater detail, more "objects of study" (Welton, 2010) to the map of adult education. The authors term their effort a "reconnaissance," "more descriptive of events, activities, and the people involved than explanatory of causes" (p. 310). They do not theorize or analyze the intersection of gender and adult learning in depth or with rigor, nor do they dwell too long on the "dark side" of educational efforts that conserve hegemonic social arrangements (Welton, 2010). Only "more informed monographs," Stubblefield and Keene write, will make it possible to "frame and answer even more questions" (1994, p. 309).

Mainstream educational historian Joseph Kett's *The Pursuit of Knowledge Under Difficulties: From Self-improvement to Adult Education in America* (1994) is a history of continuing and adult education in America told by examining several threads that link 19th century self-improvement efforts to the development of 20th century adult education: convergences with and divergences from formal education, the voluntary nature of adult learning, making knowledge relevant to adult needs, and democratic idealism.

Kett's history of adult education as self-improvement tells the story of competing visions of adult education to satisfy "popular aspirations for knowledge" (1994, p. xvi) and thus fulfill the field's designers' commitment to democratic idealism. It is a narrative that disrupts the celebratory narratives offered in the published histories prior to 1990, particularly once we move into the 20th century. Kett argues that the adult education institutions in the 20th century did not "provide a second chance for those denied formal education in their school years, because the satisfaction of 'aspirations,' the willingness to teach anyone anything anywhere, has prevented adult schools from providing a parallel or equivalent to traditional formal education" (p. xvi). Michael Welton (2010) calls Kett's history of the field "bloodless and lifeless" because Kett "fails to connect culture in interplay with class, race, and gender structures of oppression." For Welton, there are too many gaps and absences (e.g., women, African Americans, Native Americans, working-class history, slavery), and there is a failure to acknowledge his "elitist cultural hermeneutic" (p. 87).

Flawed and contentious as Kett's (1994) history is, his treatment of the self-improvement theme places more women in the adult education landscape as participants in or leaders of self-improvement efforts. Of the close to 90 references to individual women in Kett's index, roughly two thirds are connected to self-improvement efforts prior to 1920 (via lyceums, Chautauqua, women's clubs, home economics, women's academies, lecture series, libraries, etc.); a little less than a third are attached to activities in the 1920s through the 1940s (via settlement houses, labor education, parent education, libraries, writers, leisure education, writing, community theater, literacy; summer schools, university extension); and a small fraction are linked to work after 1950. In the context of professionalization and a call for lifelong learning, Kett discusses women's movement into higher education in the 1960s and 70s, coinciding with the development of institutes for women at colleges, the rise of feminism, and women's strategic efforts to enter gender-segregated careers.

In summary, both Kett's (1994) and Stubblefield and Keene's (1994) histories demonstrate awareness of gender consciousness, but neither dramatically disrupts or redresses the invisibility and marginalization of women and others underscored by the adult education professorate at the

1992 Saskatoon AERC conference. Stubblefield and Keene come closer than Kett through their compensatory approach to writing women back into adult education history and their invitation to others to ask new questions and do further research. However, in both narratives, mention of women's experiences as learners and leaders in nonformal and formal adult education thins out after the New Deal period in the 1930s.

Welton's (2010) assessment is that "the energy for historical studies (critical and mainstream) dissipated" after the publication the two 1994 texts discussed above. However, more inclusive, gender-sensitive historical research on the education of adults has a small but resilient foothold in the field's graduate education programs and professorate in Canada and the United States. Between 1989 and 1993, the Kellogg Project at Syracuse University, Syracuse, New York, hosted a series of three adult education history conferences to promote the use of the university's extensive adult education archives. Gender, race, and class were central to many presentations (Hiemstra, 1993; Welton, 2010). Stubblefield and Keene were active participants in these conferences.

Almost 10 years after the Saskatoon AERC Conference call for a more inclusive view of the field, Sheared and Sissel (2001) produced a book-length compilation of articles that made space for "women, and people of different races, voices, realities, and circumstances" who have been left out of the discourses about adult education and lifelong learning (p. 5). Several authors used historical research informed by feminist, postmodern, and critical theories to contextualize and explicate the interplay between hegemonic and counter-hegemonic practices and structures in the education of adults (Chapman, 2001; Hugo, 2001; Schied, 2001; C. A. Smith, 2001).

Similarly, the AERC Conference has been a space in which researchers could introduce, test, and refine more inclusive and/or critical historical work (see for example, Grace, 2000; Imel, 2010; Parrish, 2002; Ross-Gordon & Gyant, 1993; Thompson, 1993; see AERC proceedings for 1993-2012 on Forum for Adult Educators at http://www.adulterc.org/Proceedings.htm).

MECHANISMS OF WOMEN'S INVISIBILITY

As I argued in 1990 (Hugo, 1990), women's visibility in the historical adult education narratives was negatively influenced by three factors. First was the focus from the 1930s onward on defining and establishing adult education as a profession and a distinct educational tier on a par with the education of children. As such, its foundation needed to be in universities and required building an academic knowledge base that certified professionals for practice. Second was the privileged position of men in this period of organizational and institutional legitimization. In general, men held the positions of power and women shared in these circles by accepting the gendered terms and conditions of their relevance to men's work (D. Smith, 1987). Third was the tendency of historians of the field to draw on data sources that told of the story of the field becoming more clearly defined as "purposeful" and "systematic." As editors of journals and the U.S. adult education handbooks used "more rigorous criteria" (R. M. Smith, Aker, & Kidd, 1970, p. xxii) to define what should be included and drew on research done in university settings, many types of adult education work became marginalized and their records were not collected as part of the field's work. As a result, to tell the story of adult education in the 20th century, historians of the field relied on a narrow selection of organizational or institutional records and uncritically reinscribed the gender biased place of women in the practice and profession of adult education.

Scholars point to two other intellectual currents that supported women's invisibility as historical actors in adult education. The first is the reliance of the field on psychology to establish a scientific or empirical foundation for our practice (Rubenson, 2000; Wilson & Hayes, 2000). Rubenson (2000) believes that this influence resulted in a focus on characteristics of learners governing research efforts and a promotion of a research focus on the individual. However, the profession of adult education was blind to its gender and race biases (Johnson-Bailey & Cervero, 2000). It wasn't until the late 1960s that the second-wave feminist movement began to challenge gender and later race assumptions across the social sciences. Furthermore, Wilson and Hayes (2000) foreground the field's reliance on rational empiricism and contend that, for most of the 20th century, the adult education field looked to professionalization and scientific understandings to provide "the most reliable and suitable solutions to human problems" (p. 11). Consequently, adult education defined itself more as an "applied technical science" and less as a "social practice of practical and prudent action" (p. 12). To the degree that women's engagement with adult education as a practice was studied with a flawed epistemological lens and/or their activities were invisible to the mainstream profession because of their race, class, gender, or sexual orientation or because the work they did in corrections, libraries, and community-based social action agencies was not considered mainstream adult education, women would be invisible (Imel, Brockett, & James, 2000; Merriam & Brockett, 1997)

A second current contributing to women's invisibility has been a reluctance or slowness of U.S. adult education academics to borrow or learn from other disciplines (Rubenson, 2000; Welton, 1987). The adult education professorate was slow to draw on the development of feminist theories articulated in women's studies, gender studies, African American studies, and women's history specialties in the 1970s, 80s and 90s, and the parallel developments of critical theory, postmodernism, and social history that scholars brought into sociology, history, and education and the development of cultural studies. These theoretical frameworks are the source of new questions about the historical and cultural construction of gender roles, differences among women, and the ways power structures and inequalities are supported by language and discourse (Ware, 2001). As noted earlier, a number of professors drawing on these theoretical frameworks began to challenge the status quo in the 1990s. Today, these theoretical traditions are more integrated into adult education professional preparation, but gender has remained "largely unexamined" or "an afterthought in research and praxis" (Johnson-Bailey, Baumgartner, & Bowles, 2010, pp. 342–343).

MORE LESSONS FROM WOMEN'S HISTORY

Developments in the field of women's history continue to offer insights into what can be illuminated when we introduce gender as a category of analysis into our work in order to reframe what I had described in 1990 as the "normative male approach to adult education history" (Hugo, 1990, p. 10). Taking a compensatory history approach or a critical history approach were the two approaches I discussed in my 1990 article, as if the solution were an either/or proposition, when even then, the two approaches marked a continuum. Scott (1988) and Ware (2001) remind us that what's important is to not stop at compensatory history, that is, an "add and stir" history which adds women to men's histories without asking what's at the root of their omission in the first place. Historians, therefore, must also push toward the "how" and "why"—an analysis of the interrelated mechanisms and power relationships that create the contexts for women, or a group of women, to be omitted, valorized, victimized, marginalized, silenced, presented as representative of all women, or, using Dewar's (1998) imagery, to be "covered in a blanket of snow" (p. 360).

Women's history has developed an extensive scholarship base in the United States and internationally, undergone theoretical shifts, sparked intellectual controversies in its own ranks, given rise to new academic areas such as gender history and cultural history, been viewed on a continuum of acceptance to disdain, "changed canonical practice" (Frederickson, 2010), and faced criticisms such as postmodern elitism, racism,

"American exceptionalism," and presentism (see for example, Frederickson, 2010; Sangster, 2011; B. G. Smith, 2010).

Out of this work have come lessons and new directions that are shaping women's history and have the potential to inform the writing of adult education history. I offer a sample of five here.

1. The need for feminist historical scholarship continues. Much about women's past remains unexplored. In addition, women's history or gender history have not been mainstreamed; it is too often seen as not important except as filler in material that the historical record has missed (B. G. Smith, 2010).

2. Women's history has thrived by participating in theoretical debate, crossing discipline borders, and testing new approaches. At the same time, some scholars caution against building a professional discourse that equates progress with "new" approaches and obsolescence with "old" approaches (Sangster, 2011).

3. The concept of "whiteness" has been an important tool to look at the embedded racism within women's history in the United States. Women historians also draw on multicultural approaches in an effort to recognize differences among women and the diversity of their experiences, incorporating concepts of borderlands, intercultural borders, frontiers, and contact zones (Ware, 2001).

4. World or global history has emerged to challenge the privileged position of American or European historical narratives. There is a call to move to an approach that "focuses on international connections, facilitates comparisons, and traces personal, cultural, and intellectual relationships across national borders and cultural boundaries" (Frederickson, 2010, p. 171).

5. In the process of rewriting histories that "seemed settled or fully explored," it's not enough to know that women were active, but rather one needs to ask how they were active in order to surface the assumptions and premises about race, gender, class, and ethnicity that women bought into, negotiated, or resisted (Ware, 2001).

When applied to adult education's history, each of the above would contribute lines of research that help craft a more complete story of adult learning and the adult education profession in relation to myriad other social endeavors that are woven into the fabric of North American society: work, family, politics, citizenship, religion, war, peace, education, immigration, art, health, identity formation, social change, and leisure.

SUMMARY

This discussion of adult education history and gender has drawn on images of maps, border crossing, cartography, boundaries, intersections, contours, creating spaces, and reconnaissance. This isn't accidental or original. As a profession, adult education in North America has been concerned with definition and its identity since its emergence began in the 1920s. The vocabulary of mapmaking applies to writing history as well. The historian explores, delineates, represents, names, arranges, locates, and connects past events or phenomena in a historical narrative.

In my 1990 article and in this update, I contend that we have barely scratched the surface of women's roles in adult education as learners or professionals. Though improved slightly, our mental maps of our field remain incomplete and distorted, due in part to gender-blindness and gender-bias and the lack of a critical mass of historical research. To improve the situation, adult education professors and practitioners need to include gender consistently as one of their categories of analysis, support more historical research, and do more interdisciplinary work with feminist scholars in order to cross-fertilize historical scholarship.

To paraphrase pioneer historian Gerda Lerner (1981), anything that explains a world in which men are at the center of the human enterprise and women are at the margins "helping" them, explains a world that does not exist and never has. Is this any less true for the adult education enterprise? "Men and women have built society and have built the world. Women have been central to it," said Lerner. "This revolutionary insight is itself a force, a force that liberates and transforms" (Lerner, 1981).

REFERENCES

Adams, J. T. (1944). *Frontiers of American culture: A study of adult education in a democracy.* New York: Charles Scribner's & Sons.

Armstrong, D. P. (1968). *Corbett's house: The origins of the Canadian Association for Adult Education and its development during the directorship of E.A. Corbett, 1936–1951* (Unpublished master's thesis). University of Toronto, Toronto, Canada.

Butterwick, S. (1998). Lest we forget: Uncovering women's leadership in adult education. In G. Selman, M. Selman, M. Cooke, & P. Dampier (Eds.), *The foundations of adult education in Canada* (2nd ed., pp. 103–116). Toronto, Canada: Thompson Educational.

Chapman, B. S. (2001). Northern philanthropy's ideological influence on African American adult education in the rural south. In V. Sheared & P. A. Sissel (Eds.), *Making space: Merging theory and practice in adult education* (pp. 109–123). Westport, CT: Bergin & Garvey.

Corbett, E. A. (1950). A brief history of adult education in Canada. In J. R. Kidd (Ed.), *Adult education in Canada* (pp. 2–10). Toronto: Canadian Association for Adult Education.

Dewar, T. (1998). Women and adult education: A postmodern perspective. In G. Selman, M. Cooke, M. Selman, & P. Dampier (Eds.), *The foundations of adult education in Canada* (2nd ed., pp. 103–116). Toronto, Canada: Thompson.

Dunlop, W. J. (1936a). Notes & comments. *Adult Learning, 1*(2), 16.

Dunlop, W. J. (1936b). Editorial. *Adult Learning, 1*(1), 3.

English, L. M. (2011). Adult education on the Newfoundland coast: Adventure and opportunity for women in the 1930s and 1940s. *Newfoundland and Labrador Studies, 26*(1), 25–54.

English, L. M. (2012). Teaching the "morally and economically destitute": Nineteenth century adult education efforts in Newfoundland. *Acadiensis: Journal of the History of the Atlantic Region, 41*(2), 66–88.

Fisher, D. C. (1927). *Why stop learning?* New York, NY: Harcourt, Brace & Company.

Fisher, D. C. (1930). *Learn or perish.* New York, NY: Horace Liveright.

Frederickson, M. E. (2010). Going global: New trajectories in U.S. women's history. *The History Teacher, 43*(2), 169–189.

Grace, A. (2000). The modern practice of Canadian and US academic adult education during the brief American century (1945–1973): People, politics, and ideas shaping an emerging field. In T. J. Sork, V. Chapman, & R. St. Clair (Eds.), *Proceedings of the 41st annual Adult Education Research conference, June 2–4, 2000* (pp. 139–144). Vancouver: University of British Columbia.

Grattan, C. H. (1955). *In quest of knowledge: A historical perspective on adult education.* New York, NY: Association.

Hiemstra, R. (1993). Kellogg Project final report (September 1, 1986 to August 31, 1993). Syracuse, NY: Syracuse University. Retrieved from http://www-distance.syr.edu/kelrpt1.html

Hugo, J. M. (1990). Adult education history and the issue of gender: Toward a different history of adult education in America. *Adult Education Quarterly, 41*(1), 1–16.

Hugo, J. M. (1996). *"Perhaps it is the person first and the subject matter second": Social relationships and the construction of cultural and civic curricula in a women's study club 1885-1985* (Unpublished doctoral dissertation). Syracuse University, Syracuse, NY.

Hugo, J. M. (2001). Creating an intellectual basis for friendship: Practice and politics in a white women's study group. In V. Sheared & P. Sissel (Eds.), *Making space: Merging theory and practice in adult education* (pp. 89–108). Westport, CT: Bergin & Garvey.

Imel, S. (2010). Lucy Wilcox Adams: Early advocate of discussion-based adult education. In *Proceedings for the 2010 Adult Education Research conference.* Retrieved from http://www.adulterc.org/applications/ClassifiedListingsManager/inc_classifiedlistingsmanager.asp?ItemID=1441&CategoryID=171

Imel, S., Brockett, R. G., & James, W. B. (2000). Defining the profession: A critical appraisal. In A. L. Wilson & E. R. Hayes (Eds.), *Handbook of adult and continuing education* (pp. 628–642). San Francisco, CA: Jossey-Bass.

Jensen, G., Liveright, A., & Hallenbeck, W. (1964). *Adult education: Outlines of an emerging field of university study.* Washington, DC: Adult Education Association.

Johnson-Bailey, J., Baumgartner, L. M., & Bowles, T. A. (2010). Social justice in adult and continuing education: Laboring in the fields of reality and hope. In C. E. Kasworm, A. D. Rose, & J. M. Ross-Gordan (Eds.), *Handbook of adult and continuing education* (pp. 339–349). Los Angeles, CA: Sage.

Johnson-Bailey, J. & Cervero, R. M. (2000). Race and adult education: A critical review of the North American literature. In T. J. Sork, V. Chapman, & R. St. Clair (Eds.), *Proceedings of the 41st annual Adult Education Research conference, June 2–4, 2000* (pp. 201–205). Vancouver: University of British Columbia.

Kasworm, C. E., Rose, A. D., & Ross-Gordan, J. M. (Eds.). (2010). *Handbook of adult and continuing education.* Los Angeles, CA: Sage.

Kett, J. F. (1994). *The pursuit of knowledge under difficulties: From self-improvement to adult education in America, 1750–1990.* Stanford, CA: Stanford University Press.

Kidd, J. R. (Ed.). (1950). *Adult education in Canada.* Toronto: Canadian Association for Adult Education.

Kidd, J. R. (Ed.). (1963). *Learning and society.* Toronto: Canadian Association for Adult Education.

Knowles, M. (1977). *A history of the adult education movement in the United States* (rev. ed.). New York, NY: Robert E. Krieger.

Lerner, G. (1981, September). "Gerda Lerner on the Future of Our Past," interview by Catharine R. Stimpson, *Ms.* 10: pp. 94–95, quoted in S. Ware (2001). "Introduction." In *American women: A library of congress guide for the study of women's history and culture in the United States. Washington, DC: Library of Congress,* (para 8). A topical essay retrieved from http://memory.loc.gov/ammem/awhhtml/awintro/awintro.html

Merriam, S. B., & Brockett, R. G. (1997). *The profession and practice of adult education: An introduction.* San Francisco, CA: Jossey-Bass.

Parrish, M. M. (2002). Creating a place for learning: Dorothy Day and the Catholic Worker movement. In *Proceedings for the 2002 Adult Education Research conference.* Retrieved from http://www.adulterc.org/applications/ClassifiedListingsManager/inc_classifiedlistingsmanager.asp?ItemID=766&CategoryID=139

Peters, J. A., Jarvis, P., & Associates (Eds.). (1991). *Adult education: Evolution and achievement in a developing field of study.* San Francisco, CA: Jossey-Bass.

Ross-Gordon, J., & Gyant, L. (1993). Anna Cooper and Nannie Burroughs: Educating head, heart, and hand in the early 20th century African American community. *Proceedings for the 1993 Adult Education Research conference.* Retrieved from http://www.adulterc.org/applications/ClassifiedListingsManager/inc_classifiedlistingsmanager.asp?ItemID=72&CategoryID=121

Rouillard, H. (1952). *Pioneers in adult education in Canada.* Toronto, Canada: T. Nelson & Sons.

Rubenson, K. (2000). Revisiting the map of the territory. In T. J. Sork, V. Chapman, & R. St. Clair (Eds.), *Proceedings of the 41st annual Adult Education Research conference, June 2–4, 2000* (pp. 397–401). Vancouver: University of British Columbia.

Sangster, J. (2011). *Through feminist eyes: Essays on Canadian women's history*. Edmonton, Canada: Athabasca University Press.

Schied, F. M. (2001). Struggling to learn, learning to struggle: Workers, workplace learning, and the emergence of human resource development. In V. Sheared & P. Sissel (Eds.), *Making space: Merging theory and practice in adult education* (pp. 124–137). Westport, CT: Bergin & Garvey.

Scott, J. (1988). *Gender and the politics of history*. New York, NY: Columbia University Press.

Sheared, V. & Sissel, P. A. (Eds.). (2001). *Making space: Merging theory and practice in adult education*. Westport, CT: Bergin & Garvey.

Smith, B. G. (2010). Women's history: A retrospective from the United States. *Signs, 35*(3), 723–747.

Smith, C. A. (2001). The African-American market woman: Her past, our future. In V. Sheared & P. A. Sissel (Eds.), *Making space: Merging theory and practice in adult education* (pp.73–88). Westport, CT: Bergin & Garvey.

Smith, D. (1987). *The everyday world as problematic: A feminist sociology*. Toronto, Canada: University of Toronto Press.

Smith, R. M., Aker, G. F., & Kidd, J. R. (Eds.). (1970). *Handbook of adult education in the United States*. New York, NY: Macmillan.

Stewart, D. (1988). [Review of the book *Towards a history of adult education in America* by H. Stubblefield]. *Lifelong Learning: An Omnibus of Practice and Research, 12*(2), 27–28.

Stubblefield, H. (1988). *Towards a history of adult education in America: The search for a unifying principle*. London, UK: Croom Helm.

Stubblefield, H., & Keane, P. (1994). *Adult education in the American experience: From the colonial period to the present*. San Francisco, CA: Jossey-Bass.

Thompson, M. M. (1993). The rhetoric of leadership in the history of adult education: Implications for the acceptance of women as leaders. In *Proceedings for the 1993 Adult Education Research conference*. Retrieved from http://www.adulterc.org/applications/ClassifiedListingsManager/inc_classifiedlistingsmanager.asp?ItemID=72&CategoryID=121

Ware, S. (2001). Introduction. In *American women: A library of congress guide for the study of women's history and culture in the United States*. Washington, DC: Library of Congress. Retrieved from http://memory.loc.gov/ammem/awhhtml/awintro/awintro.html

Weir, J. (2007). Undan Snjóbreiðunni (What Lies Beneath the Snow): Revealing the contributions of Icelandic pioneer women to adult education in Manitoba 1875–1914 (Master's thesis). University of Manitoba, Winnipeg. Retrieved from http://umanitoba.ca/faculties/education/media/Weir-08.pdf

Welton, M. R. (Ed.). (1987). *Knowledge for the people: The struggle for adult learning in English-speaking Canada, 1828–1973*. Toronto, Canada: Ontario Institute for Studies in Education Press. Symposium Series/18.

Welton, M. R. (2010) Histories of adult education: Constructing the past. In C. E. Kasworm, A. D. Rose, & J. M. Ross-Gordan (Eds.), *Handbook of adult and continuing education* (pp. 83–91). Los Angeles, CA: Sage.

Wilson, A. L. & Hayes, E. R. (Eds.). (2000). *Handbook of adult and continuing education*. San Francisco, CA: Jossey-Bass.

PART II

PROFILES OF 26 WOMEN

Lucy Wilcox Adams with the Navajo Education Committee, Window Rock, Arizona (Photo courtesy of Ernest Adams).

CHAPTER 3

LUCY WILCOX ADAMS

Proponent of Discussion-Based Adult Education

Susan Imel

No Small Lives: Handbook of North American Early Women Adult Educators, 1925-1950,
pp. 37–45

Lucy Wilcox Adams became involved in adult education in 1929 when she was hired as secretary-organizer of the California Association for Adult Education (CAAE). Working with CAAE director Lyman Bryson, Lucy participated in the expansion of the association that was made possible with grants from the Carnegie Corporation (American Association for Adult Education, 1934). Between 1929 and 1935 when she resigned, Lucy played a key role in the association, moving from secretary-organizer to associate director and finally to director. In 1933, when Carnegie support for CAAE ceased, Lucy took a position in the Division of Adult Education, California State Department of Education in the Workers' Progress Administration-funded workers education program. However, she still retained the title of CAAE director. After the untimely death of her husband, William A. Adams, Lucy became the sole support of her two young sons; she left California and the CAAE and was employed by the Office of Indian Affairs, U. S. Department of Interior. That position was the beginning of a long career in government service (Miscellaneous Obituaries of Anthropologists, n.d.; E. Adams, personal communication, 2008).

EARLY YEARS

Lucy was born in San Francisco in 1898 shortly after her parents immigrated to the United States from Australia. Her father attended a technical institute, became a civil engineer, and then secured work in the oil industry; the family moved around California. In 1913, at the age of 15, Lucy made her first trip outside of California when she traveled to London, England, to spend a year with her grandparents, where she was enrolled in a private girls school.

Upon her return to the states, Lucy finished high school in Los Angeles. Due to changes in the oil industry, her family's financial conditions were tight, so she took a job as a live-in housekeeper and enrolled in Los Angeles Junior College (LAJC). At the end of her freshman year, she was encouraged to apply to Stanford by one of her employers and an instructor at the LAJC. Knowing she would need to support herself, she temporarily left the junior college to enroll in a 6-month business course, learning secretarial skills. She finished junior college and enrolled at Stanford, supporting herself by working as a secretary. Early in 1922, she left Stanford one semester prior to graduation to take a position in England as a secretary and researcher with Francis Hirst, a former editor of the *Economist*, who had been in California lecturing (E. Adams, personal communication, 2008).

While in England, Lucy became engaged to William (Bill) Forbes Adams, whom she married in 1925. He was a Stanford graduate and had gone to England as a Rhodes Scholar in 1921. She had known Adams prior to moving to England but he had been engaged to someone else. When that relationship broke off during the period Lucy and Bill were both in England, they began seeing each other. Bill returned to the United States and enrolled at Yale, working on his doctorate in history. After they married in 1925, they lived in New Haven, Connecticut, and Lucy gave birth to their two sons, Ernest W. (1926) and William Y. (1927). In 1929, Bill received his PhD and accepted a position at UCLA as an assistant professor. Hence, Lucy got back to California (E. Adams, personal communication, 2008).

LUCY'S YEARS WITH THE CALIFORNIA ASSOCIATION

In 1927, the California Association for Adult Education (CAAE) was organized to provide some structure to the activities in adult education that had been underway for a number of years through the California State University's Extension Division, the public schools, and private agencies (AAAE, 1934). Initially funded through private contributions and lecture fees, in 1929, CAAE received a grant of $5,000 from the Carnegie Corporation and Lucy was hired. Grants of $7000 in both 1930 and 1931 allowed expansion of its programs (AAAE, 1934). During this period, the CAAE developed programs designed to provide adults opportunities to participate in open group discussion and study under trained leaders to promote awareness of public issues and participation in individual or community action. A confluence of factors, including the Depression, the emergence of communism in Russia, the New Deal, and unrest in Europe and Asia, meant that many adults were eager to engage in discussion on public issues (E. Adams, personal communication, 2008).

CAAE Director Lyman Bryson was willing to share responsibility for developing the CAAE, so the job offered Lucy many opportunities for development and, with Bryson's encouragement, she was soon leading groups. As she prepared to lead her first group consisting of eight sessions titled "Crisis in Democracy," Lucy was very apprehensive; Bill Adams drove her around the neighborhood of the library where the group was to be held, went in with her, and then asked the first question to get the discussion launched; after that initial nervousness, Lucy was fine and went on to become a trainer of leaders (E. Adams, personal communication, 2008).

Because it was difficult to train enough leaders to keep up with the rapidly growing demand for discussion programs, Bill Adams was recruited as a leader (E. Adams, personal communication, 2008). In a piece titled "A Cross-Section Round Table" (W. F. Adams, 1933), Bill described the group as an ongoing discussion group that drew from a cross-section of the Los Angeles waterfront area; the group continued for 3 years. According to Bill's obituary, "His broad and accurate knowledge of current affairs and their historic background, and his deep sympathy with the desires of the less privileged to better their lot, made those meetings memorable for their stimulation of thoughtful and profitable discussion" (University of California, n.d.).

Lucy's activities in the California Association were many and varied. In 1930, she was an instructor at adult education institutes held at Occidental College in Los Angeles and at Hansford Hall, Berkeley for the purpose of training leaders. She taught a course titled, "The Unpublished Review," that organized the participants into staff members of a weekly journal of opinion that included contributions from all summer school students. The course was continued at subsequent summer schools in 1931–1933. Bill sometimes lectured at the institutes, which were directed by Lyman Bryson. The institutes were designed to train leaders for the new type of discussion-based adult education that encouraged exchanges between the leaders and participants. In 1932, Lucy started a radio discussion on current political and social issues in which Lyman Bryson also participated (E. Adams, personal communication, 2008).

In 1933, the Association sponsored a summer session for workers, similar to the Bryn Mawr School for Workers that had pioneered worker education in the United States. The school was proposed by two young women who were part of the large migration of garment workers from New York to the Los Angeles area. After several weeks of meetings and negotiation, a 3-week course devoted to the problems of labor and labor history was agreed upon. Lucy was named the director of the school, due to Lyman's absence from California during the period. At this particular time, the *Los Angeles Times* was conducting a very vigorous anti-union campaign and fear of communism was rampant in the area. The school itself attracted diverse participants, including active communists (split among followers of Trotsky, Lovestone, and Lenin), socialists, some conservative labor union types, and those supporting the New Deal. The resulting infighting among the students, plus efforts to take over the school and boycott two of the instructors, created havoc for Lucy's job as director. However, despite some repercussions, such as Lucy being named as a prominent Red in one newspaper, the experiment with workers education was considered a success and a recommendation made to continue it (E. Adams, personal communication, 2008).

The final year of the Carnegie Corporation Foundation grant to the California Association was 1933, and, in September, Lyman Bryson left for Iowa where he became director of the Des Moines Forums. Lucy became acting director for the balance of the year but then funds ran out.

Lyman recruited Bill to spend part of his sabbatical in Des Moines as a forum discussion leader; at the beginning of 1934, Lucy spent 2 months in Des Moines with Bill. When Lucy returned to California, she began work in the Workers Progress Administration-funded workers' education program within the California State Department of Education, Division of Adult Education, although she still maintained the title of Executive Director of the CAAE. Lucy's work enabled many previously unserved groups to have access to adult education. In 1934, a second summer session for workers was held, although it nearly cost Lucy her job since some students picketed and distributed inflammatory material. When she went to meet with the state superintendent about the incident, Bill accompanied her and, due to his defense of workers education, her job was saved (AAAE, 1936; E. Adams, personal communication, 2008).

In her capacity as CAAE director, Lucy administered an additional Carnegie grant of $7,500 for the year 1934–35. The money was earmarked for a series of projects, including a survey of adult education activities in Los Angeles. The Association also continued to carry on radio programs and "several dozen local forums" (AAAE, 1936, p. 61).

In 1935, just as Lucy was finalizing plans for the summer sessions at Berkeley and Occidental, Bill died after surgery to repair a duodenal ulcer. Thus, Lucy's career in adult education in California ended. Her salary was very small and because she lacked a degree, she knew she would have to seek other employment (E. Adams, personal communication, 2008). According to Lucy's obituary, "His [Bill's] untimely death ... left his widow with two young sons and very few resources" so she secured a position with the Soil Conservation Service in Albuquerque (Miscellaneous Obituaries of Anthropologists, n.d.).

Lucy went on to have a long career in public service, including work with the War Relocation Authority, the agency responsible for relocating 110,000 Japanese Americans from the West Coast; resettling refugees and displaced persons in Germany and Hungary for the UN Relief and Rehabilitation agency following WWII; and then with USAID, where she worked in Iran and as assistant director for the USAID in Korea. She ended her career with USAID in Washington, DC, when at the age of 65 she was forced to retire. She then became an adjunct professor at University of California-Berkeley in a special program for training foreign-aid personnel. She was finally forced to retire at age 70. She died in 1996 at the age of 98 (Miscellaneous Obituaries of Anthropologists, n.d.).

LUCY'S CONTRIBUTIONS TO THE LITERATURE

Between 1932 and 1942, Lucy authored five articles that appeared in the *Journal of Adult Education* (Adams, 1932b, 1933, 1935, 1938, 1941). She also contributed a piece titled "The Talk of the Town" (1932a), which appeared in the "Why Stop Learning" section of the *Journal*, which was reprinted in *Adult Education in Action* (Ely, 1936) under the section on Public Forums. The four articles (1932a, 1932b, 1933, 1935) published while Lucy was with the CAAE focused primarily on discussion-based adult education, a technique that was the basis for the forum movement.

The first of these articles, "Talk of the Town" (1932a), described the CAAE's use of public libraries "as places for discussion of ideas as well as the circulation of books" (p. 61). The article begins with the following observation:

> Good talk, an English statesman said, is the essence of good living. It is a statement which many people might be disposed to question, particularly in America, where talk has come to be associated with talkers, and the dismal professions of lecturing and politics. (p. 60)

Lucy went on to observe that when a friend asked Morley, the Englishman responsible for the statement, what he meant by good talk, he said "that it should be like good gossip. It should be informed, it should be lively, it should draw in all opinions, and it should be enjoyed for its own sake" (p. 60). Surely these were the aims the CAAE had for its library-based discussion groups.

The article describes several successful discussion groups and goes on to note two impediments in expanding the groups: funding and lack of leadership. Initially, the hope was "that participation in discussion would develop leadership within the group" but leaders did not materialize from the groups and finding "people qualified by training and temperament to assume leadership" was difficult (Adams, 1932a, p. 62). According to Lucy, the leaders who worked the hardest and those who succeeded "are those that go as scientists and investigators, and not those that have a body of facts to deliver" (1932a, p. 63). The participants in groups with good leadership may learn "to contribute in some measure to that free and informed discussion of public affairs which is the life blood of democracy" (1932a, p. 64). Lucy observes that "It would be easy to exaggerate the importance of these library discussion centers ... no great syntheses have been achieved. Nobody has changed overnight into a student or philosopher; nobody has done anything about anything, and perhaps nobody will" (1932a, p. 63).

Subsequent *Journal* articles (Adams, 1932b, 1933, 1935) echoed the themes found in "Talk of the Town," as Lucy continued to write about the connection between adult education and democracy, group leadership, the learning environment, and the purpose of education. In the 1930s, the forum movement was a predominant form of adult education, not only in California but in other areas of the country as well (Imel, 2012). Sometimes called civic education, this form of adult education was designed to prepare adults to participate in a democratic society. In "Salvaging Democracy" (1933), Lucy proposed a national civic education movement that would, among other things, engage in the "development of intelligent cooperation in the carrying out of public policies … [and the] creation of a public critically hospitable to new ideas" (p. 414).

The purpose of education and group leadership were two other themes that Lucy returned to. She felt that education for a specific purpose was the same as propaganda (1932b, 1933), and that the purpose of education should be to provide "the freedom and opportunity for men and women to satisfy their intellectual and artistic wants and to enlarge their horizons" (1932b, p. 142). Unfortunately, good leaders were difficult to attract, and many of the existing leaders were timid or ineffective in their group leadership techniques, leading to the breakdown of groups (1933, 1935). Lucy characterized the type of leaders adult education tended to attract as "the popularizer, the man or woman with an inexhaustible fund of moral enthusiasm, who substitutes emotional appeal for depth of understanding" (1933, p. 411).

Finally, Lucy wrote about the learning environment; she believed that discussion groups should be characterized by the informal exchange of opinion—what she termed "good talk," and all that entailed (1932a, p. 60). In "A Mirror of Minds," she said that discussion groups "should provide a neutral meeting place and testing ground for warring opinions" (1935, p. 25). She also noted the emotional aspects of group discussion, observing that too little attention has been paid to the importance of emotions in learning (1935).

Lucy developed an increasingly critical perspective about discussion-based adult education during the period she was in California. Her initial article (1932a) describing library-based groups was somewhat optimistic. In "Mirror of Minds"—an article that traced the development of forums from 1929 to 1934—she expressed disillusionment, saying that the later forums have "ceased to be educational bodies and have become propaganda groups or platforms for the rehearsal of prejudice" (1935, p. 24). Despite this, she still remained a believer in the importance of public discussion groups as vehicles that could provide a neutral place for free speech. In "Why Forums?" a national study of the forum movement, Mary Ely (1937) referred to "Mirror of Minds" as an "exceedingly thoughtful and interesting study of the forums of Southern California" (p. 138).

The last two articles by Lucy that appeared in the *Journal* were written after she left California and was working for the US Department's Office of Indian Affairs. The first of these articles, "Indians Go to School" (1938), describes how adult education on the Navajo Indian Reservation in Arizona and New Mexico takes place "without classes, without a schedule, and largely without teachers" primarily through conversations among the adults who come to the schools that function as community centers and serve as a gathering place with kitchens, bathhouses, and health clinics (p. 149). According to Lucy, "this largely self-initiated, self-directed form of adult education … offers almost unlimited possibilities for new learning" (p. 153). The second article, "Indians on the Peace Path," proposes the type of adult education program that would be most appropriate for implementation on reservations. It would include the same kind of training opportunities offered to youth, tap into the tribal councils that use a deliberative process that leads to consensus, and link the development of skills to specific projects (1941).

Despite Lucy's contributions to the field's literature, she remains virtually unknown in adult education. She appears to have a much more lasting legacy in the field of anthropology because of her work on overseeing the development of a system of orthography for writing the Navajo language and commissioning a study of Navajo place-names (Obituary of Anthropologists, n.d.). An analysis of Lucy's *Journal* articles (Imel, 2010) demonstrated that Lucy's ideas about group discussion were consistent with those of both historical and contemporary sources. Although she left Stanford one semester short of graduation, she was obviously a brilliant woman who had a remarkable career.

REFERENCES

Adams, L. W. (1932a). Talk of the town. *Journal of Adult Education, 4*(1), 60–64.

Adams, L. W. (1932b). What do we want of education. *Journal of Adult Education, 4*(2), 141–142.

Adams. L. W. (1933). Salvaging democracy. *Journal of Adult Education, 5*(4), 409–414.

Adams, L. W. (1935). A mirror of minds. *Journal of Adult Education, 7*(1), 21–27.

Adams, L. W. (1938). Navajos go to school. *Journal of Adult Education, 10*(2), 149–153.

Adams, L. W. (1941). Indians on the peace path. *Journal of Adult Education, 13*(3), 243–248.

Adams, W. F. (1933). A cross-section round table. *Journal of Adult Education, 5*(1), 61–63.

American Association for Adult Education (AAAE). (1934). Annual report of the director, 1932–33. New York, NY: Author. Retrieved from http://archive.org/stream/annualreportofdi1934amer#page/28/mode/2up

American Association for Adult Education (AAAE). (1936). Annual report of the director, 1935–36. New York, NY: Author. Retrieved from http://ia600502.us.archive.org/22/items/annualreportofdi1936amer/annualreportofdi1936amer.pdf

Ely, M. L. (Ed.). (1936). *Adult education in action*. New York, NY: American Association for Adult Education.

Ely, M. L. (1937). *Why forums?* New York, NY: American Association for Adult Education.

Imel, S. (2010, May). *Lucy Wilcox Adams: Early advocate of discussion-based adult education*. Paper presented at the Adult Education Research Conference, San Francisco, CA. Retrieved from http://www.adulterc.org/Proceedings/2010/proceedings/imel.pdf

Imel, S. (2012). Civic engagement in the United States: Roots and branches. In L. Munoz & H. S. Wrigley (Eds.), *Adult civic engagement in adult learning. New directions for adult and continuing education, no. 135*. San Francisco, CA: Jossey-Bass.

Miscellaneous Obituaries of Anthropologists. (n.d.). Lucy Wilcox Adams. Retrieved from http://www.obitcentral.com/obitsearch/obits/misc/anthro8.htm

University of California. (n.d.). In Memoriam, 1935–36. Williams Forbes Adams, History, Los Angeles. Retrieved from http://texts.cdlib.org/view?docId=hb9q2nb5z2&doc.view=frames&chunk.id=div00001&toc.depth=1&toc.id=

Nora Bateson
(Photo courtesy of Vanessa Osgood)

CHAPTER 4

DON'T SHUSH ME!

Nora Bateson, Activist Librarian

Sue Adams

No Small Lives: Handbook of North American Early Women Adult Educators, 1925-1950,
pp. 47–54
Copyright © 2015 by Information Age Publishing

Though libraries have long been tacitly acknowledged as sites of adult education, remarkably little in the literature identifies librarians themselves as adult educators. Nora Bateson can without apology be situated at the intersection of these two identities. She became a leader in public library promotion internationally, established regional libraries, taught in library schools, and published in both adult education and library journals. Her collaboration with leaders of the Antigonish Movement in Nova Scotia, Canada, deepened her commitment to adult education for personal and community development linked with social justice: she developed libraries as an integral element in that process. While Nora Bateson's accomplishments were impressive, her influence—especially in North America—has seldom been acknowledged. Historian Peter McNally has called her "one of the great under-appreciated figures in Canadian library history" (1996, p. 11). Her absence from the history of adult education is perhaps even more striking, and this brief account attempts to recover some of that inspiring story.

FORMATIVE YEARS

Nora Bateson, born in England in 1896, seems to have been shaped by a convergence of progressive factors. She grew up in Westhoughton, a coal and cotton town northwest of Manchester, in an area known for the strength of its cooperative movement. The family lived only a block from the Westhoughton Mechanics' Institute, and in 1908 a Carnegie Cultural Hall and Library opened in the town. Adult education no doubt contributed to the Bateson family prospects as Nora's father advanced gradually through the skilled ranks in the mines, from surveyor's assistant to chief engineer.

The rise of Labour politics in Britain gave new prominence to the concerns of the working classes, and the folk of Westhoughton responded heartily at the polls. It's perhaps not surprising that Nora Bateson, raised in this political environment, was in later life regarded as displaying inconvenient "socialist political leanings" (Coughlin, 1966, p. 169).

In 1914 Nora entered the University of Manchester's History School. There, her professors served as leaders in the university's settlement movement and the Workers' Educational Association (Tout, 1932). In Nora's hall of residence, warden Phoebe Sheavyn was enthusiastic in the struggle for women's suffrage (S. Griffiths, personal communication, October 7, 2008). With pamphlets, articles, public lectures, and marches, the suffragists carried on a campaign of adult education which sparked considerable public debate on women's rights, not all of it within the bounds of polite discourse. Although university records do not shed much light on Nora's extra-curricular activities, she certainly was immersed in a thriving adult education milieu.

EARLY WORK

Following graduation, employment as a teacher, coupled with a lively sense of adventure, brought Nora to Canada in 1920. She quickly abandoned the life of a schoolmistress, however, and discovered her true métier in the world of libraries, where a different sort of education evidently captured her heart. Nora spent a decade grounding herself in library practice at the Ontario Legislative Library, then in 1929 obtained formal qualifications from the Pratt Library School in Brooklyn. She was quickly hired to teach a summer course at the library school of McGill University, and then by the University of British Columbia to serve as reference librarian.

Only a year later, in 1930 Nora was attracted to the world of public libraries, which was to become her abiding passion and the channel for most of her adult education work. Dr. Helen Gordon Stewart was implementing a Carnegie-funded project to establish a regional library system in the Fraser River Valley of southern British Columbia. This was to be Canada's first regional library, and Helen Stewart was the woman to do it. Using adult education methods and a community development approach, Dr. Stewart focused on libraries as "the most potent agency amongst all educational institutions" (Morison, 1953, p. 49). Although Nora stayed with this project only briefly, its influence was profound. She and Dr. Stewart corresponded for years, and Nora based much of her later library development work on Stewart's Fraser Valley model (Coughlin, 1966, p. 105).

In 1931, drawn back east, Nora became an instructor in the McGill University Library School. Here her teaching methods were experiential and somewhat unconventional: she worked with her students to improve the American Library of Congress classification system for Canadian historical materials (McGill University Library School, 1932). While this might seem a rather impudent undertaking, Nora was herself completing a master's degree in Canadian History from McGill at the time.

A LIFE IN LIBRARIES AND ADULT EDUCATION

In 1933, a life-changing opportunity arose for Nora. The Carnegie Corporation funded a 3-year project to develop a regional public library system in Prince Edward Island, Canada's smallest province. Nora was selected to direct the project and pounced on the opportunity with enthusiasm and skill. Within two months on the island, she had made numerous presentations to community organizations such as the Women's Institutes, Home and School associations, farmers' groups and cooperatives, exciting the participants about the potential of public libraries. She became known as a popular, animated, and engaging speaker. While promoting library development, she also spread the idea of study clubs inspired by the social change-oriented Antigonish Movement in the nearby province of Nova Scotia. Coughlin (1966) suggests that "largely through Bateson's influence, thirty-five study clubs were formed during the winter of 1933–34" alone (p. 112). Ned Corbett, Director of the Canadian Association for Adult Education, reported that "adult education is finding a place in Prince Edward Island as a natural outcome of the establishment of an adequate library service" (Rogers, 1938, p. 262).

As word of the ambitious Carnegie project spread throughout eastern Canada, libraries became a topic of presentations at adult education gatherings. Nora addressed three of the annual conferences sponsored by the Antigonish Movement and left the participants inspired. Her energy seems to have been boundless. By 1936, Prince Edward Island had a flourishing library system, with 42,000 volumes in 22 rural branch libraries supporting the province's study clubs, schools, and community-based organizations. Today's librarians and adult educators alike will recognize this as a stunning achievement in only 3 years!

Despite this success, provincial politicians were lukewarm in offering financial support for the libraries. This became a deep source of frustration for Nora, and though friendly and popular with the Island's ordinary folk, she tended to clash openly with those in power. Her colleague John Croteau (1951) noted, "Her trouble was that she had no awe of persons in high places; Ministers of the Crown … do not like to hear unflattering descriptions of their intellectual equipment uttered in public meetings" (p. 17).

A positive development during the early 1930s was Nora's growing friendship and collaboration with Father James Tompkins in Nova Scotia. Father Tompkins was an adult educator with a passion for libraries, and Nora, a librarian fervent about adult education. Their dynamic partnership bore fruit in both areas. In their 1936 co-authored pamphlet, *Why Not a Co-operative Library?* they outlined a vision of public libraries' contribution to educational, economic, and cultural development in communities of all sizes. Nora clearly felt that "the public library … could potentially be a centre of adult education in its community" (Bruce, 2010, p. 124). Tompkins' role on the executive of the Canadian Association for Adult Education, and Nora's as Canadian representative with the Extension Division of the American Library Association kept their joint vision prominent in both professional organizations.

In late 1938, Nora Bateson was invited to become the first Director of Libraries for the Province of Nova Scotia. As in Prince Edward Island, her task was to develop a regional library system; unlike her previous assignment, however, this project came with no substantial funding. With only one assistant, but apparently undaunted, Nora was "a gallant figure as she carried her message and sense of urgency from one end of Nova Scotia to the other" (Henson, 1985, p. 5). She met with local government officials, influential figures, unions, and community groups, educating them on the potential of libraries as powerful agents of continuing education, and personal and community development.

Enthusiasm for libraries was building, but just as it seemed a breakthrough was imminent, Canada's entry to World War II realigned government priorities. Nora was seconded to the Canadian Legion Education Service and charged with establishing libraries for the educational and recreational needs of armed service personnel in the Atlantic region. Although no doubt disappointed that the public library work was postponed, Nora took on the new task with customary vigor. She and her assistant Marion Gilroy, later to become a renowned library pioneer in her own right, developed a collection of 25,000 books, which they distributed via dozens of small libraries linked with the training programs of the armed forces (Nova Scotia Regional Library Commission, 1944).

PUBLICATION AND INTERNATIONAL WORK

This wartime period was clearly a frustrating one for Nora, as her correspondence indicates (Bateson, 1942). The constraints of military bureaucracy grated on her impatient spirit, and she focused her energy on publication and work with professional associations. Nora had previously written mainly for library journals; now she turned more directly toward an adult education audience. Her articles in the Canadian Association for Adult Education's journal *Food for Thought* highlighted libraries' role in preparing an active citizenry for the return of peace.

In 1944, an opportunity arose to carry the message of adult education through libraries further abroad. The British Council provided funds for a library plan for Jamaica, a colony advancing toward self-government, and Nora seized the opportunity. In a 10-month period she conducted an island-wide survey of the library situation: wherever she went she also spoke of the achievements of the Antigonish Movement in Canada, with its emphasis on adult education, cooperatives, and credit unions. Her *Library Plan for Jamaica* (1945) noted a "real awakening among the people" that would lead them to a new, self-governing society (p. ii). The adult education role of the library in this emerging nation would be to "meet the living needs of the people concerned: to meet their known interests and to provoke them to new ones" (p. 2). Within this service, "librarians should be real advisors, and they have a unique opportunity of taking part in an informal way in the education of the people" working in "co-operation with other adult education activities" (p. 10). This document, which became known as the "Bateson Plan," served as the foundation for Jamaica's public library service.

LATER CAREER

Having completed her Caribbean assignment, and at the height of her career and reputation, Nora returned to Nova Scotia in March 1945, eager to resume the work sidelined by the war. Public anticipation of an end to hostilities was running high, and libraries were being considered as war memorials. Nora revitalized community interest, drawing on the forward-looking energy she had encountered in Jamaica. Her zeal, combined with a habitual lack of discretion, proved her undoing. Addressing a public meeting, she was reported to have contrasted the "library desert" of Nova Scotia with verdant Jamaica, where people's eagerness to learn made them "too intelligent to swallow election propaganda" (Bateson says, 1945, p. 3). The Premier of the province quickly demanded her resignation; she refused, and was subjected to a humiliating public dismissal. Only a month after her departure, a former colleague, Guy Henson, was appointed Director of Adult Education for Nova Scotia. He was also informally given responsibility for library development—perhaps an eloquent (though ironic) testimony to Nora's success at linking libraries and adult education in the public mind.

Although she left Canada, Nora Bateson's career was far from over; she was still to have an impact on adult learners in both the United States and New Zealand. She was quickly offered a position as head of the Home Reading Department of the Detroit Public Library, where interacting with library patrons on their learning projects was likely a welcome change from navigating political and bureaucratic minefields. Two years later, in 1947, she was invited to New Zealand as an instructor in a new library school. After only a few months, she replaced the outgoing Director of the New Zealand Library School, and in this role helped shape the adult learning curriculum of the emerging institution for 5 years.

In 1953, at the age of 57, Nora retired to the British Isles where she and two sisters shared a small house in Wales until her sudden death 3 years later. Upon her passing, philosopher George Grant described

Nora's "zest in the cause of education," and her spirit as "a shining sword, which never faltered in the faith that it is only the truth which makes men free" (1956, p. 4). Over the next months, stirring memorials appeared in Canadian adult education and library journals alike, as Nora might well have wished.

CONCLUSION

Librarians historically seem to have found difficulty justifying their role as adult educators. Tompkins (1936), for example, suggests that Nora's effort to depict librarians as leaders in adult education might be considered "evidence of an extremely naïve or absurdly overconfident attitude" (p. 867). Yet in addition to responsibilities typically associated with library work in the public mind, Nora Bateson's career exemplified adult education practice. She addressed community groups and gatherings of adult educators, published articles in the professional and popular press, promoted the development of study clubs, developed curriculum, and educated new librarians.

Today, many public libraries are enthusiastically reclaiming and reshaping their identities as community-builders and vital centers of adult learning; perhaps librarians themselves can do more to name and celebrate their own roles as adult educators. Adult education professionals might broaden their view, from a focus on libraries as venues for adult education to librarians as agents. As a first step, recognition is due to the pioneering influence of early librarian adult educators, of whom Nora Bateson is but one bright example.

REFERENCES

Bateson, N. (1942, October 20). [Letter to M. Gill]. Library and Archives Canada (MG 28, Series T-197, File 92-24), Ottawa, Canada.

Bateson, N. (1945). *Library plan for Jamaica*. Kingston, Jamaica: Government Printer.

Bateson says Nova Scotia is a 'literary [sic] desert'. (1945, April 15). *Morning Chronicle* (Halifax, Canada), p. 3.

Bruce, L. D. (2010). *Places to grow: Public libraries and communities in Ontario, 1930–2000*. Guelph, Canada: Author.

Coughlin, V. L. (1966). *Larger units of public library service in Canada: With particular reference to the provinces of Prince Edward Island, Nova Scotia and New Brunswick*. Metuchen, NJ: Scarecrow.

Croteau, J. T. (1951). *Cradled in the waves: The story of a people's co-operative achievement in economic betterment on Prince Edward Island, Canada*. Toronto, Canada: Ryerson.

Grant, G. (1956, January 26). Library pioneer [Letter to the editor]. *Chronicle-Herald* (Halifax, Canada), p. 4.

Henson, G. (1985). Can Tompkins' objectives for the Nova Scotia regional library system be revitalized? A historical review. In G. Henson & K. McRae (Eds.), *Libraries and community development* (pp. 1–11). Halifax, Canada: Dalhousie University Department of Education.

McGill University Library School. (1932). *Library of Congress Classification, British North America - Canada F 1001-1199: Expanded by the 1932 class in advanced classification of the McGill University Library School under the direction of Nora Bateson.* Montreal, Canada: Author.

McNally, P. F. (1996). Canadian library history in English and French to 1964: A survey and evaluation. In P. F. McNally (Ed.), *Readings in Canadian library history 2*, (pp. 3–20). Ottawa, Canada: Canadian Library Association.

Morison, C. K. (1952). Helen Gordon Stewart. In H. Rouillard (Ed.), *Pioneers of adult education in Canada* (pp. 49–54). Toronto, Canada: Thomas Nelson.

Nova Scotia Regional Libraries Commission. (1945). Annual report. In *Annual report of the Superintendent of Education for Nova Scotia for the year ended July 31st, 1944* (pp. 164–169). Halifax, Canada: King's Printer.

Rogers, F. S. (1938). Regional libraries in Prince Edward Island. *Journal of Education (Nova Scotia),4th series,9*(2), 258–263.

Tompkins, J. J., & Bateson, N. (1936). *Why not a co-operative library?* Antigonish, Canada: Extension Department, St. Francis Xavier University.

Tompkins, M. D. (1936). Librarians as leaders in adult education. *Bulletin of the American Library Association, 30*(9), 867–872.

Tout, T. F. (1932). *The collected papers of Thomas Frederick Tout* (Vol. 1). Manchester, UK: University Press.

Nannie Helen Burroughs
(From 1995 Nannie Helen Burroughs School Calendar)

CHAPTER 5

NANNIE HELEN BURROUGHS

Religious Leader, Educator, Activist

Opal Easter-Smith

No Small Lives: Handbook of North American Early Women Adult Educators, 1925-1950,
pp. 55–64
Copyright © 2015 by Information Age Publishing

Nannie Helen Burroughs was a Black woman religious leader, school founder, and an activist for social change. She devoted her entire life to the education and leadership training of Black women and girls. For 61 years (1900–1961) she led, influenced, taught, and mentored millions of Black Baptist women as an officer of the Woman's Convention (WC), Auxiliary to the National Baptist Convention. She was also active in the major political movements for social change and justice that took place during her lifetime.

Burroughs was born in 1879 in Virginia. At an early age, her mother brought her to Washington, DC, so that she could receive a better education in the Negro schools there. Burroughs attended the M Street High School. She studied business and domestic science and was an excellent student. After graduation, Burroughs was unable to find a teaching job in the colored public schools in Washington and eventually went to work in Philadelphia as Associate Editor for *The Christian Banner*, a Baptist newspaper (Fletcher, 1980).

Later she returned to Washington. Although she passed the test, she could not find employment as a civil service clerk because of her race. She worked for a while as a janitress before becoming the bookkeeper and editorial secretary for Rev. L. G. Jordan, Corresponding Secretary to the National Baptist Convention's Foreign Mission Board. She moved to Louisville, Kentucky, when the Board's offices moved there (Fletcher, 1980).

THE WOMEN'S INDUSTRIAL CLUB

It was in Louisville that her first adult education efforts began. Involved in the women's club movement of the day, she established a Women's Industrial Club. Burroughs began to offer evening classes in typing, shorthand, hat-making, domestic science, sewing, and bookkeeping for the group. These business courses were the first to be offered to Negro women in Kentucky. The program was so successful and highly respected that she was able to secure financial help to hire teachers and become the program administrator (Washington, 2006).

THE WOMAN'S CONVENTION, AUXILLARY TO THE NATIONAL BAPTIST CONVENTION

The National Baptist Convention (NBC)[1] was formed in 1895 from three organizations of Black male Baptist ministers. Black Baptist women had their own state conventions and were allowed to attend the men's annual convention. They were able to meet separately and present reports on their activities to the men, but had no voting rights. For some time, they had been requesting their own convention (Brooks, 1984). This would be a separate organization controlled by the women so they could discuss issues important to them, make their own decisions, raise money for the missions, and control their own finances.

Finally in 1900, with support from some of the men and a dynamic speech by Burroughs in which she told the men they were hindering the women from helping to spread God's word, the men approved the establishment of the Woman's Convention, Auxiliary to the National Baptist Convention. Ms. S. Willie Layton was elected president of the WC and Burroughs, corresponding secretary (Brooks, 1984). Burroughs was 21 years old at the time and held the office for 48 years.

The new Convention's motto was "The Work for Christ. Woman arise. He calleth thee." The objectives of the organization were to (a) facilitate the growth and activities of existing women's societies at all levels, (b) organize new societies, (c) disseminate knowledge, (d) raise money for education and missions at home and abroad, and (e) raise up women (Easter, 1995, p. 29). The WC met annually and consisted of pastors' wives and delegates from missionary societies and state organizations.

According to the by-laws, the corresponding secretary duties were to gather and compile the activities from each state organization or society into a report given at each annual convention. She was responsible for the correspondence of the executive committee of the WC and authorized to organize societies (Easter, 1995, p. 30).

Burroughs sent letters to the state organization encouraging them to join the Woman's Convention. In her first year, she reported sending "tracts, cards, report forms, envelopes and coin mailers to hundreds of local women's missionary societies. She traveled 22,125 miles, delivered 215 speeches, organized 12 societies, wrote 9,235 letters and received 4,820 letters" (Easter, 1995, p. 30). The organization that began with 38 members and raised $15 grew. By 1920, the WC represented over a million Black Baptist women. By 1930 they had raised over $884,000 for the missions (Daniel, 1931, p. 113). Children's bands and new missionary and education societies had been organized in the 48 states. Missionaries had been sent to and supported in Africa, Haiti, the West Indies, and South America (Daniel, 1931, p. 112).

Burroughs knew the women of the WC could be moral and social change agents in both their churches and communities. She was passionate about the development of their knowledge and skills to be effective leaders. Seeing that they needed training and information, she wrote "how to" guides for leaders of missionary and young peoples' societies. The guides informed and called for action. They always included something on Negro history and articles on what could and should be done by

the Negro people to improve their lives and situations. There was also a
list of books and other resources to assist the leader. Her guides included

- *How: A Guide to the Missionary Society* (n.d.a)—"This booklet
  included everything one would need to know to organize and sustain a missionary society. The need for, the purpose of, and the
  structure of the society were explained. There was information on
  how to: organize, find talent, begin the first meeting, prepare programs, put everyone to work, renew a society, and resurrect a dead
  one." (Easter, 1995, p. 33)
- *Red Circle Guide for Christian Young People* (n.d.b)—This was a handbook for leaders of Red Circles and Young Women's and Young
  Matrons Leaders/Auxiliaries of the church. The Red Circles served
  junior girls ages 9–13 and senior girls ages 14–16. The Young
  Women's group served unmarried women ages 17–25. The Young
  Matrons served married women up to the age of 35. Like *How*, it
  contained everything one needed to know to establish and sustain
  these organizations. The agenda and activities for each meeting
  from September to May were given. These activities included book
  discussions, personal health issues, opportunities for Christian service in daily life, and Bible study questions. (Easter, 1995, pp.
  33–34)
- *Making Your Community Christian* (1975)—Burroughs believed that a
  church must serve the community in which it is located. She writes,
  "A Christian is responsible for his Community because he is saved
  to save others.... A Christian is as responsible for the actual needs
  of humanity as he is for his own life" (p. 9). This book included
  assessment tools for urban and rural communities, and what
  actions the churches could take to address the spiritual and social
  needs of their communities through the missionary societies' Community Welfare Committees.

In 1934, in cooperation with the Woman's Missionary Union (WMU) of
the Southern Baptist Convention,[2] Burroughs published, *The Worker: A
Missionary and Educational Quarterly.* This magazine was another teaching
tool to provide the leader with everything needed to conduct the weekly
missionary meetings for each quarter. Every issue contained the agenda,
the theme, the devotion, an article for discussion, and an editorial. The
articles were on different aspects of Christian living, and the editorials
were on issues affecting the everyday lives of the Negro people. Burroughs was editor-in-chief of *The Worker* and wrote each editorial from
1934 to 1961, which she completed on her deathbed. The circulation at

the time was 103,000 per quarter (Downey, 1984, pp. 11–12). The magazine is still in publication.[3]

Burroughs also taught through her corresponding secretary reports at the WC's annual convention. In addition to reporting the activities of the missionary societies, she kept them informed of the political issues of the day and suggested ways to improve the organization. She suggested forming an education department to write and distribute literature, and offering early morning classes prior to the start of the convention's official day. The School of Methods began at the 1941 convention with over 500 women in attendance (Easter, 1995, p. 42). These classes became a permanent part of the annual conventions and were attended by both women and men.

Burroughs became the president of the Woman's Convention in 1948 and served until 1961. In her first address as president, she stressed that "the supreme purpose of the Convention was to raise women. Without women of vision, devotion and unselfish interest this organization ... will be ineffective in national service" (Burroughs, 1949, p.13).

THE NATIONAL TRAINING SCHOOL FOR WOMEN AND GIRLS

Beginning in 1901, Burroughs began to urge the WC to establish a school for women and girls. The school was to train women to be Sunday School teachers, missionaries for work at home and abroad, and women to give better domestic service[4] and to be better homemakers (Wilson, n.d.). Burroughs explained,

> Our purpose is to send girls out with skills in their hands, common sense in their heads, and with the ambition and spirit to go to work and render efficient service in their homes and communities ... to lift as they climb. (Washington, 2006, p. 68)[5]

The National Training School for Women and Girls[6] opened in 1909 with Burroughs as president, a position she held when she died. It was the first school established by a national organization of Black women, for Black women and girls, and paid for with donations primarily from the Black community. It was open to women and girls, of any income level, with good moral character and in good health. The School offered a strong academic curriculum and also trades. Every student had to take Black history, public speaking, and at least one trade course so they had an employable skill upon graduation. The first class consisted of seven students from three states and included two from South Africa (Daniel, 1931, pp. 115–116).

By 1926, the School's enrollment was 102 students from 23 states, the District of Columbia, Liberia, and Puerto Rico. It had a seventh- and eighth-grade division, a 4-year high school, a 2-year normal school, and a 2-year junior college. Trade courses included waitressing, dressmaking, beauty culture, home nursing and public health, school dining room management, interior decorating, printing, and those needed to be professional domestic servants (Easter, 1995, pp. 65–66).

Burroughs' papers at the Library of Congress contain articles from Black newspapers throughout the country praising the quality of the school's graduates. They were exceptional workers and many were successful entrepreneurs. The school also "educated more African and other foreign girls for mission service than any other Negro school in America. Thirty-four non-American young women trained as missionaries at the school between 1909 and 1956" (Easter, 1995, pp. 61–62).

Summer Institutes

Burroughs philosophy was that "you could not teach unless you knew and you could not know unless you studied" (Easter, 1995, p. 32), so she held a 3-week Summer Institute program at the school beginning in 1934. It provided training to Sunday School teachers, State Convention officers, missionary society members and officers, and other women interested in church leadership (Easter, 1995, p. 73). Women of all denominations came from across the country. Course topics included the Bible, building Christian communities, pageantry, parliamentary procedures, public speaking, church music, and youth programs (Easter, 1995, p. 74). The Summer Institutes were offered each year until 1985.

The School Today

In 1964, the school became an elementary school for Black children and was renamed the *Nannie Helen Burroughs School*. Its mission is to "provide high quality education to children in a Christian environment and foster high academic achievement" (D. Robinson, personal communication, February 12, 1992). In 1991, the School was declared a Historical Landmark by the District of Colombia and the street named after Burroughs. The school is still in operation.

ACTIVIST FOR SOCIAL CHANGE

Burroughs said, "Education and justice are democracy's only life insurance. There is no substitute for learning ... it is the investment of our hopes and dreams for the generations that are to come" (Johnson, 2000, p.65).

Burroughs used her secretary reports, her presidential addresses, and various speakers to keep the women abreast of the social and political issues affecting the Negro race. These efforts were to move the women to fight the economic, social, and political conditions that oppressed the Negro people. She said, "It is no evidence of Christianity to have people mock you and spit on you and defeat the future of your children. It is a mark of cowardice" (Easter, 1995, p. 107). She urged the women to support the vote for women. Her message "calling for an anti-lynching law and for the repeal of the separate [railroad] coach law" led both the WC and NBC "to send it to President Hoover, the U.S. Congress, and to the governors of the states" (Easter, 1995, p. 41).

Burroughs worked closely with the Woman's Missionary Union to help build up Negro missionary societies and to end racial discrimination in the South. She was an active member and officer of the National Association of Colored Women (NACW) (Easter, 1995, p. 100), the Washington, DC branch of the National Association for the Advancement of Colored People (Easter, 1995, p. 107), and the National Urban League (Salem, 1990, p. 195). She was the link between these organizations and the WC and encouraged the women to become members. She spoke at their gatherings and invited speakers from these organizations to address the WC. These organizations worked cooperatively on many initiatives for the betterment of the Negro people (Easter, 1995, p. 100). Each organization has an active education committee.

In 1920, Burroughs and Mary Talbert, NACW president, along with community activist Lugenia Hope and educators Mary McLeod Bethune, Mary Church Terrell, Charlotte Hawkins Brown, and Margaret Murray Washington (the wife of Booker T.) formed the International Council of Women of the Darker Races of the World (ICWDR). Per Article II of its constitution, the purpose of the organization was

> The dissemination of knowledge of peoples of color the world over in order that there may be a larger appreciation of their history and accomplishments and so that they themselves may have a greater degree of respect for their own accomplishments and a greater pride in themselves. (ICWDR, n.d.)

This was done through study programs for adults and children in the United States and abroad.

Concerned about the needs of working women, Burroughs suggested to the NACW that a conference be held to discuss their problems. In 1922, the National Association of Wage Earners was formed. Its purposes were the development of efficient workers and to provide a forum for the discussion of issues of just wages, working conditions, grievance resolution, legislation to protect working women, and better living conditions. Burroughs was the President; Bethune was Vice President; banker Maggie L. Walker was Treasurer; and Talbert was the Chair of the Advisory Board (Easter, 1995, p. 102).

A lifelong Republican, Burroughs along with Terrell, Walker, Brown, and journalist Ida Wells Barnett formed the National League of Republican Colored Women. They set about educating the electorate about the selection of Black leadership, pending legislation and political matters affecting Republican women and the Negro people (Easter, 1995, p. 106).

IMPACT

Burroughs was a remarkable woman of deep faith and trust in God. She had a deep sense of God's call on her life to equip women to serve God and to lift themselves, their families, communities and, by extension, the Negro race and society as a whole. This call permeated her life and everything that she did for 61 years from 1900 until the day she died in May of 1961.

She was described as a woman "far above the average in quick intelligent thinking. She was courageous, charming, and dynamic to the point that she was irresistible to the open minded and contemptible to the jealous and prejudiced" (Harrison, 1956, p. 10). William Pickens, NAACP field secretary, said,

> No other person in America has so large a hold on the loyalty and esteem of the Colored masses as Nannie H. Burroughs. She is regarded all over the broad land as a combination of brains, courage, and incorruptibleness.... We know of no woman of any race in Washington whose unsupported individual influence can move as many people in this country as can that of Miss Burroughs. She is naturally sought in aid of every cause of colored people. (Washington, 2006, p. 83–85)

Her 61 years of service to the Woman's Convention and her publications continue to contribute to the leadership training of Black women, men, youth, and children to this day. Many of her publications are as relevant today as they were when first published. The Woman's Day program she established to raise leadership and public speaking skills in the missionary society women is celebrated yearly in most Christian denominations. Burroughs is still written about by scholars studying different aspects of women in the Black Church.

NOTES

1. By 1928, the National Baptist Convention represented 22,000 churches, 19,800 preachers, and a total membership of over 3 million. It is still the largest organization of Black Baptist ministers in the country.
2. The WMU was an organization of White Baptist women.
3. *The Worker* is now published by the Progressive National Baptist Convention, www.pnbcinc.com/aboutus/theworker.htm
4. The majority of jobs for Black women were as domestic servants and in agriculture.
5. Quotes from the Story of Nannie Helen Burroughs by S. Washington, 2006, Birmingham, AL: Copyright (2006) by Woman's Missionary Union, SBC. Reprinted with permission.
6. The name changed to the National Trade and Professional School for Women and Girls in 1934.

REFERENCES

Brooks, E. (1984). *The women's movement in the black Baptist church 1880–1920.* (Doctoral dissertation). Retrieved from UMI Dissertation Services.

Burroughs, N.H. (n.d.a). *How: A guide to the missionary society.* Burroughs Papers, Library of Congress.

Burroughs, N.H. (n.d.b). *Red circle guide for Christian young people.* Burroughs Papers, Library of Congress.

Burroughs, N. H. (1949, September 8) *The first message of Miss Nannie Helen Burroughs to the woman's convention.* Los Angeles, CA.

Burroughs, N. H. (1975). *Making your community Christian* (6th ed.). Washington, DC: Nannie Helen Burroughs Publications.

Daniel, S. I. (1931). *Women builders.* Washington, DC: Associated.

Downey, A. R. (1984). Dr. Nannie Helen Burroughs 1905–1961 or a span of life of over 56 years. *The Worker, 54*(196), 11–12.

Easter, O. V. (1995). *Nannie Helen Burroughs.* New York: Garland Publishing, Inc.

Fletcher, J. (1980). Burroughs, Nannie Helen. In Barbara Sickerman (Ed.), *Notable American women: The modern period* (pp. 125–127). Cambridge, MA: Belknap Press of Harvard University Press.

Harrison, D. E. (1956). *The dream and the dreamer.* Washington, DC: Nannie H. Burroughs Literature Foundation.

International Council of Women of the Darker Races (ICWDR). (n.d.). *International Council of Women of the Darker Races of the World.* Burroughs Papers, Library of Congress.

Johnson, K. A. (2000). *Uplifting the women and the race.* New York, NY: Garland.

Salem, D. (1990). *To better our world: Black women in organized reform, 1890–1920.* New York, NY: Carlson.

Washington, S. (2006). *The story of Nannie Helen Burroughs.* Birmingham, AL: Woman's Missionary Union, SBC.

Wilson. E. A. (n.d.). *History of the Woman's Convention 1900–1955*. Burroughs Papers, Library of Congress.

CHAPTER 6

MAESTRA MARAVILLOSA

Fabiola Cabeza de Baca Gilbert

Rosalie C. Otero

The mediocre teacher tells. The good teacher explains. The superior teacher demonstrates. The great teacher inspires.

—William Arthur Ward (n.d.)

Fabiola Cabeza de Baca (Gilbert) told, explained, demonstrated, and inspired individuals during her long career as an educator and author. Not many women could lose a leg at the age of 38 and continue to work enthusiastically to educate New Mexico's rural poor on methods of preparing nourishing and delicious food. Fabiola Cabeza de Baca Gilbert was that remarkable home economist and educator who traveled the expanse of her native New Mexico demonstrating innovative cooking techniques and teaching women how to improve various domestic tasks such as sewing and refurbishing furniture. She was an exceptionally popular, well-respected extension agent.

FABIOLA'S EARLY LIFE

Fabiola represented a small but growing group of Hispanic women who attained education and launched careers. She was born on May 16, 1894,

No Small Lives: Handbook of North American Early Women Adult Educators, 1925-1950, pp. 65–71

into a prominent Hispanic ranching family of the *rico* (rich) class at La
Liendre, New Mexico Territory. One of four children, she was raised by
her paternal grandmother Estefanita Delgado Cabeza de Baca and her
father Graciano Cabeza de Baca, after her mother died in 1898. Estefanita served as a role model for her granddaughter because, as a wife of a
patrón, Estefanita held an important place in the community. She taught
her granddaughters to sew, embroider, and cook (Cabeza de Baca Gilbert,
1954, p. 60).

When the children were old enough to go to school, the family moved
to Las Vegas, New Mexico where the girls attended the Loretto Academy.
In her memoir, *We Fed Them Cactus* (1954), Fabiola describes how she
refused to take on the expected role of a Spanish lady and spent summers
at the family ranch riding horses and tending the fields and animals.
After some disagreement, Fabiola left the Loretto Academy and completed her education at a public high school run by New Mexico Normal
(later Highlands University). In 1906, at the age of 12, she spent a year in
Spain studying language and history. She graduated in 1912 with a teaching certificate. At the age of 16, Fabiola began her teaching career in a
one-room school house 6 miles from her father's ranch. She describes the
joys and struggles of teaching in a country school in *We Fed Them Cactus*.

EARLY WORK AND PERSONAL CHALLENGES

In 1921, she earned a BA degree from New Mexico Normal and a second
degree in 1927 in home economics from New Mexico State University.
Fabiola then embarked on a 30-year career as an extension agent during
the Great Depression and into the late 1950s. She was the first Spanish-
speaking agricultural extension agent, which was an important asset for
the New Mexico Extension Service since 60% of the state's population was
Hispanic (Sullivan, 1991).

In 1931, Fabiola and Carlos Gilbert, a divorced man, eloped to Mexico
despite her family's objections. He was an insurance agent and activist in
the League of United Latin American Citizens (LULAC). The couple
divorced after 10 years. It was likely that because of Gilbert's position
within LULAC, Fabiola became involved in the early Hispanic civil rights
movement. In the late 1930s and early 1940s, an increasing number of
women's clubs endorsed the Equal Rights Amendment. Fabiola became a
leader for the national organization and served as president of the Santa
Fe Ladies Council of a local chapter for the group. In 1939, she became
the director of junior LULACs for the New Mexico region (Sullivan,
1991). Throughout her life, Fabiola participated in community organizations. She was a member of the New Mexico Museum Board, the Red

Cross, the Girls Scouts, the Santa Fe Opera Guild, and La Sociedad Folklórica de Santa Fe, a group devoted to the preservation of the Spanish language and Hispanic culture.

In 1932, a train hit her automobile, injuring one of her legs, which was eventually amputated. Except for the 2 years of hospitalization and recuperation, Fabiola strapped on her wooden leg, donned her apron, and continued her work traversing the northern part of the state training the Hispanic, Anglo, and Indian women of the county. Even during the 2 years of convalescence, she continued her work by writing extension articles on canning and food preparation.

PIONEER EXTENSION WORKER

Although agricultural extension goes back to the early years of this country, the Smith-Lever Act of 1914 formalized extension by establishing partnerships between the land-grant agricultural colleges and the U.S. Department of Agriculture (USDA). Agricultural agents taught farmers more efficient crop and livestock practices, and they taught farmer's wives lessons in food preservation and preparation (USDA, 2011).

Fabiola began her work as an extension field agent in Rio Arriba and Santa Fe Counties. Her work took her to farms and homesteads that were many miles apart, keeping her continually on the road. She wrote in the *Journal of Home Economics* in 1942 that the extension service first reached Hispanic women in rural areas of New Mexico in 1929 and that the first Spanish bulletins on canning were issued in 1930. Until then, she pointed out, Hispanic women used traditional drying methods (Cabeza de Baca, 1942).

Fabiola was appointed as the first agent assigned to Pueblo people and worked in Taos, San Ildefonso, and Pojoaque Pueblos. Later she was promoted to agent-at-large for Los Alamos, Sandoval, and Santa Fe counties. Fabiola gave demonstrations in women's homes and eventually began to organize women into extension clubs. She was especially successful in organizing Rio Arriba women, who had little experience with formal community organizing. She wrote in one report, "Outside of dances, Church festivals, and weddings, they never get together for social activities" (Jensen, 1985, p. 250). Fabiola's position included helping families obtain necessary equipment such as tin can sealers, jars, and sewing machines, as well as teaching women how to use the equipment properly. She also procured other useful materials such as patterns for clothing and household items. The pressure cooker was the most useful and desired item. Not only could it be used to make meals more quickly, preserving flavor and nutrients, but it could be used for pressure canning. Often individual families could not afford a pressure cooker, so several households pooled their few resources and purchased a "communal" pressure cooker.

During the Great Depression, Fabiola taught rural women how to can surplus foods, how to plant vegetable gardens, and how to sew—skills that helped many farm families survive the years of economic depression and drought. She trained women to use herbs and spices to *guisar* or season food for more flavorful meals.

> *Guisar*, which has no exact English equivalent, is the most popular word in the native homemaker's vocabulary. Roughly translated, it means to dress up food, perhaps only by adding a little onion or a pinch of oregano; good food always deserves a finishing touch. (Cabeza de Baca Gilbert, 1970, p. 1)

From her work in the Taos and Española valleys, she became well informed of the indigenous pueblo cultures of northern New Mexico. She often translated government bulletins into Spanish, Tiwa, and Tewa languages. In addition to bringing rural families new home-management techniques, Fabiola also valued the traditional ways. She helped people combine tradition with new modern information to better their lives. "By 1938 she had helped organize thirteen adult clubs, and it is estimated that she was reaching eighty percent of farm families" (Jensen, 1982, p. 178).

During World War II, Fabiola continued to work with farmers and their families, along with 4-H club members, to secure the production increases essential to the war effort. As a community organizer, she helped found many associations and clubs for women and children and organized food canteens for working mothers. Fabiola also helped plant Victory Gardens by providing seeds, fertilizer, and simple planting tools for the gardeners.

In homes and community centers, Fabiola taught new home industries. "For those she could not reach directly, with group demonstrations or individual home visits, she provided a 'Ciencia Domestica' column in the weekly newspaper *El Nuevo Mexicano* and bulletins in Spanish" (Jensen, 1982, p. 179). She is probably the first American-trained nutritionist to combine progressive scientific principles with cultural values and traditions implicit in a regional ethnic cuisine. Her ethnicity, coupled with her reverence for the traditional ways, contributed to her success as an extension agent.

In 1951, Fabiola's success as an extension agent led her to establish home-economics programs in Mexico through the United Nations Educational, Scientific, and Cultural Organization (UNESCO). She developed food preservation and cooking techniques among the Tarascan Indians in the Mexican state of Michoacán. Some of the food-processing and fish-drying techniques she introduced in the Lake Pátzcuaro region are still in use today. Fabiola established 18 training centers throughout northern Mexico and instructed agents from other Latin American countries in her techniques as well (Rudnick, 2012; Sullivan, 1991).

Fabiola won many awards for outstanding achievement in her field, including a National Home Demonstration Agents Association Distinguished Award for Meritorious Service and a U.S. Department of Agriculture Superior Service Award. She was also honored in 1976 by the American Association of University Women with the inclusion of her works in the New Mexico Bicentennial Exhibit featuring the role of women in New Mexico history (Sullivan, 1991).

FABIOLA'S PUBLICATIONS

Fabiola believed that next to hands-on, personal instruction, writing was one of the most effective forms of social action and education. During the 1930s, she began to compile copious notes about village traditions. She collected recipes, folklore, herbal remedies, religious rituals, and planting practices. She sent these recipes and articles to *The Santa Fe Scene* and the *New Mexican* Santa Fe newspapers. She also hosted a bilingual weekly radio program on KVSF (Rudnick, 2012). Literacy not only enhanced Fabiola's ability to act upon her world, it made her an example of independence and scholarship. Her ability to blend the genres of personal memoir and social history with New Mexican cuisine was unique and effective.

Los Alimentos y su Preparación, published in 1934, and *Boletín de Conservar*, published in 1935, provided a more progressive discourse. Fabiola introduced *Los Alimentos* instructional manual with an assertion that is half apologetic, half imperative: "*Cada día hay una nueva invención y nuevos descrubimientos de la ciéncia y todos estamos listos para adoptarlas*" [Every day there is a new invention and new scientific discoveries, and we should be ready to adopt them] (Jensen, 1982, p. 175). Both of these circulars provided detailed instructions for home food preservation. Fabiola encouraged a change from some of the provincial methods to modern American ways.

A cultural and historical artifact, credited with the popularization of New Mexican cuisine, *Historic Cookery* (1970) first appeared in 1931, was repeatedly reprinted, and has sold more than 100,000 copies (Rudnick, 2012). From her fieldnotes and observations in Hispanic, Indian, and Anglo-American kitchens across New Mexico, Fabiola developed the first definitive collection of authentic New Mexican recipes. She invites her readers to try the recipes and "think of New Mexico's golden days, of red chili drying in the sun, of clean-swept yards, outdoor ovens, and adobe houses ... because good food and good cheer are natural *compadres*" (Cabeza de Baca Gilbert, 1970, p. 1).

Fabiola also published two other books. *The Good Life: New Mexico Traditions and Foods* published in 1949 focused on the Turrieta family. In this book, Fabiola brings to life the folklore and folkways of a traditional, yet contemporary, northern New Mexico village by fictionalizing the biography of a local family. The cycles of seasons and fiestas reveal the cultural wealth in a village. Fabiola centers the story in the kitchen by lavishing details on the cultural context and folklore associated with the recipes included in the book, such as frijoles, tamales, and chile rellenos.

Fabiola will probably be best remembered for her classic folk history of the Llano Estacado of eastern New Mexico, *We Fed Them Cactus*, published in 1954. In this book, Fabiola preserved the unique expressions of Hispanic culture by chronicling her Hispanic family in its historical and domestic context. As a participant and observer, she blends her own memories with family history, interviews, and archival materials into a captivating synthesis of autobiography, folklore, and history.

After her retirement in 1959 Fabiola continued to deliver lectures and serve as a trainer and consultant for the Peace Corps. She died in Albuquerque on October 14, 1991, at the age of 97 (Sullivan, 1991, p. 3).

A LIFETIME OF HELPING OTHERS

Hard work, resourcefulness, and a ferocious independence characterized Fabiola. New Mexico farmers, housewives, laborers, and communities benefited from Fabiola's expertise and experience. She was a successful extension agent because she was a strong motivator and a patient teacher, willing to traverse the state countless times in order to promulgate innovative skills. Fabiola was equally well liked and respected by poor rural homesteaders, small village folk, as well as by the elite of places like Santa Fe. People called her *comadre* and welcomed her visits with warmth and hospitality. She mediated judiciously between the federal government's desire to force modern ways of cooking and eating on rural Hispanos and Pueblo people. She introduced new methods of canning and cooking, but she preserved the old ways that complemented the cultural desires and the nutritional needs of the people. Besides her tireless work with individual families and community groups, her pioneer documentation of New Mexico cuisine and the cultural context of which it is a part have played an important role in adult education.

REFERENCES

Cabeza de Baca, F. (1934). *Los alimentos y su preparación.* Circular No. 129. State College of New Mexico: New Mexico Agricultural Extension Service. (NMSUES). Retrieved from http://www.csrees.usda.gov/qlinks/extension.html

Cabeza de Baca, F. (1935). *Boletín de conservar.* Circular No. 133. NMSUES. Retrieved from www.csrees.usda.gov/qlinks/extension.html

Cabeza de Baca, F. (1942). New Mexican diets. *Journal of Home Economics, 34,* 668.

Cabeza de Baca Gilbert, F. (1949). *The good life.* Santa Fe, NM: San Vicente Foundation.

Cabeza de Baca Gilbert, F. (1954). *We fed them cactus.* Albuquerque: University of New Mexico Press.

Cabeza de Baca Gilbert, F. (1970). *Historic cookery.* Santa Fe, NM: Ancient City

Jensen, J. M. (1982). Canning comes to New Mexico: Women and the Agricultural Extension Service 1914–1919. *New Mexico Historical Review, 57*(4), 1–26.

Jensen, J. M. (1985). "I've worked, I'm not afraid of work": Farm women in New Mexico 1930–1940. In J. M. Jensen & D. A. Miller (Eds.), *New Mexico women: Intercultural perspectives* (pp. 227–255). Albuquerque: University of New Mexico Press.

Rudnick, L. (2012). La fabulosa Fabiola: First lady of New Mexico cuisine. *El Palacio, 117*(4), 72–75.

Sullivan, M. A. (1991). *Cabeza de Baca, Fabiola.* New Mexico Office of the

State Historian, Santa Fe, New Mexico. Retrieved December 2012, from http newmexicohistory.org/filedatais.php?fildID=547

United States Department of Agriculture (USDA). (2011). *About us.* Retrieved from http://www.csrees.usda.gov/qlinks/extension.html

Ward, W. A. (n.d.). *BrainyQuote.com.* Retrieved January 2, 2014, from http://www.brainyquote.com/quotes/quotes/w/williamart103463.html

Olive Dame Campbell
(Photo courtesy of the John C Campbell Folk School Fain Archives)

CHAPTER 7

OLIVE DAME CAMPBELL

An Appalachian Social Activist
and Adult Educator

Carol E. Kasworm

No Small Lives: Handbook of North American Early Women Adult Educators, 1925-1950,
pp. 73–79
Copyright © 2015 by Information Age Publishing

Notable for her many contributions in adult education and community development, Olive Dame Campbell, "was one of the leading women social reformers of the period and part of the Progressive movement in America" (McCutchen Williams, 2012, p. 120). This profile will provide background of the life of Olive Dame Campbell with a particular focus on the development of the John C. Campbell Folk School, her related earlier travels throughout Appalachia and the folk schools of Scandinavia, and her leadership in community development through mountain crafts.

COMING TO KNOW THE PEOPLE, THEIR STRENGTHS, AND THEIR STRUGGLES

As context to her eventual contributions to adult education and the Appalachian region's sociocultural development, there were three key experiences that appear to form and focus her interests: her marriage to John C. Campbell, an educator committed also to progressive education and community development; her relocation to the Appalachian region and her significant engagement in the improvement of its people, traditions, and culture; and her fascination and collection of English folk ballads, aligned with her advocacy for mountain crafts. Olive Arnold Dame was born in Massachusetts in 1882, graduated from Tufts College in 1903, and taught in the public schools. Her interest in adventure led her to travel with her sister to the British Isles in 1906, meeting an older gentleman, John Campbell, on the voyage, and eventually to marriage approximately one year later. Prior to these travels in Scotland, John C. Campbell had been president at Piedmont College in Georgia, spending a decade in the southern highlands of Appalachia, to both gain greater understanding of the culture and provide future improvement to this region (McCutchen Williams, 2012; Whisnant, 1983).

Upon their return and marriage, John sought out sponsorship of a newly formed Russell Sage Foundation to conduct a study of the conditions in the Appalachian region. As context, during the time of this study and eventual development of the John C. Campbell Folk School, this region of the United States was deeply impoverished and declining. As noted by Eller (1982),

> In 1929, Olive Dame Campbell reported that the average income of the small farmers in western North Carolina was between $85 and $90 per year.... By 1936, over 47 percent of all mountain families were on federal relief rolls. A gutted economy, an impoverished population, and a growing dependence on federal relief programs increasingly characterized mountain life. (pp. 238–240)

Beginning in 1908, this couple spent more than 10 years traveling over 1,500 miles and visited over 70 schools—independent, church, and public schools. They "collect[ed] data about rural life, health conditions, educational issues, and denominational friction" (McCutchen Williams, 2012, p. 8). Specifically, they desired to identify the "best methods" for creating collaboration and cooperation among the various agencies now working in the mountains (Whisnant, 1983, p. 107).

During the period of 1908–1918, Olive bore two children, both of whom died. And with the untimely death of her husband, John, in 1919, Olive focused on many unfinished projects started by John. In particular, she wrote most of the final report of their studies, *The Southern Highlander and His Home*, published in 1921 by Russell Sage Foundation (J. C. Campbell, 1969, 2003; Smith & Wilson, 1999), naming husband John C. Campbell as author in honor of his leadership and contributions.

During this period of their travels through southern Appalachia, Olive was also drawn to "all things native and fine," exemplifying the handicrafts she saw and the ballads she heard (Smith & Wilson, 1999, p. 255). While conducting the Sage study, she also began a collection of English and Scottish ballads from these mountaineers. (The 2000 film *Songcatcher* was loosely based upon her work as a musicologist.) Eventually with collaboration from Cecil Sharp, she published what would be known as the "best scientific ballad collection of English Folks Songs" (O. D. Campbell & Sharp, 1917, p. 105; Whisnant, 1983). Beyond the documentation of these ballads, Olive strongly valued maintaining the tradition of mountain ballads, with many of the folk schools and settlement schools using music as a start to their daily educational activities.

During their study travels, Olive met with Tennessean Philander P. Claxton, executive secretary of the Conference for Southern Education (and later to become US Commissioner of Education). Along with her husband, John C. Campbell's interests, Claxton also suggested they consider exploring Scandinavian folk schools, focused upon establishing "the grown-up schools of Denmark and Sweden" (Whisnant, 1983, pp. 127–128). Subsequently, Olive received an American-Scandinavian Foundation fellowship to study *Folkehöjskole*, Scandinavian folk schools. Campbell maintained journals of her trip and eventually wrote a book regarding the variety of activities, based upon the principles of Danish folk schools. This study would provide her foundational perspectives for the co-founding and directing of the John C. Campbell Folk School in Brasstown, North Carolina (McNelley, 1966; Whisnant, 1983).

As a social activist and adult educator in her later years, she also guided the early work of the Conference of Southern Mountain Workers. These efforts included the development of various Scandinavian folk school efforts focused on various agricultural and handicraft cooperatives, inspired by her previous study of the Scandinavian folk school efforts focused on craft skills and which would contribute to the social and economic reconstruction in western North Carolina, similar to its impact on Denmark (Whisnant, 1983). Lastly, she was known as one of the founders of the Southern Highland Handicraft Guild in the 1920s, which was the formal establishment of a guild that both preserved the traditions of the mountain handicrafts, while functioning as a major change agent toward entrepreneurial business development of the Appalachian crafts industry (Eaton, 1973, p. 163; Whisnant, 1983).

Olive retired in 1946. Noting that she did not wish to get in the way of a new director, she returned to Massachusetts, dying on June 14, 1954, in her 72nd year (Smith & Wilson, 1999).

JOHN C. CAMPBELL FOLK SCHOOL—
AN INNOVATIVE ADULT EDUCATION INSTITUTION

After John's death, Olive and her friend and colleague, Marguerite Bidstrup Butler of the Pine Mountain Settlement School, explored Denmark and other Scandinavian countries. They spent 14 months investigating the folk school movement, noting the value of these schools focused on rural living skills and community-oriented development (McCutchen Williams, 2012). Her experiences were brought together into a book, *The Danish Folk School: Its Influence in the Life of Denmark and the North*, focused upon serving not only the targeted region but also, "the great field of rural education, adult education especially" (O. D. Campbell, 1928, p. viii). In particular, she was taken by the focus of the folk school and Gruntvig's philosophy, noting in her book that the folk school was

> a meeting place away from the pressure of the necessary and commonplace, and where youth, stirred by an inner impulse, could assemble and catch a glimpse of what life may mean.... It was absolutely necessary to break away from the book standard of education if the deeper importance of human development were to be made clear. (O. D. Campbell, 1928, p. 61)

Through the work of many individuals, the John C. Campbell folk school was based upon pledge cards with promises regarding donations of land, money, and labor. These pledge cards were solicited and received by Fred Scroggs, a local storekeeper and Marguerite Bidstrup Butler, with the addition of funding coming from surrounding churches and the Carnegie Corporation. In 1925, Olive and Marguerite established the John C. Campbell Folk School in Brasstown, North Carolina, finally "fulfilling one of their dreams—a school to teach adults how to preserve their native heritage and to function and even prosper at the same time"

(McCutchen Williams, 2012, p. 11). But it was also grounded in the practical. "Here in Brasstown the teaching lay in the practical work itself in a seldom out-spoken, but very clear goal setting: from goal to goal, from ditch to field, from poor earth to rich" (McNelley, 1966, pp. 2–3).

During her 40 years as researcher, progressive adult educator, and community organizer, Olive shared her wealth of experience. In particular, as an administrator and teacher at John C. Campbell Folk School, she had a "love of the folk ways and dances, and has steadfastly maintained her confidence and respect for the stalwart characters of the people of Appalachian" (McNelley, 1966, p. 49). She believed in the individual and in the individual's power to grow, once stimulated and given opportunity.

> The young person left her class with a new vision of his own area and a broader conception of the part he may play in its growth.... It may well be said that "Where ever Olive Campbell touched life she enriched it." (McNelley, 1966, p. 47)

Also she had her hand and eye on regional improvement. As noted in her biography, "She was esteemed for her wise and practical approach to sometimes controversial social and educational issues" (McCutchen Williams, 2012, p. 13).

With its beginnings in 1925, the John C. Campbell Folk School was initially focused upon youth (viewed as adults, because they were out of high school, most without a high school education) and was focused upon daytime activities that included various groups within the community. From the 1930s to the 1960s, the John C. Campbell Folk School concentrated its program on farming skills, crafts, and recreation. The folk school never gave grades or diplomas, but functioned as a social settlement center, perceiving needs and establishing programs in response. To address concerns within the community, the school established a credit union, a creamery, a farmers' cooperative, a club for homemakers, and an organization for craftsmen, musical dances, lectures, and other recreational programs, which provided the school and its surrounding community with leisure activities (Alvic, 2003). In January 1950, the School focused upon returning veterans.

> Today, the veterans who are, and will be major factors in the development of the region, are one of our greatest challenges. A group of sixty ... are enrolled in the school through the cooperation of the Veterans Administration, and there is a long waiting list. (McNelley, 1966, p. 18)

In 1958, the school started a program of literacy teaching and subsequently moved to a first-time offering a craft-vacation course in August with creative classes in the mornings, after-noons free for relaxation, and some group activities at night ... In addition to the courses in creative recreation and crafts, the Folk School conducts a "little Folks School" for the neighborhood children; it also takes a very active part in the Craftsman's Fair, which is sponsored by the Southern Highland Handicraft Guild. (McNelley, 1966, pp. 18–19)

This focus on crafts and particularly mountain crafts became the more dominant mission of the School:

Crafts had a prominent place in the school, viewed both as a way to supple-ment farm income and as a leisure pursuit.... As the crafts program grew in importance, the school's cooperative social activities became absorbed into the local economy of the nearby town of Murphy, North Carolina. The J. C. Campbell Folk School redirected its mission toward teaching adults, while still preserving some of the adapted Danish folk school ideas. (Alvic, 2003, p. 121)

In this current era, the John C. Campbell Folk School has gained the distinction as a special residential adult education facility for both the production and teaching of craft skills, and was named as a Historic Dis-trict with the National Register of Historic Places on August 22, 1983. As of 2001, the John C. Campbell Folk School offered

crafts classes and a few other specialty courses to students from all over the country. The students live on campus in a variety of buildings and dine together in a central facility [Olive Dame Campbell dining hall]. A changing faculty of over 350 experts teaches over 450 single-week sessions through-out the year. Most of the teachers come from outside the mountains, although some live in the area.... The school also still provides recreation to the local community in the form of music, dance, and an annual craft festi-val. (Alvic, 2003, p. 121)

As of 2013, the School offers 860 classes in 47 subject areas, to include blacksmithing, ceramics, weaving, woodcarving, woodworking on a lathe, furniture construction, book arts, painting, garden art, gardening, land-scaping, cooking, masonry, storytelling, writing, singing, and others. With its motto, "Singing Behind the Plow," it continues to sponsor a Friday night music concert series and every other Saturday community dances. The School's current website is https://folkschool.org/index.php

REGIONAL DEVELOPMENT THROUGH MOUNTAIN CRAFTS—
SOUTHERN HIGHLANDS HANDICRAFT GUILD

As part of her effort to bring about further community development, as well as enhancement of the lives and financial well-being of the region,

Olive Dame Campbell also espoused the idea of a cooperative for mountain crafts, eventually leading to the organization of the Southern Highland Handicraft Guild. The idea of a cooperative organization for mountain crafts was inspired during her and Marguerite's visit to a Finnish folk school and cooperative crafts shop (McNelley, 1966). In his authoritative work, *Handicrafts of the Southern Highlands* (1973), Eaton drew attention to Olive's part in the promotion of crafts, as did Philis Alvic in the more recent *Weavers of the Southern Highlands* (2003). In particular, Alvic championed Olive's work with the Conference of Southern Mountain Workers and stated that many of the "most progressive ideas concerning crafts development can be traced back to her" (Alvic, 2003, p. 19; Eaton, 1973).

Olive Dame Campbell was a remarkable woman adult educator, a "songcatcher," a supporter of regional cultural activities of both song and craft, and an organizer for adults to seek out a better life through their talents in mountain crafts and in Appalachian traditions. Although she is sometimes judged to have done little to improve social or economic conditions for the mountaineers (Whisnant, 1983), others believe that Olive Campbell made a substantial contribution to the betterment of mountain lives (McCutchen Williams, 2012). Her contributions continue through the vibrant learning environment of the John C. Campbell Folk School.

REFERENCES

Alvic, P. (2003). *Weavers of the Southern Highlands.* Lexington: University Press of Kentucky.

Campbell, J. C. (1969, 2003). *The Southern Highlander and his homeland.* Lexington: University Press of Kentucky. (Original work published 1921)

Campbell, O. D. (1928). *The Danish folk school: Its influence in the life of Denmark and the north.* New York, NY: Macmillan.

Campbell, O. D., & Sharp, C. J. (1917). *English folk songs from the Southern Appalachians, comprising 122 songs and ballads, and 323 tunes.* New York, NY: Putnam.

Eaton, A. H. (1973). *Handicrafts of the Southern Highlands.* New York, NY: Dover. (Original work published 1937)

Eller, R. D. (1982). *Miners, millhands, and mountaineers: Industrialization of the Appalachian South, 1880–1930.* Knoxville: University of Tennessee Press.

McCutchen Williams, E. (2012). *Appalachian travels: The diary of Olive Dame Campbell.* Lexington: University Press of Kentucky.

McNelley, P. (Ed.). (1966). *The first 40 years: John C. Campbell folk school* (1st ed.). Atlanta, GA: McNelley-Rudd.

Smith, M. S., & Wilson, E. H. (1999). *North Carolina women making history.* Chapel Hill: University of North Carolina Press.

Whisnant, D. E. (1983). *All that is native and fine: The politics of culture in an American region.* Chapel Hill: University of North Carolina Press.

Jessie Allen Charters, 1929.
(Photo courtesy of The Ohio State University)

CHAPTER 8

JESSIE ALLEN CHARTERS

"Giving the Best We Know to Mothers and Fathers"

Constance E. Wanstreet

No Small Lives: Handbook of North American Early Women Adult Educators, 1925-1950,
pp. 81–89
Copyright © 2015 by Information Age Publishing

"Am I spoiling my baby?"
"What should a child eat?"
"Why do my children congregate downtown?"

Such questions formed the curriculum of the Parental Education Department headed by Jessie Allen Charters at Ohio State University. She and her staff addressed those concerns by "giving the best we know to ... mothers and fathers who may be hoping to hear something of value to them" (Charters, 1930a, p. 943).

Established in 1928 as a joint service of the Ohio Department of Education and Ohio State University, the mission of the department was to prepare citizens and preserve communities by making current knowledge and educational methods available to parents (Arps, Clifton, Charters, & Nelson, 1928). For the next 5 years, Charters and her staff worked prodigiously to organize adult study groups throughout Ohio, train discussion leaders, provide study materials, produce a bulletin with practical information for parents, conduct twice-weekly radio programs, and run a demonstration preschool in Columbus. However, during the height of the Great Depression, after the Ohio Department of Education withdrew funding, the Ohio State University board of trustees determined that the university was no longer able to finance adult education (W. W. Charters, 1931). According to the university's payroll records (n.d.), Jessie Charters' position ended on June 30, 1933. Table 8.1, provides a more complete timeline for the career and life of Jessie Allen Charters.

This chapter reflects progressive adult education through the lens of Jessie Charters' work at Ohio State. Ten journal articles, a compilation of nine radio lectures, and 15 issues of the *Better Parents Bulletin* published while she was at the university provide insight into her philosophy of parental education and her approach to "help parents make better homes and to bring up better and happier children" (Charters, 1929a, p. 6).

WIFE AND MOTHER

The mother of four children, Charters was known nationally for her work in parent education when she came to Ohio State (Geyer, 1992). She led the development of parenting skills in the United States and influenced its development in Scotland, India, China, and Myanmar (Karlovic, 1993). As Jessie Allen, she was the first woman from the Pacific coast to receive a PhD (see Table 8.1). She began to specialize in woman's psychology while in California and Pennsylvania but concluded that problems girls have in school stem from problems at home (Imel, 1993). Education to prepare mothers and fathers for their jobs as parents became her career focus.

Table 8.1.   Timeline: Jessie Blount Allen Charters

Year	Event
1880, Sept. 23	Born Jessie Blount Allen in Canton, Texas
1890	Family moved to Seattle
1899	Received bachelor's degree from the University of Washington
1901	Received master's degree from the University of Washington
1904	Received PhD in philosophy from the University of Chicago; studied under John Dewey
1907	Married Werrett Wallace Charters (b. 1875 in Hartford, Ontario; earned PhD from the University of Chicago in 1904)
1910–27	Affiliated with the University of Missouri, Columbia; Carnegie Institute of Technology, Pittsburgh; and the University of Chicago.
1928	Founded the Department of Adult Education at Ohio State University, Columbus, as an assistant professor earning $4,000 per year; also held the position of director of the Department of Parental Education for the Ohio Department of Education.
1928	Began fieldwork with parent study groups by partnering with the Ohio Congress of Parents and Teachers.
1928, October	Began radio programming on Ohio State University station WEAO with two half-hour programs each week.
1929	Joined 36 educators from 19 colleges and universities to develop the Ohio Plan of Leadership Training to develop adult study groups as symbols of modern democracy.
1929, September	Opened the Parents' Pre-School Laboratory in Columbus where parents could observe and write reports on activities of the students and teachers and have individual conferences with staff about their children.
1929, December	Began publishing the free *Better Parents Bulletin* to disseminate information of value to parents. The small bulletins were generally between 14 and 16 pages and were printed as a class project by the Ohio State School for the Deaf.
1930 Census	Both Jessie, 48, and Wallace, 53, list their occupations as professor at Ohio State University. Their family includes Margaret A., 19; Aileen J., 18; Jean C., 15; and Wallace II, 8.
1931	Dean George Arps, College of Education, informed W. W. Charters that the university expected to eliminate the department of adult education due to financial constraints during the Great Depression and dismiss Jessie from the faculty. After strenuous objection by W. W., she was retained but her pay was cut to $2,000 per year.
1931, Spring	Ohio Department of Education terminated staff contracts; fieldwork with parents' study groups ended; production of the *Better Parents Bulletin* and radio programming ended; leadership training institute and Parents' Laboratory Pre-School closed.

(Table continues on next page)

Table 8.1. Timeline: Jessie Blount Allen Charters

Year	Event
July 1928– April 1932	Charters and staff of between four and six women addressed 342 meetings; held 63 courses and institutes of one to three days in length for 27,017 attendees; conducted 295 radio programs; attended 59 state and national conferences; and received an estimated 3,906 letters and sent out 3,586 letters.
1933	Ohio State Board of Trustees did not approve a salary request of $1,500. President George W. Rightmire wrote that the university was no longer able to finance the work of adult education. College of Education Dean George Arps wrote Charters, "This distresses me more than any of the distressing things with which I have been confronted."
1934	Named director of intercounty groups, which include juvenile court and probation offices throughout Ohio for the Ohio Probation Association.
1952, March 8	Werrett Wallace Charters died.
1971, Oct. 22	Jessie Allen Charters died in Northport, Michigan.

Note: Sources include Jessie A. & W. W. Charters Papers 1922–1953, the Adult Education History Project, Syracuse University Library Archives; the Ohio State University Archives, Werrett Wallace Charters Papers; U.S. Census records; the Social Security Death Index; the *Columbus Citizen*; the *Better Parents Bulletin*; and Jessie Charters' publications in the *Educational Research Bulletin*, the *Journal of Adult Education*, and *Education on the Air.*

When her spouse, W. W. Charters, became the director of Ohio State University's Bureau of Educational Research, Jessie was hired to undertake an experiment in parent education for the Ohio Department of Education and the university (Imel, 1993). W. W. Charters (1931) wrote that they came to Ohio State because it represented an opportunity for Jessie to

> return to her career. She was a brilliant young doctor of philosophy in 1904, taught successfully for three years, and thereafter gladly spent fifteen years rearing her family. With the family cared for, I backed her desires to return to active professional work for which she was eminently qualified.

Geyer (1992) and Karlovic (1993) offer additional insight into Charters' home and professional life before and after her time at Ohio State.

DIRECTOR AND DEPARTMENT HEAD

In 1928, Charters was named head of the Division of Adult Education at Ohio State University and director of the Department of Parental Education at the Ohio Department of Education (Charters, 1929a). She explained that the purpose of her office was "to keep to the practical, helpful, and vital issues in our work, and not float above ground in the rarefied atmosphere sometimes regarded as the native element of college departments" (Charters, 1929a, p. 8). Study groups and in-home projects were at the core of parental education, and Charters' department was set up to support them via leadership training, study materials, and a preschool that served as a "training center for the parents as well as for the child" (Nelson, 1930a, p. ii).

Charters initially employed a staff of five women: a psychologist who supervised the demonstration preschool, two "well-trained mothers" who taught in the preschool, one field worker who assisted parents' study groups, and a "loyal, hard-worked secretary" (Charters, 1929b, p. 10). Because her staff could not reach all parents in Ohio through their own efforts, Charters partnered with civic organizations, state bureaus, and local libraries to provide materials and leveraged radio and parent-teacher associations as training spaces. She undertook what she described as her first "experiment" in providing service to those interested in parental education by working with the Ohio Congress of Parents and Teachers (Charters, 1930b, p. 202). That organization had district chairs of parental education who gave talks, held conferences, met study-group leaders, secured study material, and otherwise assisted the program. Initially, Charters (1930b) worked with district chairs in Athens, Hillsboro, New Concord, Springfield, Swanton, and Youngstown.

Based on early success, Charters recommended expanding this type of outreach so that every community would have someone whose primary interest was developing opportunities for parents to study. Charters (1930b) felt that the opportunity would appeal to

> the imaginative and constructive thinking of those leaders who may have found the rewards of club work or social leadership inadequate, or who have graduated from the school of practical parenthood with honors and are ready to use their experience in service. (p. 202)

Although Charters (1930d) claimed that Ohio had hundreds of parent study groups, her department undertook a systematic effort to determine that number in Ohio during 1929–30. Of 1,500 questionnaires sent to parent-teacher association presidents and parents who attended two leadership institutes, only 136 were returned. Four groups in Youngstown, for example, were identified in the questionnaires. However, the department knew of 14 groups in that city, making even an estimate of the number of groups in Ohio "out of the question" (Schlesinger, 1930, p. 10).

DISCUSSION AS A SYMBOL OF DEMOCRACY

So convinced was she of the educational value of group discussion that Charters (1930d) said she would "stand or fall by study programs.... These study groups, groping and exploring and questioning and reading, are learning" (p. 175). Joining with others to learn "has advantages for modern civilization," including fostering discussion and exposing group members to multiple perspectives, and is a "significant symbol of modern democracy" (Charters, 1929a, 1930c, p. 16). Charters (1930c) rejected formal lectures delivered by teachers because "the average layman looks up to an expert with great respect, and tends to accept his lightest state-ment as an authoritative dictum" (p. 17). Such "hero worship" supports the "antiquated idea that education is given *to* pupils *by* teachers who have it" (Charters, 1930c, p. 18; italics in original). On the contrary, Charters (1929d) considered dissent a "healthy sign of original thinking" (p. 3) and actively sought criticism of her department's programs and materials.

More important than content expertise from experts who "tend to be remote ... and not necessarily able to lead" (Charters, 1929e, p. 219) was leadership ability (Charters, 1930c). Trained leaders who emerged from the study group could transform academic information into practical material for parents to use in solving their problems (Charters, 1929e). A group leader must have "personality, poise, and training" (Charters, 1930e, p. 4), be familiar with the study materials, and be willing to learn "more and more with the group; she should know how to manage group discussion and how to get results" (Charters, 1930e, p. 1).

In 1929, study group leaders could secure leadership training from the University of Cincinnati; Cleveland College, the continuing education division of Case Western Reserve University; Akron University; Witten-berg College; and Otterbein College (Charters, 1929b). Those institutions were part of a consortium of 19 colleges and universities that developed the Ohio Plan of Leadership Training (Charters, 1930c). Leadership training covered group organization, program planning, securing materi-als, and teaching methods. Training was supplemented with letters and conferences (Charters, 1929b) and helped leaders overcome difficulties associated with parents who "gossip about their family troubles," use their children as an excuse for not attending or being late, or "usurp all the time talking" (Charters, 1930e, pp. 3–4).

A popular training supplement was the *Better Parents Bulletin,* which grew from 1,000 to 4,000 free subscriptions in 18 months. The bulletin was designed to assist study groups and leaders by demystifying scientific findings to help mothers and fathers excel at their jobs as parents. In addition, each issue featured a study lesson, book and magazine recom-mendations, news about the demonstration preschool, and a list of upcoming radio programs. From practical advice about how to organize a parents' study group—"write a few of your friends to meet in your home" (Charters, 1930e, p. 1)—to what to tell children about Santa Claus— "never tell a child an untruth" (Nelson, 1930b, p. 4)—the bulletin helped readers "carry on their own education better" (Charters, 1929b, p. 10).

Charters was less certain of the success of her radio outreach efforts. She envisioned radio as a way to reach all of the parents in Ohio and took to the airwaves in 1928 with two half-hour programs each week supplemented with study guides (Charters, 1929b). However, the direct lecture format of the radio programs did not represent Charters' (1930d) idea of parental education because of the absence of "group stimulus" and the "solitariness of the student" (p. 177). Despite nagging doubts about who was listening and what difference radio lectures made in parents' lives, Charters continued radio programming until her department's funding was cut, producing a total of 295 programs (Charters, 1932).

HOME PROJECTS AS EVIDENCE OF EDUCATION

Despite her enthusiasm for study groups, Charters (1929c) predicted that they would be "done to death" without an ongoing series of "vital subjects" to discuss (p. 210). Further, a study group that did not prompt home or community projects was "a barren enterprise unworthy [of] the name of education" (Charters, 1931a, p. 2). A home project was a plan to form or break a child's habit or to change an attitude, and it involved retraining children as well as their parents (Charters, 1931a).

Parents were encouraged to develop projects around brushing teeth, washing hands, and bathing by making check marks on a chart; to enliven dinner conversation by having older children read stories or articles to relate at the table; and to involve children in planning parties or setting daily schedules (Stone, 1931). Planting a garden, making presents, and sharing amusements such as the *Amos 'n' Andy* radio program were other examples of home projects that could be "instructive and important as well as a great deal of fun for everybody" (Stone, 1931, p. 11).

AN ENDING AND RESOLVE

In the fourth annual report of her department's activities, Charters (1932) acknowledged the financial problems that would result in a "vain effort to preserve some part of the enterprises" (p. 1). In the spring of 1931, however, the Ohio Department of Education cut funding, effectively eliminating staff, fieldwork with study groups, the *Better Parents Bulletin*, radio programming, leadership training, and the preschool. The last vestiges of parental education disappeared by the summer of 1933 when Charters' contract was not renewed (Geyer, 1992).

Although privately her spirit may have been broken (Karlovic, 1993), in public Charters (1931b) was optimistic about the future:

> I am sure that in this trying period of world war and financial depression we are about to take a great positive and decisive step forward, impelled by the fundamental urge to preserve the home and promote the best good of the family. (p. 649)

ACKNOWLEDGMENTS

My thanks are due to Gretchen Bersch for beginning the development of the Jessie Blount Allen Charters timeline and to Susan Imel for sharing her research and insight. Portions of this research were funded by the Kellogg Project at Syracuse University and reported in the *Adult Education Colloquium* newsletter, Spring 1993, Ohio State University.

REFERENCES

Arps, G. F., Clifton, J. L., Charters, J. A., & Nelson, A. K. (1928). Courses in parental education. *Educational Research Bulletin, 7*(13), 283–291.

Charters, J. A. (1929a, December). What is a department of parental education? *Better Parents Bulletin, 1*(1), 5–8.

Charters, J. A. (1929b). The responsibility of the state for education of parents. *Adult Education: Official Organ—Department of Adult Education N.E.A., 5*(2), 8–10.

Charters, J. A. (1929c). Problems in adult education. *Educational Research Bulletin, 8*(10), 207–211.

Charters, J. B. A. (1929d). *Bringing up children.* Columbus: Ohio State University Press.

Charters, J. A. (1929e). Leader versus teacher. *Educational Research Bulletin, 8*(10), 218–220.

Charters, J. A. (1930a). The radio as an educational force. *Religious Education: The Official Journal of the Religious Education Association, 25*(10), 938–943.

Charters, J. A. (1930b). Parental education. *Educational Research Bulletin, 9*(7), 201–204.

Charters, J. A. (1930c). The training of leaders for adult study groups. *Journal of Adult Education, 2*(1), 16–21.

Charters, J. A. (1930d). Parental education by radio. In J. H. MacLatchy (Ed.), *Education on the air: First yearbook of the Institute for Education by Radio* (pp. 168–179). Columbus: Ohio State University.

Charters, J. A. (1930e, March). Organizing parents' study groups. *Better Parents Bulletin, 1*(4), 1–4.

Charters, J. A. (1931a, January). Home projects. *Better Parents Bulletin, 2*(5), 2.

Charters, J. A. (1931b). Obligations of the home in this mechanistic age. *Religious Education: The Official Journal of the Religious Education Association, 26*(8), 644–649.

Charters, J. A. (1932). *Fourth annual report of adult education.* Jessie A., and W. W. Charters Papers, Special Collections Research Center, Syracuse University Library.

Charters, W. W. (1931). [Letter to George Arps]. Ohio State University Archives (RG: 40/p/117, Box 1), Columbus, OH.

Geyer, C. K. (1992). Dr. Jessie A. Charters: Reclaiming her role in adult education. *Journal of the Midwest History of Education Society, 20,* 101–112.

Imel, S. (1993, Spring). Jessie Allen Charters. *Adult Education Colloquium* (pp. 1–2). Ohio State University.

Karlovic, L. (1993). Jessie Allen Charters. *Adult Learning, 4*(5), 13–14, 26.

Nelson, A. K. (1930a, February). Pre-school education, an editorial. *Better Parents Bulletin, 1*(3), 13–14.

Nelson, A. K. (1930b, December). Children and Santa Claus. *Better Parents Bulletin, 2*(3), 3–5.

Ohio State University Payroll Records. (n.d.). Inactive: R6/c-13/Roll 2, 1881–1940.

Schlesinger, E. (1930, October). Ohio's study groups, 1929–1930. *Better Parents Bulletin, 2*(1), 1–10.

Stone, D. V. (1931). Examples of home projects. *Better Parents Bulletin, 2*(5), 9–11.

Jean Carter (standing) at Bryn Mawr Summer School for Women Workers
(Photo courtesy of School of Management and Labor Relations, Rutgers University)

CHAPTER 9

JEAN CARTER OGDEN— THESE THINGS WE'VE TRIED

Democracy and Adult Education

Susan J. Barcinas

Jean Carter Ogden was an important adult educator whose distinguished career included contributions as an author, teacher, extension educator, community development specialist, workers' education movement activist, and as a leader in local, regional, state, and national education organi-

No Small Lives: Handbook of North American Early Women Adult Educators, 1925-1950,
pp. 91–97
Copyright © 2015 by Information Age Publishing
All rights of reproduction in any form reserved.

zations. Born in 1897 in Rochester, New York, early information about Jean Carter's career begins in 1931. At that time, she served as a high school teacher at Benjamin Franklin High School in Rochester, New York. An early syllabus (Carter, 1931) utilized by Carter indicates that she was involved in the workers' education movement during that time period. This offers a lens into Carter's early developing philosophical and educational leanings. Workers' colleges, particularly for women, were established in the 1920s and 1930s and served as a valuable site for democratic education and represented a breakdown of social class barriers. Factory and other types of blue-collar workers became temporary residential students, learning via intensive summer experiences at nearby colleges. Early on, Jean Carter became involved with Bryn Mawr College as a teacher and then directed a similar summer program at Oberlin College. Under the direction of Hilda Worthington Smith, Bryn Mawr educated approximately 1,700 working class women from 1921 to 1938, with a social justice movement agenda which was progressive, at times radical, and a catalyst for women leaders in the workers movement. It cultivated students' development as thoughtful, political thinkers and doers through studying academic subjects such as English, literature, the arts, physical education, music, economics, and encouragement to collectively analyze and articulate views on a broad range of social, economic, and political issues. It was also known for experiential pedagogies that included the use of drama, music, and literature as a way to examine challenging societal issues (Heller, 1990; Hollis, 1995). This embodied approach to adult learning became a focal point during Jean Carter's career, along with her desire for democratic participation, capacity building, inclusion of the arts, and informal as well as formal forms of teaching and learning.

In her own educational work teaching English and Latin at Bryn Mawr, Carter drew upon a syllabus developed in 1930 by a group at the Bryn Mawr Summer School for Women Workers and incorporating materials in her teaching and administration at Oberlin. The syllabus, entitled, "This America; A Study of Literature Interpreting the Development of American Civilization," combined with Carter's role as the Director of the Summer School for Office Workers at Oberlin College, was a part of her early dedication to breaking down class barriers via democratic pedagogies and to a community capacity building orientation. Carter wrote about the pedagogies and teaching techniques and goals of the workers education movement in an article (Carter & Smith, 1934) on educating workers and further shared her educational and community work experiences via an Affiliated Schools for Workers publication, the *Scrapbook* (Carter, 1937).

THE YEARS WITH THE AMERICAN ASSOCIATION
FOR ADULT EDUCATION

In 1937, Carter joined the study staff of the AAAE, the American Association for Adult Education. The AAAE was founded in 1926 to promote continuing education and education for adults at-large. As a part of her early involvement with the AAAE, Carter wrote frequently for its *Journal of Adult Education* on topics such as creative expression as a form of learning, drama/plays, and workers education. Jean Carter authored five articles in total (Imel & Bersch, 2012). In 1938, the AAAE sponsored a series, *Studies in the Social Significance of Adult Education in the United States*; two volumes in the series were authored or co-authored by Jean. The first was on parent education, *Parents in Perplexity* (Carter, 1938). The second, co-authored with her future husband, Jess Ogden, presents results from a study on noncommercial theater and its role in education and is entitled, *Everyman's Drama: A Study of the Noncommercial Theatre in the United States* (Carter & Ogden, 1938). Jean Carter and Jess Ogden wrote about the importance drama plays as a "conveyer of ideas and emotions" (Carter & Ogden, 1938, p. 1) and their belief that noncommercial theater serves as a holistic site for adult learning and education and is evidence of a desire for the integration of intelligent, creative activities for adults.

Jess Switzer Ogden and Jean Carter married in 1941. Jess Ogden was born in 1894 in Rockland, Massachusetts, and he attended graduate school at the University of Rochester and New York University. He was a veteran, having served in the army during World War I. Ogden's educational background includes time teaching English and drama (in high school), work as a field representative for the AAAE, and in addition as a director of adult education at the Hull House in Chicago, Illinois. Ogden's background in art, drama, and in democratic community capacity building was a good fit for his long-standing professional working relationship with Jean Carter.

DEMOCRATIC COMMUNITY WORK
AT THE UNIVERSITY OF VIRGINIA

Newly married, Jean Carter Ogden and Jess Ogden began employment at the University of Virginia as field directors in the extension division (Imel & Bersch, 2012). Historically, university extension divisions play a strong role in the field of adult education, serving as a site for outreach, community engagement, and community building and as a bridge of academic theory to practice and practice to theory, referred to as praxis. Pedagogically, extension work parallels earlier frameworks in Carter Ogden's work, drawing upon democratic community development techniques as well as a commitment to reflective practice and the sharing of professional experiences for the purposes of encouraging interested adults to participate in adult education activities as facilitators, leaders, and learners. Both Jean Carter and Jess Ogden were known as energetic, outspoken, down-to-earth, and committed to democratic participation. Ogden was bald and stocky, and Carter had a small build and was known for her greenish blue eyes (Whitman, 1946). At first, they elected to live in Greene County, Virginia, in the mountains, to get to know the communities where their early projects would be based.

The Ogdens' new role at UVA included a special project which was focused upon better understanding how communities can become active, engaged, and vibrant. One newspaper reporter when featuring their work in Virginia described how his interactions with them influenced him personally: "I hope it will give you, as it gave me, a new zest for the democratic way. What Jess and Jean are doing for Virginia can be done in your own state and your own town" (Whitman, 1946, p. 7). According to Whitman, the Ogdens were true adult educators, and he writes that community members describe them as *hypo-dermickers*, people who serve as democracy's spark plugs. They began their community outreach work in the rural Blue Ridge Mountains, and they attended church, festivals, community meetings, and became a part of the communities in which they were working. Their approach to education included the use of movies, art, and media in order to share what the faraway world was like and illustrate to local residents that people share common issues and challenges. For the Ogdens, local participation was a key to a happy and productive community. They covered topics such as agriculture, travel, nutrition, family studies, economics, and politics. They talked about culture, fairness, equity, and cultivated a meeting place that community members could meet to talk, learn, and develop ideas for shared projects (Whitman, 1946).

The Ogdens' work in Virginia was high profile and painstaking in the sense that they wanted not only to succeed in the communities that they were working with, but they were charged with developing models or best practices strategies to share with adult educators or community development specialists throughout the country. They ultimately wrote a book, *These Things We Tried: A Five-Year Experiment in Community Development Initiated and Carried Out by the Extension Division of the University of Virginia* in 1947. The foreword to the book, written by George Zehmer, an extension director at UVA, explains that good community development isn't rooted in a magical formula nor is it neat and tidy; instead it stems from "having faith in people and in the democratic way of life; extensive training and experience in working with people; mastery of techniques without slavish adherence to patterns of procedure" (Ogden & Ogden, 1947, p. ix) and calls for exceptional patience and hard work that is marshaled to serve a collective rather than individual purpose.

The book is reflective of contemporary adult education writings with discussion of the importance of being aware of what is obvious versus the unwritten ways of doing things that permeate adult education activities. For instance, Ogden and Ogden (1947) describe experiences with success that grow to the point of becoming impersonal and describe dogged intentionality in consciously including community members in directly working on issues that impact their lives and avoiding rapid, explosive growth that pulls community members too far from their needs or contexts. During an age of printed materials (as compared to information access via the Internet), they caution that there is a danger in using generic information and state their belief that it is worth the time and expense to identify, collect, and share information that is specific to the community context. They held the firm belief that specific, relevant information and building personal relationships were more effective and sustainable than massive marketing or generic informational campaigns, even though scaling up was tempting.

They suggest the role of extension staff and adult educators as "middlemen" who translate, bridge, and engage discussions in making meaning out of the wealth of academic and other expert information as it is applied in communities and the role of community members as translators who inform academics, researchers, and experts about what works and what doesn't and why. They advocate for a two-way engagement process, praxis, that has stood the test of time and is currently considered an imperative in university-community partnership activities. According to Imel and Bersch (2012), the project included information about community-based extension programs shared through bulletins called "New Dominion Series." The bulletins focused upon describing the process and the community members rather than on the project content. It was distributed to over 4,000 addresses via a regional mailing list. Their belief was that the sharing of information on how to build community capacity as well as information on who participated offered the most significant ingredients and motivation for those community members who might want to step up and become involved within their own communities.

The Ogdens co-authored an article on community responsibility (Ogden & Ogden, 1952), which was a precursor to the current literature on university-community partnerships in terms of the core principle of mutuality between partners and the importance of avoiding the notion that universities are experts that need to fix or resolve problems for communities in a top-down or expert-to-novice approach. It argues, primarily for the idea of cooperative inquiry, for the acceptance of any general national or statewide plans provided the plans were flexible and designed so that local communities would have the ability to customize and adapt to their local contexts and self-defined needs and goals. Interestingly, they make the argument that even in 1952, change and information sharing happens so rapidly, that what we know is only as good as "*day-before-yesterday, figuratively speaking*" (emphasis in original) (Ogden & Ogden, 1952, p. 100) and calls for a vision that incorporates adaptiveness and flexibility to keep up with technology, societal change, and communities whose members will have ever-increasingly informed and aging citizens.

OTHER PROFESSIONAL CONTRIBUTIONS

In 1951, the AAAE, the American Association for Adult Education, merged with the Adult Education Association of the United States, known as AEA. According to memoirs by Roger Hiemstra (2003), a major figure in adult education, Jean Carter Ogden and Jess Ogden were instrumental in the establishment of the AEA, and Jean Carter Ogden was a delegate to the National Organizational Committee. To give some sense of the importance of the AEA during that time period, Milton Eisenhower, the President of Pennsylvania State College (now Penn State University) and brother to the President of the United States, was interested and involved in the topic of older adult learners and college, and Thurman White, an early President of the AEA and long-standing editor of the major journal of the field, *Journal of Adult Education*, were a part of the early collaborations with the Ogdens and other key leaders of the field. Jean Carter Ogden was one of the few women elected as a delegate-at-large of AEA in 1951, and served alongside major contributors in the field such as Malcolm Knowles, Cy Houle, Howard McClusky, Alice Sowers, and numerous delegates and executive board members from the National Education Association, the U.S. Department of Agriculture, the International Garment Workers Union, the Washington DC Public Libraries, and major universities from across the country (Hiemstra, 2003).

In 1953, the Ogdens accepted an invitation from the University of England and spent several months on a comparative adult education program study in West Africa and England. Subsequently, they were awarded the first Delbert Clark Award in Adult Education by the West Georgia College, which is considered a prestigious national award (Jarvis, 2003; McClusky, 1958). Jean Carter Ogden was promoted by the University of Virginia to an assistant professor of extension teaching in 1946, and she resigned her position in 1957 due to ill health (Imel & Bersch, 2012). Jess Ogden passed away in February 1958; little is known about Jean Carter

Ogden's life after 1957, and she passed away in April 1974 in Rochester, New York (Imel & Bersch, 2012).

REFERENCES

Carter, J. (1931). *This America, a study of literature interpreting the development of American civilization*. New York, NY: Education Department, Affiliated Schools for Workers.

Carter, J. (1937). Snapshots of workers' education here and abroad. *Affiliated Schools Scrapbook, 1*(3/4).

Carter, J. (1938). *Parents in perplexity*. New York, NY: American Association for Adult Education.

Carter, J., & Odgen, J. (1938). *Everyman's drama*. New York, NY: American Association for Adult Education.

Carter, J., & Smith, H. W. (1934). *Education and the worker-student*. New York, NY: Affiliated Schools for Workers.

Heimstra, R. (2003, March 7). *Founding of the AEA of USA, 1949–1955*. Presentation at 2003 International Adult and Continuing Education Hall of Fame Conference.

Heller, R. (1990, November). *The women of summer: The Bryn Mawr summer school for women workers, 1921–1938*. Paper presented at Syracuse University Kellogg Project's First Visiting Scholar Conference in the History of Adult Education, Syracuse, NY. Retrieved from http://www-distance.syr.edu/heller.html

Hollis, K. L. (1995). Autobiography and reconstructing subjectivity at the Bryn Mawr summer school for women. *Women's Studies Quarterly, 23*(1/2), 71–100.

Imel, S., & Bersch, G. B. (2012, June 1–3). *Who were the women? In-depth analysis of four additional early women adult educators*. Roundtable paper presented at the Adult Education Research Conference, Sarasota Springs, NY.

Jarvis, P. (Ed.). (2003). *Adult and continuing education: Teaching, learning, and research*. Retrieved from http://books.google.com/books?id=DL-ITGH1io0C&pg=PA226&lpg=PA226&dq=Delbert-Clark+award+in+adult+education&source=bl&ots=7JGrtL97mV&sig=XUFp7-S8YJM7ac5V0OYkH9INvrI&hl=en&sa=X&ei=EmK-T5aYLoTk6QGsyNhb&ved=0CHAQ6AEwBQ#v=onepage&q=Delbert-Clark%20award%20in%20adult%20education&f=false)

McClusky, H. (1958). *A tribute to Jess Odgen*. Retrieved from http://oakdene.org/OgGateWeb/ogden/ogde998.htm

Odgen, J., & Ogden, J. (1946). *Small communities in action: Stories of citizen programs at work*. New York, NY: Harper & Brothers.

Odgen, J., & Ogden, J. (1947). *These things we tried: A five-year experiment in community development initiated and carried out by the Extension Division of the University of Virginia*. Charlottesville, VA: University of Virginia Extension.

Ogden, J., & Ogden, J. (1952). Sharing community responsibility. *Annals of the American Academy of Political and Social Science, 279*, 98–105.

Whitman, H. (1946, August 24). Virginia pioneers. *Spokesman Review*, 7–12.

CHAPTER 10

EVE CHAPPELL

A Fine Italian Hand

Susan Imel

Eve Chappell was a freelance writer, editor, and former newspaper reporter who was a prolific contributor to the *Journal of Adult Education*. Between 1932 and 1941, she authored a total of eight articles (1934a, 1934b, 1935a, 1935b, 1936, 1937, 1939, 1940). A ninth article (1937) listed "Cooperative," as the author, but credit was given to Eve, who was identified as a freelance writer. In addition to her contributions to the *Journal*, Eve was also the co-author of *Women in Two Worlds* (Ely & Chappell, 1938), a book that was part of the series Studies in the Social Significance in Adult Education in the United States published by the American Association for Adult Education. Shortened versions of four of her *Journal* articles were reprinted in *Adult Education in Action* (Ely, 1936). Despite using a number of search strategies and consulting different sources, I was only able to locate one other article by Eve. The article, "Kate Gleason's Careers," appeared in *The Woman Citizen* in 1926 and has been reprinted in Layne (2009).

Eve was born on November 22, 1874, in Andrew County, Missouri (Passport Applications, 1924). She was the daughter of William O. and Sarah A. Simmons. In the 1897 Denver City Directory, she was listed as an assistant

No Small Lives: Handbook of North American Early Women Adult Educators, 1925-1950,
pp. 99–105

librarian at the Denver Public Library (Ballanger & Richards, 1897), where she met her future husband, Robert Henry Chappell. Chappell was an attorney, and Eve and he were married in May 1905. They lived in Mexico during May and June of the same year; Robert Chappell died in 1913. Eve's 1924 passport application indicates that she was a widow, currently living at 23 Bank Street in New York City. According to passenger lists, Eve went abroad three times, sailing back into New York from London in 1925; Cherbourg, France, in 1919; and Le Havre, France in 1931.

EVE'S CONTRIBUTIONS TO THE *JOURNAL OF ADULT EDUCATION*

It is unclear when Eve moved to New York City; apparently, however, she had been living there for at least a decade before her first article appeared in the *Journal* in 1934. According to information in the "Our Contributors" section of the *Journal*, "After having done newspaper work in both Denver and San Francisco, Mrs. Chappell came to New York and established herself as a free lance writer" (1937, p. 113).

Most of the other information about Eve comes from the "Our Contributors" sections of the *Journal* issues in which her articles appeared, including the following:

- Eve Chappell, who makes her first contribution to the Journal with her story of the New York emergency education dramatic classes, is a free-lance writer who owes her keenness of observation perhaps to her training as a reporter on the *Rocky Mountain News* and other newspapers. Her ability to see beneath the surface of things has not been acquired; it is her own gift. (1934a, p. 245)
- Eve Chappell is a free-lance writer who though not directly engaged in adult education, is coming to be known as one of the most understanding and sympathetic chroniclers of the movement. (1936, p. 232)
- Eve Chappell, newspaper woman, trained observer and recorder of observations, has upon several occasions performed for us the important service of helping us to see ourselves as others see us. The time she tells us, what, as she sees it, adult education is doing for Negroes [sic] in the Harlem district of New York City. (1935b, p. 474)
- Eve Chappell is one of our most faithful and regular contributors.... One grateful author, whose manuscript she had revised, said of her that no one could fail to recognize her "fine Italian hand" [subtlety] in anything she had touched. We think the delicate trac-

ing of that hand was never more apparent than in the beautiful story of Louis Pasteur and his father, which she has written for this issue of the Journal. (1937, p. 113)

- Eve Chappell, a frequent contributor to the *Journal*, writes of many things; but her chief interest is in people, and she is at her best, we think, in her biographical sketches, such as the present one on Walter J. Damrosch and the one on Louis Pasteur, published in the *Journal* for January 1937. (1940, p. 456)

The articles that Eve wrote for the *Journal* followed its general policy to publish articles that described and appraised various programs in adult education. In other words, they were primarily descriptive in nature. Her articles covered a variety of topics, including adult education programs offered in Harlem; the School for Adult Jewish Education; labor institutes that were organized by the Workers Education Bureau with funding from the Recovery Act; drama classes taught by out-of-work Broadway actors with emergency funding from the New York program of adult education; and the handicraft movement in New England.

"Tonic Hunger of the Mind" (1935a), an article that described high school institutes for adult education, provides an example of Eve's understanding of adult education as well as her journalistic skills. This particular article describes institutes in two different locations: one in Maplewood, New Jersey, and the other in the Bronx at DeWitt Clinton. It opens with the following paragraph:

No longer are our high schools devoted solely to the service of adolescents. Parents and grandparents are going back to school. By the dozens and by the hundreds they swarm up the steps to take advantage of the opportunity for instruction; some to renew interest in a subject in which they have grown rusty; some to begin a study that has long been a dream, dusty in a mental pigeonhole marked *Some Day* or *Too Late*. (p. 150; emphasis in original)

To develop the article, Eve visited the two programs and observed and talked to the participants and the administrators. She skillfully compares and contrasts the two programs, noting that each is developed to meet the needs and interests of the participants as well as the economic status and level of education of the particular area. In conclusion, she says "The institutes I have described are types. Types and models" (1935a, p. 154), and then she briefly enumerates other institutes that followed the examples of those described in the article. She notes that a common denominator among all the institutes is the fact that they are voluntary on the part of the schools that house them, the teachers that staff them, and the participants themselves.

Two of Eve's articles were biographical sketches. "Study, *con amore*" (1937) described the loving efforts of Louis Pasteur to help his father, Jean Joseph Pasteur, make up for the education he had missed out on as a youth. Eve uses letters from a biography written by Pasteur's son-in-law (Vallery-Radot & Devonshire, 1923) to illustrate how Louis used letters as a means of correspondence education for his father. Although Eve does not comment directly on the nature of this type of informal learning— other than to refer to it as correspondence study—she surely recognized it to be a form of adult education.

In her second biographical sketch "Music and life appreciation" (1940), Eve focuses on Walter Damrosch, who was for many years the music director for the National Broadcasting Company and developed the Music Appreciation Hour, a radio program designed for children. Compared to the article on the Pasteurs, in discussing the Music Appreciation Hour, Eve is much more overt in her discussion of the adult education aspects of Damrosch's work. Even though the program was developed for and aimed at children, it had a "multitudinous adult following," (p. 379) that resulted in a large volume of mail with correspondence from as far away as Australia and New Zealand and South Africa. Eve comments that "to me at least, it was apparent that the lessons in music appreciation were also lessons in life appreciation. And that is adult education at its finest" (p. 382).

CO-AUTHOR OF *WOMEN IN TWO WORLDS*

Women in Two Worlds (1938), the book Eve co-authored with Mary Ely, is a study of women's organizations. In the book's Foreword, Mary explained that she and Eve followed the advice of several to restrict the study to "a very few organizations that might be considered representative of the larger number" (p. v). The study was divided into two major parts: "The Man's World," authored by Mary and "The Woman's World," authored by Eve. Mary's section covered three fields in which women were in direct competition with men: higher education, business and the professions, and politics. Eve's section focused on the activities of women's clubs. Recognizing that women had recently made strides in gaining emancipation, the two writers were concerned with how "women have used their dearly bought opportunities" (p. 4).

For her section of the book, Eve visited a number of clubs and then chose three to use as brief case histories. Of greater interest, however, is the chapter "The Present Scene," in which she describes the diversity in clubs stating, "attempts at generalization are futile as is the search in a crowd for the hypothetical, nonexistent creature, the average man. There is no representative composite" (1938, p. 142). In another chapter, she focuses on the type of club achievements highlighting educational efforts.

The book ends with a discussion of the relevance of the study for the field of adult education. Mary (writing for both herself and Eve) comments on the vast range of club programs and wonders if the study has revealed any social significance in the women's club movement. In ruminating on the vast differences among the club programming, she contemplates the ongoing tension between offering only what adults want versus developing programs based on values that reflect what "we are seeking in education" (1938, p. 167).

MUCH ABOUT EVE REMAINS A MYSTERY

Although Eve was a freelance writer, only one other article by her was located: a profile of Kate Gleason, the first woman to qualify for full membership in the American Society of Mechanical Engineers. The article appeared in 1926 in *The Woman Citizen*, the publication of the American Woman Suffrage Association. In the article that was reprinted in Layne (2009), Eve describes Ms. Gleason's determination to follow in her father's footsteps and become an engineer. Because he was a friend of Susan B. Anthony, he supported her desire and allowed her to work along side of him from the age of 11—despite the disapproval of friends and neighbors.

Based on the limited information about Eve as well as her writing, the following conclusions (or inferences) have been formulated:

- Since Eve was a freelance writer, she probably received payment for her articles that appeared in the *Journal of Adult Education*. She may also have received support for collecting information for articles; for example, for the article on high school institutes for adult education (1935a), she visited two locations.

- It appeared that Eve also preformed editing services for the *Journal*. This assumption is based on the contributor information that referred to her "fine Italian hand," in editing another author's submission.

- She was also employed by the Association to do the work and writing for the study of women's clubs. This involved a large amount of travel around the country as well as sifting through correspondence, writing up findings, and developing her section of the book.

- Although Eve was not an adult educator, she understood the field and adult learning. This is evident in the articles she authored. She also appeared to be an adult learner herself. In the article on Walter Damrosch, for example, she refers to her participation in the 1939–1940 music appreciation series; perhaps that is what led to the development of the article.

- Finally, I believe that Eve was a feminist. I base this conclusion on the fact that she was a widow making her living as a freelance writer, her article on Kate Gleason that appeared in the publication of the American Woman Suffrage Association, and her work on the study *Women in Two Worlds*.

Eve Chappell made significant contributions to the literature during the field's formative years. Many of the details of her life, however, remain a mystery. The last listing for Eve in Manhattan City Directory was 1949, when she would have been approximately 75 years of age. Despite scouring various online records, no record can be found of her death, leading to the conclusion that she may have died in 1949 or shortly thereafter.

ACKNOWLEDGMENT

A version of this chapter was presented by Susan Imel as an unpublished handout at the 2011 Adult Education Research Conference for the Roundtable "Who Were the Women? In-Depth Analysis of Some Additional Early Women Adult Educators" presented by Gretchen Bersch and Susan Imel at 2011 AERC and CASAE Conference

REFERENCES

Ballenger & Richards. (1897). *Twenty-fifth annual directory*. Denver, CO: News Printing Company.

Chappell, E. (1926, January). Kate Gleason's careers. *The Woman Citizen*, 19–20, 37–38.

Chappell, E. (1934a). Depression's drama. *Journal of Adult Education*, 6(2), 167–170.

Chappell, E. (1934b). Scholar and worker. *Journal of Adult Education*, 6(3), 263–267.

Chappell, E. (1935a). Tonic hunger of the mind. *Journal of Adult Education*, 7(2), 150–157.

Chappell, E. (1935b). Toward universal values. *Journal of Adult Education*, 7(4), 399–404.

Chappell, E. (1936). Conservation of Jewish culture. *Journal of Adult Education*, 8(2), 153–157.

Chappell, E. (1937). Study, *con amore*. *Journal of Adult Education*, 9(1), 10–14.

Chappell, E. (1939). Imponderables and money returns from handicrafts. *Journal of Adult Education, 11*(1), 36–39.

Chappell, E. (1940). Music and life appreciation. *Journal of Adult Education, 12*(4), 379–382.

Cooperative. (1937). Aesthetic need and utilitarian purpose. *Journal of Adult Education, 9*(2), 171–174.

Ely, M. L. (Ed.). (1936). *Adult education in action.* New York, NY: American Association for Adult Education.

Ely, M. L., & Chappell, E. (1938). *Women in two worlds.* New York, NY: American Association for Adult Education.

Layne, M. E. (Ed.). (2009). *Women in engineering: Pioneers and trailblazers.* Reston, VA: American Society of Civil Engineers.

Passport Applications. (1924, August 20–21). Passport Applications, January 2, 1906–March 31, 1935. Roll 2625 – Certificates 469850-470349, 20 Aug 1924–21 Aug 1924. Pages 250–252.

Vallery-Radot, R., & Devonshire, R. L. (1923). *Life of Pasteur.* Garden City, NY: Doubleday.

Mary L. Ely
(Passport photo, 1923, from Ancestry.com)

CHAPTER 11

MARY L. ELY

Dedicated Adult Educator

Gretchen T. Bersch

Unlike Dorothy Canfield Fisher, a public figure and published author, Mary L. Ely was a behind-the-scenes worker bee in the early adult education movement. She edited the *Journal of Adult Education*, authored adult education books and articles, worked as an educator and research assistant. She was at the center of the adult education association and early movement for almost three decades.

No Small Lives: Handbook of North American Early Women Adult Educators, 1925-1950,
pp. 107–113

MARY'S EARLY YEARS

Mary Lillian Ely was born in Dayton, Ohio, to John C. and Lillian I. Ely on September 28, 1881. Mary attended college, studying Latin and Greek, among other subjects. The 1900 and 1910 U. S. Census both show her living at home with her parents. Mary's early career was as librarian at the Dayton Public Library. Dayton City Directories show that Mary worked as a librarian from 1904 to 1917. In her late 30s, she moved to New York City to do graduate study at Columbia University, completing her master's degree there (Ely, 1919). By the next year, she was working as a writer/advertiser for an advertising agency (1920 U.S. Census). Soon after she became education director and general secretary for the National League of Girls Clubs, working from 1920 to 1927 (AAAE Staff, 1941). Among other activities, she taught social history to club girls.

She applied for a passport in June 1923. Eve Chappell signed as witness on her application, declaring they had known each other 3 years. Mary and Eve probably met not long after Eve arrived in New York. They lived near one another, continued to have a close working relationship and probable friendship for many years. That summer, Mary sailed to Great Britain to study summer schools and to vacation in France. She must have loved to travel. According to ship records of arrivals in New York City, Mary took five more trips to Europe and three trips to Bermuda between 1929 and 1937 (New York Passenger Lists, 1820–1956). Each gives her New York City address, born September 28, with birth years ranging from 1887 to 1891.

Mary worked as the education director involved with women's clubs. About this period she wrote,

> After several intellectually drab years following graduation from high school, I had entered college and experienced there an intellectual awakening that literally made the world over for me, and I could conceive of no more satisfying purpose in life than to pass on to others some of the intense joy that I found in my new intellectual interests. My opportunity to do this seemed assured when, in the early years of the adult education movement, I was made the first educational director of a league of working women's clubs, the activities of which had previously been largely social and recreational. The head of the league was a women of vision and unconquerable optimism, who shared to the full my hopes for the new venture. (Ely & Chappell, 1938, p. 43)

MARY'S WORK WITH THE
AMERICAN ASSOCIATION OF ADULT EDUCATION

With Mary's degree from Columbia University, writing/editing work, and her experiences as secretary and education director, she was well suited to work for Morse Cartwright and the new American Association for Adult Education. The Association, centered in New York City and closely connected to Columbia University, established adult education as a field. It was directed by Cartwright, assisted by Mary L. Ely. Mary served as publications editor for the Association beginning in 1928. The *Journal of Adult Education* was initiated in 1929, edited primarily by Ely until its end in 1941. As journal editor, she would have had ties to many of the early women in the field. In his annual report, Cartwright (1931, p. 6) stated the *Journal* "is far and away the most important single activity of the Association," the voice of AAAE nationally/internationally. Mary served on the AAAE council for a term ending September 30, 1929 (Cartwright, 1929, p. 338). In summer 1930, Mary was one of four who taught a course at Columbia University, entitled "Adult Education: Proposals, Undertakings, and Accomplishments" (Cartwright, 1931, p. 21).

Cartwright and Ely published a pamphlet, *Adult Education in the United States of America* (1929). It first appeared as a paper for the Third General Session of the Institute of Pacific Relations, held in fall 1929 in Kyoto, Japan. It gives a short description of AAAE and brief descriptions of 15 different aspects of adult education in the United States.

Through the 1930s Mary continued to edit the *Journal*. She wrote *Retrospective and Forecast* for the Association's 10th Anniversary (Ely, 1936a). She edited *Adult Education in Action*, a book that included 162 chapters, condensed versions of articles that had been published in the *Journal* (Ely, 1936b). Mary wrote one chapter, "Teachers at a World Convention," reporting on the first international conference of the World Association for Adult Education she and others attended in Cambridge England in July 1929. She sailed from Liverpool back to New York City on the *Antonia* in September 1929. Charles A. Beard wrote the foreword to the book:

> Miss Ely is more than a collector of papers. She has been long associated with the adult education movement. She is a source herself—a living document. So we have the marvel of a living source selecting sources for the permanent record! Miss Ely's volume is not "the next best thing" to a comprehensive history. It is better than a history or text written by a single hand. In selection and organization, it represents the work of a discriminating mind, experienced in the field of adult education; and at the same time, in content, it reflects the thought of many other minds also concerned with the ideas, interests, and activities of the movement. (Beard, 1936, p. ix)

In May 1936, the *New York Times* reported Mary was among those who gave informal addresses about adult education at the AAAE meeting at the Hotel Astor; speakers included Dorothy Canfield Fisher, John Finley, Frederick Kappel, and Mary (Newspaper Held Best Broadcaster, 1936, p. 21).

The Association announced in November 1936 that it planed to undertake a 5-year study of adult education, creating the series Studies in the Social Significance of Adult Education in the United States. In 1937, Mary took a one-year leave as journal editor and transferred to the study staff. Mary Ely wrote "To Our Readers" in the *Journal* describing the program:

> Mr. Cartwright, who originated the plan and who is to direct the study [said], "the emphasis formerly placed by the Association upon experimentation and demonstration is to be shifted in the next five years to the study program.... During the years 1936–1941, therefore, the funds granted by the Corporation to the Association ... will be directed toward the improvement of existing fields..." The findings of the study will be issued at irregular intervals over the five year period in a series of books and pamphlets that will deal with the social significance of adult education. (1937a, p. 74)

Each book in the series focused on an aspect of adult education. Studies were to be made by those familiar with adult education but not employed in the specific area to be studied. Of the 28 books in the series, 10 were written by women.

Mary authored *Why Forums?* published in 1937 as part of this series (Ely, 1937b). Her book reported that at the time there were more than 1,500 forum projects in the United States. She narrowed those she selected to include public meetings designated as forums, which met regularly over a period of time, which started with a speech by a leader and included active audience participation and discussion. She spent 3 months visiting forums from one end of the country to the other. She included chapters on over 20 forums. She discussed what makes forums successful or not successful, including organization, speakers, publicity, finances, and having someone good at managing or chairing the forum.

Mary Ely and Eve Chappell co-authored *Women in Two Worlds* (1938), also part of the series, focusing on women's organizations. Mary and Eve divided the book into two parts: "The Man's World," which Mary wrote, and "The Women's World," authored by Eve. Part I, "The Man's World," included organizations in which women were in direct competition with men. This included higher education, business and professions, and politics. Part 2, "The Women's World," focused on the activities of women's clubs. To gather the information for the book, Mary and Eve visited clubs, attended meetings, talked with clubwomen in restaurants, on trains, and in the street. They provided background and history as well as references. They traveled widely, including the South and the West Coast.

Mary became a freelance writer, but she continued to edit the *Journal* and to be involved with the Association. She served on the Committee on Future Policy, appointed by the AAAE Executive Board, chaired by Miriam Tompkins. Eight members—Miriam, Mary, and six men—worked to investigate all phases of the Association activity and programs and were charged with making recommendations for the future needs of the organization (Cartwright, 1947). Their final report prompted the Executive Board to decide their ideas were so important that they appointed a Ways and Means Committee to plan for implementation of the ideas.

The *Journal of Adult Education* ceased publication in 1941. In the "Editors' Note Book" in the final edition, Cartwright and Mary Ely wrote,

> This last issue of the Journal of Adult Education can be sent out without regrets. Thinking of the precarious foothold that adult learning held in the educational world only fifteen years ago, and of the well-established position that it occupies today; recalling the strangeness, the lack of understanding, that workers in adult education felt toward one another then, as contrasted with the warm fellowship that unites them now, we, the Editors of the Journal are encouraged to believe that our periodical, having been responsible in part at least for these changes, has done some work that need never be done again. (Cartwright & Ely, 1941, p. 430)

By 1948, Mary was in her late 60s and still working for both the Association and the Institute of Adult Education at Columbia University, where Morse Cartwright was the executive director. She edited the 1948 *Handbook of Adult Education in the U.S.* It was an ambitious effort, gathering chapters from more than 50 authors. Cartwright wrote in the Preface,

> This *Handbook* is chiefly the work of its editor, Mary L. Ely, formerly the editor for eleven years of the *Journal of Adult Education* and the compiler and editor of the omnibus volume, *Adult Education in Action*. In her double capacity of Research Associate both of the Institute and of the Association, she has given unstintedly of her time far beyond any recompense, to the compiling and editing of this extensive volume. The *Handbook* represents almost two years of Miss Ely's life. It has been largely a labor of love for her, and whatever intrinsic merit the book possesses is attributable to her care and marked abilities. (Cartwright, 1948, p. xii)

MARY'S IMPACT ON THE FIELD

Mary died in New York City after a short illness on May 27, 1950, four months shy of her 70th birthday. The *Adult Education Journal* wrote in July,

> Few persons have served the cause of adult education in the United States as conscientiously, ably and selflessly as Mary Ely.... The many hundreds of American adult education workers who knew Mary Ely personally and counted her among their friends will feel a keen sense of loss in her passing.

Particularly will this be true of the members of the American Association for Adult Education which Miss Ely served first as editor and later as a member of the Council. At the time of her death Miss Ely had just been nominated for vice-presidency of the Association. (AAAE, 1950, p. 97)

It was a challenge to sort out information on Mary. One of the mysteries was that she changed her age throughout her life. She consistently gave September 28 as the month and day of her birth, but the year of birth varied greatly from 1880/81 to 1891, with almost perfect progression to later as she aged. Since she was single all her life, perhaps this was a survival strategy so she could continue to work even as she neared mandatory retirement age, or just a bit of vanity.

To summarize her life work, Mary L. Ely was an author, editor, teacher, and advisor from the beginning of the new field of adult education until her death in 1950. Editing the *Journal* from its inception in 1929 until its final publication in 1941 was a major contribution. Editing the 1936 *Adult Education in Action* put her in the center of the action. Authoring *Why Forums?* and co-authoring with Eve Chappell *Women in Two Worlds* contributed to the literature of the field. The 1948 *Handbook of Adult Education* was a 2-year effort of dedication and persistence. Mary L. Ely was a key figure in the formative years of the adult education field that are the focus of this book; she was active from before 1925 until 1950.

ACKNOWLEDGMENT

Parts of this chapter were presented by Bersch in an unpublished handout for a roundtable session with Imel at the 2009 Adult Education Research Conference.

REFERENCES

AAAE Staff. (1941). The clearing house. *Journal of Adult Education, 13*(3), 455.

American Association for Adult Education. (1950). *Adult Education Journal, 9*(3), 97.

Beard, C. A. (1936). Foreword. In M. Ely (Ed.), *Adult education in action* (p. ix). New York, NY: American Association for Adult Education.

Cartwright, M. (1929, February). Annual report of the director. *Journal of Adult Education, 1*(1), 338.

Cartwright, M. (1931). *Annual report of the director in behalf of the executive board, 1930–31.* New York, NY: American Association for Adult Education.

Cartwright, M. (1947, April 10). *Annual report of the director for 1946–1947.* New York, NY: American Association for Adult Education.

Cartwright, M. (1948, January 2). Preface. In M. Ely (Ed.), *Handbook of adult education in the United States*. New York, NY: Teachers College, Columbia University.

Cartwright, M., & Ely, M. (1929). *Adult education in the United States of America*. New York, NY: American Association for Adult Education.

Cartwright, M., & Ely, M. (1941, October). The editors' note book. *Journal of Adult Education, 13*(4), 430.

Ely, M. (1919). *Some effects of overseas expansion upon industry in England during the 18th century* (Master's essay). New York, NY: Columbia University.

Ely, M. (1936a). Retrospect and forecast: Proceedings (in miniature) of the tenth anniversary celebration. *Journal of Adult Education, 8*(2), 297–298.

Ely, M. (Ed.). (1936b). *Adult education in action*. New York, NY: American Association for Adult Education.

Ely, M. (1937a). To our readers. *Journal of Adult Education, 9*(1), 74–76.

Ely, M. (1937b). *Why Forums?* New York, NY: American Association for Adult Education.

Ely, M. (Ed.). (1948). *Handbook of adult education in the United States*. New York, NY: Institute of Adult Education, Teachers College, Columbia, with cooperation of AAAE.

Ely, M., & Chappell, E. (1938). *Women in two worlds*. New York, NY: American Association for Adult Education.

New York Passenger Lists, 1820–1956. Accessed through Ancestry.com.

Newspaper held best broadcaster. (1936, May 22). *New York Times*, p. 21. Retrieved from http://search.proquest.com.proxy.consortiumlibrary.org/docview/101898924/769683904BCB4E9CPQ/26?accountid=14473

Dorothy Canfield Fisher, 1917
(Photo courtesy of the University of Vermont)

CHAPTER 12

DOROTHY CANFIELD FISHER

Strengthening Democracy
Through Adult Learning

Charlene A. Sexton

No Small Lives: Handbook of North American Early Women Adult Educators, 1925-1950,
pp. 115–123
Copyright © 2015 by Information Age Publishing

Dorothy Canfield Fisher (1879-1958) is the author of two major works associated with the formal organization of adult education: *Why Stop Learning?* (1927) and *Learn or Perish* (1930). She authored six journal articles (Fisher, 1920, 1933, 1936a, 1936b, 1938, 1942), and led the American Association of Adult Education (AAAE) in 1932–34 as its first and only female president. She was the only woman on the Book of the Month Club (BOMC) Selection Committee (1926–1951), bringing authors like Richard Wright, Pearl Buck, and Isak Dinesen to the reading public. The Carnegie Corporation commissioned her to write *Why Stop Learning?* to disseminate and promote the idea of adult education among the general public. In *Ten Years of Adult Education*, Morse Cartwright, the AAAE Director, wrote, "The importance of Mrs. Fisher's contribution at this time cannot be overestimated. The reaction of educational leaders and the public was immediate and gratifying" (Cartwright, 1935, p.15).

Nearly 90 years have passed since publication of the books. Her contributions to adult education (Imel & Bersch, 2009; Sexton, 1993) and literature are commanding attention. She published fiction under the name "Dorothy Canfield" and, with the publication of *A Montessori Mother* in 1912, nonfiction under the name "Dorothy Canfield Fisher." Her life is examined in three biographies (Yates, 1958, 1971; Washington, 1982), a book of selected letters spanning six decades (Madigan, 1993), and selected letters of Willa Cather, which include correspondence with Fisher (Jewell & Stout, 2013). These sources provide numerous details about Fisher's multifaceted, unconventional life, and cite her contributions to adult education (Ehrhardt, 2004, p. 54; Madigan, 1993, pp. 19, 134; Washington, 1982, p.194; Yates, 1958, p. 166). Yates' 1958 biography is noteworthy because it is based on personal meetings with Fisher, who read and approved the manuscript prior to publication (Yates, 1990).

In her biography, Yates (1958) wrote, Fisher "is the result of influences around her as well as standing up to them" (p. 5). Some influences were givens or matters in which she had no choice: her parents, her birthplace, her son's death, her small stature, and deafness. Other influences resulted from personal decisions. She chose a writing career over music, marriage to John Fisher, a home in an ancestral rural community rather than New York City, a Quaker affiliation, and causes she wanted to support through her writing. The first decisive influence was her parents. She was born on February 17, 1879, the second child of James and Flavia Canfield, who named her after Dorothea Brooks, the heroine of the mid-19th century British novel, *Middlemarch*.

THE EARLY YEARS

Like the heroine in *Middlemarch*, Fisher lived during a period of social, economic, and political change (Howe, 2007) in Lawrence, Kansas, a community settled by ardent Northern abolitionists, suffragists, and Free Soil advocates (Oertel, 2009). Her parents had family roots in Vermont, were raised in ministers' families, and were teachers active on behalf of women's rights, racial equality, and universal education. Fisher's father knew "there would no longer be the necessity to fit herself into a tightly prescribed role because she was a girl" (Yates, 1958, p. 14). Because of her father's career and her mother's artistic interests, Fisher spent her childhood and adolescence in three geographically disparate and culturally distinct places: the Midwest (Kansas, Nebraska, and Ohio), rural southern Vermont, and France. These diverse environments provided unique experiences and opportunities to encounter varied social mores and ideas and meet people, some of whom were connected to adult education. She attended public schools in Kansas and spent summers with her paternal family in Arlington, Vermont. Books were a prominent feature in both households, which also prized education, music, and physical activity.

At the age of 11, Fisher went to Paris with her mother, who studied art. She attended a French school and became an indispensable guide due to her multilingual skills. This period left a deep impression on her as she read French authors like Montaigne, Rousseau, and Rabelais, whom she cited in *Why Stop Learning?* (1927). She viewed art, such as Danton's statue with its inscription, "After bread, the first need of the people is education," which reinforced ideas learned from her father (Yates, 1958, p. 44). Fisher completed preparatory school in Lincoln, Nebraska, where her father was university chancellor (1891–95); he urged her to learn fencing, boxing, and swimming as an antidote to women being too protected and unable to profit from criticism (Yates, 1958, p. 49). Her brother introduced her to Willa Cather, his college classmate, and they discovered their mutual interest in French literature, music, and art (Madigan, 1993, p. 11).

Pain in her ears persisted in Columbus, Ohio, where a doctor diagnosed a middle ear infection that would lead to deafness (Yates, 1958, p. 62). Nonetheless, Dorothy completed a bachelor's degree in French in 1899 at Ohio State University, where her father was president (1895–99). Her mother organized the Women's Clubs of Ohio into a federation and became the first president, a continuation of her efforts in Kansas to organize clubs for women whose lives were "bounded by the cookstove, the chicken coop and the crib" (Washington, 1982, p. 28). Fisher would write a chapter on women's clubs in *Why Stop Learning?* (1927). A letter written after her parents' deaths reflects her keen insight: "I was never a feminist.

It was my older generation, my father and mother, who were. I was rather (as it often goes in generations) in reaction from their extreme zeal for 'women's rights'" (Washington, 1982, p.115).

MARRIAGE AND FAMILY

While completing her PhD in French in 1904 at Columbia University, New York City, she met John Redwood Fisher (1883–1959), a fellow student from a Pennsylvania Quaker family. They married in 1907 and moved to Arlington, Vermont, and the Canfield house, a place that was the source of comfort, stability, and solitude necessary for her work. John had an "active role as collaborator in the writing of articles and as editor of her fiction" (Washington, 1982, p. 187). He introduced her to Alfred Harcourt, his college classmate, who became her publisher. When John volunteered as an ambulance driver in France during World War I, Dorothy and their young children, Sally (b. 1909) and Jimmy (b. 1913) joined him. Her French fluency was invaluable to establishing a Braille printing press for French soldiers and a safe house for children (Yates, 1958, pp. 128–133). After returning home in May 1919, she began wearing a hearing device to accommodate her hearing loss. Jimmy's death while serving in the Army Medical Corps in World War II was her greatest loss: "I am using work as an opiate—and like all opiates, it is dangerous when abused.... But now there is only intolerable pain" (Washington, 1982, p. 212).

DOROTHY AS WRITER

When she died at home of a stroke in 1958, she was known for her books, magazine articles, civic work, and numerous honorary degrees. Eleanor Roosevelt cited her as one of the 10 most influential American women. However, in a 1929 letter to her publisher, Fisher wrote, "I wish you'd put in [my biographical sketch] a little more mention of *Why Stop Learning?* I'd like not to have people forget that book. I've said some things in it I'm glad to have said" (Madigan, 1993, p. 134). At that time, she was almost 50 and had reluctantly accepted BOMC editorial board membership. She was ambivalent about selecting other people's books, but realized her father's generation erred in assuming "a spontaneous, lasting, continuous interest in books and intellectual life, which doesn't seem to exist, any more than a spontaneous interest in being good seems to animate human nature" (Washington, 1982, p. 198). She saw the opportunity to foster reading, a foundational habit for citizens of a democratic society. Earlier, she demonstrated commitment to childhood and parent education as author of *A Montessori Mother* (1912), *Mothers and Children* (1914), and *Self-Reliance* (1916); the latter was disseminated and discussed among education leaders (Johnston, 1917).

Why Stop Learning?

Fisher may not have written *Why Stop Learning?* (1927) if not for the personal request of Frederick Keppel, Carnegie Corporation President (1923–1941) and longtime family friend. It meant she gave up a year of her own writing to organize and read numerous AAAE field reports. In the foreword, Fisher stated her purpose: to present in 12 chapters "a running commentary" on new information about "attempts at education by grown-ups [by] a fairly typical American." The book "enabled her to express a conviction that had been intensifying through the years—that learning could not be confined to any one period of life, that real education was a process which, once started, went on" (Yates, 1958, pp. 165–166). In chapter one, "The Idea of Mass Education," Fisher argued that personal growth and a healthy democracy required adult education in the 20th century, just as literacy was the type of mass education required and achieved in the 19th century. "Anyone who considers for a moment the signs of the times, knows that the next battle in the campaign of democracy is going to rage around the question of the possibility and advisability of general education for the majority of grown-ups" (p. 15). The terms, *self-education* and *mass education*, are used throughout the book to connote adult education, which she distinguished from literacy: "We are merely a literate nation, not an educated one" (p. 8).

The next eight chapters focus on different types of adult education with most discussion given to workers education, followed by museums, women's clubs, and public libraries. Fisher considered the future of adult education in the final chapter, "Some Last Guesses," declaring, "It takes genuine education, not the mere acquisition of more information, to enable people to order their lives intelligently" (1927, p. 291). She included *The Meaning of Adult Education* (Lindeman, 1926) in the brief reference list. Fisher gave a historical background to each type of adult education, drawing on the AAAE reports. For example, in the chapter on correspondence schools, she noted the growth from 115 students when the first commercial school opened in 1891 to two million students, four times the enrollment in colleges, universities, and professional schools (p. 32). She cited factors influencing this development like the growth of scientific, technical knowledge, more complex machines, business competition, and fraudulent advertising. She criticized education's connection to increasing commercialism and materialism, pointing out that one large commercial school spent only three quarters of one cent of every dollar for instruction and the remainder for advertising and profit.

Fisher (1927) described free public libraries as a new institution in world history which represented the communal, cooperative impulse of society. As in other chapters, she linked institutional developments with democracy: "Both card catalogues and modern bookstacks are as direct and purposeful manifestations of the spirit of democracy as the ballot box" (p. 61). She critiqued class society and queried, "Are the masses, ordinary folks, the general public *worth* serving?" (p. 72; emphasis in original). Fisher demonstrated an understanding of adult learners' needs: "Adults based on years of actual struggle with reality don't find the books they need and written in the manner [they need]" (p. 69). She urged Americans not to become complacent, citing data that 83% of the rural population was without a local library and that one third of U.S. counties had no public libraries (p. 67). In concluding chapters, she listed 52 kinds of adult education, from study courses in prisons and the military, to genealogical societies and nature study groups, and discussed developments in other countries like the Danish folk high school.

Fisher (1927) clearly favored educational methods based on reading and grounded in "the educational axiom: Interest is the only absolutely indispensable ingredient to learn anything" (p. 141). She admitted her bias interfered with objectively discussing lyceums based on the lecture method. In the chapter titled "Parents as Students," she acknowledged "fathers have realized that they too are modern parents," (p. 124) but described women as pioneers in the footsteps of the first club women who sought rational child-rearing methods. In the "Women's Clubs" chapter, she discussed various activities like "Americanization work" with immigrants in addition to study groups. "The subject chosen is always something directly connected with personal human life. Those seem to be the subjects women turn to when they're free to choose" (p. 84).

In the parent education chapter, Fisher (1927) appeared to promote ideas contradicting her progressive views and abhorrence of racial discrimination. In lauding universities with child psychology programs, she acknowledged experts like John Dewey and listed books "that are not pretentious, popularizing or shallow [and] written by sound educators" (p. 133) including the title, "Evolution, Genetics, and Eugenics." Eugenics was a prevalent 20th century social philosophy that espoused practices to improve human hereditary traits. That she recommended this title bolsters the assertion by literary scholars that Fisher supported eugenics endeavors (Ehrhardt, 2004).

Some chapters reveal Fisher's (1927) sensitivity to gender, race, and class and the influence of changing social conditions on educational need and opportunity. She referred to "the possessing class" (p. 5), "the intelligentsia," (p. 117) or the ruling class's obstructing the aspirations of middle-class women and of working men. In the chapter "Women's Club," she cited consequences in transitioning to an industrial society: "the disappearance of enforced and absorbing occupation; physical safety which removes ... physical risk; and most of all the possession of ... leisure time" (p. 93). Women's clubs developed as a response to these new conditions (Martin, 1987). The General Federation of Women's Clubs grew from 720,000 members in 1901 to 2 million members by 1924 without the support of educators, some of whom educated former slaves, but resisted educating women: "Odd, is it not, that not one professional educator moved out of his tracks to try to set straight this army [of women] of humble, willing students, the grade of whose intelligence was so vitally important to the nation?" (Fisher, 1927, p. 103).

Learn or Perish

Fisher's focus on educators and exhortation, "We must go on learning, or perish," (1927, p. 118), were expanded in *Learn or Perish* (1930), the second monograph in the Kappa Delta Pi Lecture Series. It includes sections on the perils of the teaching profession; firsthand psychology of learning; culture and the habit of study. In relationship to educational leadership necessary to establish adult education, Fisher repeated themes discussed in *Why Stop Learning?* She reported teachers' failure to provide leadership due to attitudes toward methods other than teacher-directed classroom learning, and highlighted the significance of intrinsic motivation: "Things learned from the inside traditionally are a thousand times more living than those from the outside because they are felt, not merely seen" (1930, p. 40). Fisher hoped that presenting educators with facts from data in the AAAE field reports would lead to change, drawing on her lifelong conviction that "Truth was something to be determined by one's self when one had the facts" (Yates, 1958, p. 37).

CONCLUSION

Fisher was the result of many influences leading to her adult education advocacy and writing. In turn, she influenced the organization and practice of adult education as the only woman of 19 AAAE presidents who served between 1926 and 1950 (Knowles, 1977, p. 201). As president, she created committees on cooperation with industry and labor, Negro education, parent education, rural education, and techniques of discussion. As author of *Why Stop Learning?* (1927) and other works, she left a rich legacy for students, teachers, and researchers of adult education history and for citizens of democratic societies.

REFERENCES

Cartwright, M. A. (1935). *Ten years of adult education, A report on a decade of progress in the American movement.* New York, NY: Macmillan.

Ehrhardt, J. C. (2004). *Writers of conviction, The personal politics of Zona Gale, Dorothy Canfield Fisher, Rose Wilder Lane and Josephine Herbst.* Columbia: University of Missouri Press.

Fisher, D. C. (1912). *A Montessori mother.* New York, NY: Henry Holt.

Fisher, D. C. (1914). *Mothers and children.* New York, NY: Henry Holt.

Fisher, D. C. (1916). *Self-reliance: A practical and informal discussion of methods of teaching self-reliance, initiative and responsibility to modern children.* Childhood and Youth Series. Indianapolis, IN: Bobbs-Merrill.

Fisher, D. C. (1920). Facts versus education. *Delineator, 96* (11).

Fisher, D. C. (1927). *Why stop learning?* New York, NY: Harcourt & Brace.

Fisher, D. C. (1930). Learn or perish. *The Kappa Delta Pi Lecture Series,* (2). New York, NY: Liveright.

Fisher, D. C. (1933). Bright perilous face of leisure. *Journal of Adult Education,* (5), 237–243.

Fisher, D. C. (1936a). To meet the challenge of free choice (M. Ely, Ed.). *Adult Education in Action.* New York, NY: American Association of Adult Education.

Fisher, D. C. (1936b). My grandmother as a young mother (M. Ely, Ed.). *Adult Education in Action.* New York, NY: American Association of Adult Education.

Fisher, D. C. (1938). Will to understand. *Journal of Adult Education,* (10), 168–170.

Fisher, D. C. (1942, September). More to life than jobs. *Journal of Home Economics,34*(7), 413–15.

Howe, D. W. (2007). *What hath God wrought: The transformation of America, 1815–1848.* Oxford, UK: Oxford University Press.

Imel, S., & Bersch, G. T. (2009). *Who were the women? An in-depth analysis of some early women adult educators.* Unpublished manuscript. Adult Education Research Conference.

Jewell, A., & Stout, J. (2013). *The selected letters of Willa Cather.* New York, NY: Alfred A. Knopf.

Johnston, N. B. (1917). Book review: Self-reliance by Dorothy Canfield Fisher. *Education Administration and Supervision, 3*(3), 176.

Knowles, M. S. (1977). *A history of the adult education movement in the United States* (Rev. ed.). Huntington, NY: Robert E. Krieger.

Lindeman, E. C. (1926). *The Meaning of Adult Education.* New York, NY: New Republic.

Madigan, M. (Ed.). (1993). *Keeping fires night and day: Selected letters of Dorothy Canfield Fisher.* Columbia: University of Missouri Press.

Martin, T. P. (1987). *The sound of our own voices: Women's study clubs, 1860–1910.* Boston, MA: Beacon.

Oertel, K. T. (2009). *Bleeding borders, race, gender, and violence in pre-civil war Kansas.* Baton Rouge: Louisiana State University Press.

Sexton, C.A. (1993, March 14–18). *The influences of the turn-of-the century midwest on Dorothy Canfield Fisher's educational philosophy.* (Unpublished manuscript). Fourth Visiting Scholar conference in the History of Adult Education, Syracuse University, Syracuse, NY.

Washington, I. H. (1982). *Dorothy Canfield Fisher: A biography.* Shelburne, VT: New England Press.

Yates, E. (1958). *Pebble in a pool: The widening circles of Dorothy Canfield Fisher's life.* New York, NY: E. P. Dutton.

Yates, E. (1971). *The lady from Vermont: Dorothy Canfield Fisher's life and world.* Brattleboro, VT: Stephen Greene Press.

Yates, E. (1990). *An oral history with Elizabeth Yates/Interviewer Charlene A. Sexton.*

Mary Parker Follett

CHAPTER 13

MARY PARKER FOLLETT

A Paradox of Adult Learner and Educator

Vivian W. Mott

No Small Lives: Handbook of North American Early Women Adult Educators, 1925-1950,
pp. 125–132
Copyright © 2015 by Information Age Publishing
All rights of reproduction in any form reserved.

She was a paradox, not only as a woman in the late 19th and early 20th centuries, but as a learner and educator. Mary Parker Follett (1868–1933) has been described as holding multiple philosophical positions throughout her relatively long and undoubtedly distinguished life. Treatises by her and about her refer to both her pragmatism and idealism, and contradictorily to her feminine liberal humanism, instrumentality, and convention. Follett was said to have been "dogmatic, sometimes pedantic, and arrogant, but always provocative and stimulating" (James, James, & Boyer, 1971, p. 641). Scholars have described her as a political scientist, master analyst, and scholar of business and organizational administration decades ahead of her time. She is also noted as an "often forgotten, but still deeply instructive thinker for educators and social animateurs" (Smith, 2002). Evidence of this paradox and the complexity of her teachings and scholarship are demonstrated by the wide range of sources in which one finds her work—from early adult education literature to what some would consider fugitive literature from business, accounting, organization theory, and social justice disciplines. Although she published obscurely and relatively little, Mary Parker Follett is considered by many to be one of the most influential and relevant thinkers on community organizing, informal education, and organizational management (Graham, 1995; Hurst, 1992; Tonn, 2003).

EARLY LIFE AND FORMATIVE EXPERIENCES

Mary Parker Follett was born in September of 1868, one of two children (and the only daughter) of affluent Quaker parents in Quincy, Massachusetts. She was mentored by her father until his death and then educated at the prestigious Thayer Academy in Braintree, Massachusetts. Follett enjoyed a quiet and cultured childhood, reading several languages; she was tutored in nature and the arts, and was exceptionally well-read in sociology, psychology, history, and philosophy. In her mid 20s, as a nontraditional learner in the truest sense, Follett studied philosophy, law, economics, and government at the distinguished Society for the Collegiate Instruction of Women, later to become Radcliffe College in Massachusetts. At least two of the noted Harvard faculty, George Santayana and William James, undoubtedly impacted Follett's critical thinking and growing social consciousness (Davis, 1989; Tonn, 2003). Even though her studies were interrupted several times due to family illnesses and other responsibilities—it took her 10 years to graduate *summa cum laude*—she also enjoyed a year's study in Cambridge, England, and pursued postgraduate study in Paris (James et al., 1971; Smith, 2002; Tonn, 2003).

Follett spent most of her early working years in community organizing, most notably in the Roxbury neighborhoods of Boston. Her interests and commitments to community were influenced by her Quaker upbringing and deeply engrained beliefs that "members work together, consensus is built, and power is shared" (Feldheim, 2004, p. 341). Follett's experiences with those who were socially and economically disadvantaged also led to her interests and efforts in labor education, youth development, and political action. Her work in community and political action was no doubt influenced and encouraged by her lifelong friend and partner, Isobel L. Briggs, with whom Follett made her home until Brigg's death in 1926. Severely impacted by Brigg's death, Follett returned to London, where she lived with Dame Katharine Furse, an influential leader in the Red Cross and Women's Royal Naval Service, as she continued her lectures for the London School of Economics (James et al., 1971; Tonn, 2003).

At the height of her popularity in London, Follett returned to the United States in the fall of 1933, concerned with both her financial holdings and increasing ill health. Following surgery for an enlarged thyroid, her physicians discovered and removed several advanced tumors. Mary Parker Follett died two days later on December 18, 1933; her ashes were scattered on the hillside overlooking her beloved home in Vermont (Graham, 1995; Tonn, 2003).

FOLLETT—AN EARLY ADULT EDUCATOR

Follett's teaching and scholarship in the opening decades of the 20th century were consistent with the legacy and earliest principles of adult, community, and informal education. She is credited with helping develop the thinking of adult educators such as Eduard Lindeman, and her philosophies and ideas compared to those of John Dewey, Myles Horton, Jane Addams, and others (Smith, 2002; Stewart, 1987). Echoing many principles from classic adult education literature, Follett described adult education as the "process of engagement and encounter, where the individual thinks through his or her experience, questions its meaning and truth, relates the experience to his or herself and learns from the experience" (Feldheim, 2004, p. 344).

In her 1918 publication, *The New State*, Follett wrote of the importance of rich experience in learning and change, of self-directedness, lifelong learning, and of the integral connection between life and experience. Follett wrote that "life and education must never be separated. We must have more life in our universities, more education in our life" (Follett, 1918, p. 369). Among her most noteworthy influences was her role in the establishment of community centers in public schools that sat empty after hours and on weekends and holidays. Follett brought together youth groups, labor organizations, churches, and schools to create local networks, support citizenship training and group interaction, and to counter civic apathy (James et al., 1971; Tonn, 2003). These initiatives and her national leadership in community center associations eventually led Follett to Eduard Lindeman and her recognition in adult education. Other ideals and concepts promoted by Follett have found their way into subsequent adult education teachings as well, resulting in her work being cited as among the earliest examples of adult education scholarship (Stewart, 1987).

Even though Follett's work flourished at the opening of the women's movement in the United States, Follett did not consider herself a feminist, and there is no record of her active participation in early women's organizations. Like many female reformers of the Progressive Era, however, much of Follett's biography suggests the strong influence of other women in her life. Due to her inheritances, she was able to live independently, but shared lifelong friendships with women such as Isobel Briggs, Ella Lyman Cabot, and Dame Katharine Furse (Feldheim, 2004; Furse, 1934; Morton & Lindquist, 1997; Tonn, 2003). Her position regarding equity and participation in organizational life was counterintuitive to the "gendered or 'masculine' orientation toward expertise, leadership" (Morton & Lindquist, 1997, p. 349) that marked administrative management throughout most of the discipline's history. Morton and Lindquist and other scholars maintain, however, that Follett's work and philosophies such as emancipatory relationships, the value of experiential learning and subjective knowing, and the concept of power *with* instead of power *over* are "remarkably reminiscent of current feminist theory" (Morton & Lindquist, 1997, p. 353).

FOLLETT'S INFLUENCE
ON ADMINISTRATIVE ORGANIZATIONAL PRACTICES

Follett was perhaps less appreciated for her business acumen, undoubtedly because of her gender, but also because she spoke and wrote in the simplest, most direct manner—a manner her friend Dame Furse referred to as "Mary's indomitable power of expression" (Furse, 1934). She was said to have been an avid and accurate observer of human nature and social interaction, which led to her insightful perception where both people and organizations were concerned.

She maintained that people were at the core of any business activity, and that to resolve the concerns of people was to mediate and improve the situations present in any organization. Her work presented a more humanized and accessible approach to the male dominated, positivistic scientific management influence and work of Frederick Taylor, Max Weber, Henry Gantt, Frank and Lillian Gilbreth, and others in the early 20th century and postwar era of the 1940s (Fox, 1968; Hurst, 1992; Smith, 2002). In lecturing on the centrality of human interaction, for instance, Follett stressed, "I do not think we have psychological and ethical and economic problems. We have human problems, with psychological, ethical, and economical aspects" (Metcalf & Urwick, 1942, p. 184). Follett was also one of the early proponents of group efficacy, of the capacity for a group to produce greater results than individuals alone, even though the concept of synergy had not yet been conceived (Fox, 1968).

Follett's philosophy regarding human difference was also reflected in her work in communities and social reform. She valued diversity, especially in community groups, and maintained that integrated neighborhoods served to counter "the narrowness and exclusiveness of many more homogenized communities" (Smith, 2002, n. p.). Follett taught that "difference will make a richer content of life ... Every difference that is swept up into a bigger conception feeds and enriches society; every difference which is ignored feeds on society and eventually corrupts it" (Follett, 1918, p. 40).

Among her most important contributions to administrative thinking was her teaching on conflict resolution. According to Follett, of the three ways of "settling of differences: by domination, by compromise, or by integration" (Follett, as cited in Urwick, 1949, p. 66), only integration offers progress. Integration holds the possibility of some new outcome, while in domination, only those in power achieve what they want, and in compromise, "each side gives up a little in order to have peace" (Follett, as cited in Metcalf & Urwick, 1942, p. 32; Urwick, 1949). Follett further maintained that

> We cannot hope to integrate our differences unless we know what they are. The first rule, then, for obtaining integration is to put your cards on the table, face the real issue, uncover the conflict, bring the whole thing into the open. (Follett, as cited in Metcalf & Urwick, 1942, p. 36)

Despite her recognition in what was very much a male-dominated world, Follett never achieved mainstream acceptance and is said to have been rediscovered repeatedly in the near century since her passing (Feldheim, 2004; Fox, 1968; Hurst, 1992; Tonn, 2003). In the United States in particular, successive shifts in administrative management and strong American individualism likely resulted in benign neglect of Follett's work. Even though her ideas were not popular in America's efficiency-oriented, hierarchical, conventional management in the early and mid-20th century, Follett's ideas remained popular in Great Britain and Japan. Her writings were especially favored in Japan mid-century, where total quality management was the paradigm of choice. Industrialists and business leaders in Japan even maintained a Follett Society, which recognized leaders and innovative thinkers in business and industry. In an overview of Follett's reemerging influence in 1989, one advocate of her work wrote, "To call her the 'first management consultant' or an 'organizational consultant,' as is often done, is equivalent to describing Leonardo da Vinci as a 'graphic artist'" (Davis, 1989, p. 231).

FOLLETT'S BIBLIOGRAPHY

Mary Parker Follett wrote prodigiously during her studies at Harvard and Cambridge, while engaged in community action in Boston, and later as she lectured in the U.K. and elsewhere. Several volumes of her collected works are still in print and available to readers. Below are her key works and three principle examples of her collected lectures, accompanied by notes of their significance or history.

The Speaker of the House of Representatives (1896). This 378 page manuscript, Follett's first publication, began as her thesis while studying in Cambridge and later at Radcliffe. Credited by Theodore Roosevelt as the first comprehensive analysis of the office, Follett's inaugural scholarship was considered a valuable contribution to the understanding of constitutional law.

The New State—Group Organization, the Solution for Popular Government (1918). *The New State* (373 pages) is perhaps Follett's most quoted work and remains influential with audiences rediscovering her work. This classic work includes Follett's thoughts on dynamic democracy, self-rule, and group efficacy. Part of the appendix represents one of the earliest writings on adult education principles.

Creative Experience (1924). This publication built on Follett's experiences with groups, but shifted the focus to teamwork, learning in organizations, co-active versus coercive power, and participatory management in business, commerce, and industry. *Creative Experience* (303 pages) is considered Follett's first business-oriented publication and enjoyed an early and sustained audience in administrative circles.

Dynamic Administration: The Collected Papers of Mary Parker Follett (1942). Published shortly after Follett's death, this collection was edited by colleagues Henry Metcalf of the New York Bureau of Personnel Administration and Lionel Urwick of the International Management Institute, both of whom had helped promote Follett's lecture series. In addition to the concept of power as a commodity that can be produced, these collected papers also brought the concepts of empowerment, decentralized responsibility, and situational leadership into the lexicon of management thinking.

Freedom & Co-ordination: Lectures in Business Organization (1949). This brief volume (89 pages), also edited by Lionel Urwick, contains what are thought to be among Follett's more significant lectures on authority, influence, leadership, followership, and administrative control. It is in this collection of her papers where early mention of the principles of transformative leadership can be found, as well as her fundamental tenets of organization presented in Follett's final lecture.

Mary Parker Follett: Prophet of Management (1995). This collection of Follett's writings is the newest addition of her collected works. Edited by Pauline Graham, this 309 page volume includes 11 of what many consider to be Follett's most influential lectures, accompanied by commentaries by such notable leader-scholars as Rosabeth Moss Kanter, Peter Drucker, Warren Bennis, Henry Mintzberg, and Angela Dumas.

REFERENCES

Davis, A. M. (1989). An interview with Mary Parker Follett. *Negotiation Journal, 5*(3), 223–235. doi:10.1111/j.1571-9979.1989.tb00519.x

Feldheim, M. A. (2004). Mary Parker Follett lost and found—Again, and again, and again. *International Journal of Organization Theory and Behavior, 7*(3), 341–362.

Follett, M. P. (1896). *The Speaker of the House of Representatives*. New York, NY: Longman Green.

Follett, M. P. (1918). *The new state—Group organization, the solution for popular government*. New York, NY: Longman Green.

Follett, M. P. (1924). *Creative experience*. New York, NY: Longman Green.

Fox, E. M. (1968). Mary Parker Follett: The enduring contribution. *Public Administration Review, 28*(6), 520–529.

Furse, K. (1934). Letter to Ella Cabot Lyman. Schlesinger Library. Radcliffe College, Cambridge. Retrieved June 10, 2013, from http://oasis.lib.harvard.edu/oasis/deliver/~sch00485

Graham, P. (Ed.). (1995). *Mary Parker Follett—Prophet of management*. Boston, MA: Harvard Business School.

Hurst, D. K. (1992). Thoroughly modern—Mary Parker Follett. *Business Quarterly, 56*(4), 55–58.

James, E. T., James, J. W., & Boyer, P. S. (Eds.). (1971). *Notable American women 1607–1950: A biographical dictionary* (Vol. 1, pp. 639–641). Cambridge, MA: Harvard University Press.

Metcalf, H. C., & Urwick, L. (Eds.). (1942). *Dynamic administration: The collected papers of Mary Parker Follett*. New York, NY: Harper.

Morton, N. O., & Lindquist, S. A. (1997). Revealing the feminist in Mary Parker Follett. *Administration & Society, 29*(3), 348–371.

Smith, M. K. (2002). Mary Parker Follett and informal education. *The encyclopedia of informal education*. Retrieved May 12, 2013, from http://infed.org/mobi/mary-parker-follett-community-creative-experience-and-education/

Stewart, D. W. (1987). *Adult learning in America: Eduard Lindeman and his agenda for lifelong education*. Malabar, FL: Robert E. Krieger.

Tonn, J. C. (2003). *Mary P. Follett: Creating democracy, transforming management*. New Haven, CT; London, UK: Yale University Press.

Urwick, L. (Ed.). (1949). *Freedom & co-ordination: Lectures in business organization*. London, UK: Management Publications Trust.

CHAPTER 14

WAKING UP THE WORLD

Mae C. Hawes and Adult Education

Lisa R. Merriweather

Throughout history, there have been individuals who dared to care. In their vision for a new world, everyone had a role to play. Mae C. Hawes was such a visionary. Born in Macon, Georgia, on September 7, 1886 to Hampton B. Hawes Sr. and Janie Glover (U. S. Census Bureau, 1900), Hawes took her place within an accomplished family, which was recognized in 1959 by the *Los Angeles Tribune* as "one of Los Angeles' most distinguished families" (Dr. Hinton Developer, p. 6). Hawes' passing in 1979 at the age of 94 in New York City was punctuated by an exclamation mark, not a period, because of the significant impact she had on the lives of others.

LIVING WITH JIM CROW

Mae C. Hawes came to age during the period of Jim Crow in the aftermath of the unfulfilled promises of the Reconstruction Era. This was a time of radical change in which those who were once enslaved and considered to be three fifths of a human being were enfranchised through three

No Small Lives: Handbook of North American Early Women Adult Educators, 1925-1950,
pp. 133–139
Copyright © 2015 by Information Age Publishing
All rights of reproduction in any form reserved.

strokes of the legislative pen: the 13th, 14th, and 15th amendments (Franklin, 2013). The Reconstruction Era held out the promise of positive material and symbolic change, but the well of dignity and human rights from which African Americans had begun to dip their cups dried as quickly as it had filled.

The post-Reconstruction Era was characterized by Rayford Logan (1954) as the nadir of race relations in America. Across the nation, particularly in the South, Black people were socially, politically and economically re-disenfranchised through a variety of de facto and de jure laws and practices. For Mae C. Hawes and other African Americans, Jim Crow permeated their lives, resulting in a racial hierarchy which positioned Whites at the top and defined life for others by separation, inequity, extreme hostility, violence, and assaults on dignity.

Having spent many years in Georgia, Hawes was not a stranger to Jim Crow racism but developed strategies to decrease its mental and emotional consequences by values and examples set by her family of origin. Mae was the fifth child born to a hardworking family-oriented couple who had 13 children in all (U.S. Census Bureau, 1900, 1910). Her mother worked as a clothes presser and later as a sick nurse, and her father collected clothes for orphaned children and worked on a farm (U.S. Census, 1900, 1910). Given the times and the lack of economic benefit to do so, it is remarkable that all of the offspring went to school. Hawes' educational pedigree includes older sisters Ida and Ella, who were school teachers (U.S. Census Bureau, 1910); Hampton Jr., who studied at Lincoln Union Theological Seminary to become a minister; younger siblings DeWitt, who was a social worker (Bersch, 2011), Maxie who also worked as a social worker (Bersch, 2011) and a seamstress finisher (U.S. Census, 1930), and Bessie who was a registered nurse (U.S. Census Bureau, 1930). It was noted that her other siblings, Ada, Nellie, and Earnest, also attended school. Evidence of education as a core value was evident but equally compelling were the strong bonds the family had with each other. Janie lived with Mae's sister, Bessie (Florida State Census, 1935), and after retirement Mae relocated to California and resided with her brother, Hampton Jr. and his family (Bersch, 2011). Being present for family members was an integral component of how her family functioned. Education and family support were sources for the resiliency exhibited by Mae during the turbulent racial climate of Jim Crow.

ON BEING A TEACHER

Mae C. Hawes, throughout her lifetime, positioned herself as a cultural change agent and employed education as the vehicle through which she advanced change. Her primary vocation was as an educator in the formal education arena. As early as 1910 continuing to 1951, save the few years she spent in the nonformal education sector, Hawes demonstrated that she was a catalyst for change. She taught future leaders and teachers at Tennessee Agriculture and Industrial State Normal School (A&T) (Tennessee Board of Education, 1916) and Bethune-Cookman College in Florida (Still Hard at Work, 1968) as an instructor of mathematics; she taught children as a public school teacher in New York City (U.S. Census Bureau, 1930) and future social workers at Atlanta University (Still Hard at Work, 1968). Her educational background prepared her for teaching in both spheres. Hawes graduated from Atlanta University, earned a specialized degree from Chicago University, received a masters' degree in education from Columbia University, and completed postgraduate work in sociology (New Move For, 1931; Tennessee Board of Education, 1916).

Within the formal education structure as an administrative leader, she was also on the front line and was strategically positioned to ignite and fan the fires to ensure a positive and equitable outcome for all. She served as the department chair as well as a faculty member at Tennessee State University and was the dean of women at Cheyney State College in Pennsylvania (Still Hard at Work, 1968). In both capacities, it is certain that she recognized the significance of the racialized context in which her students, who were predominantly African American, existed. Hawes recognized the importance of formal education as a vehicle for helping others to help themselves and to help each other. Her actions showed that improving society through racial uplift was a priority on her agenda. Undoubtedly, Hawes had an illustrative career as a servant leader in arenas of public school and higher education, but she also was an influential actor in the adult education scene.

WAKING UP THE WORLD THROUGH ADULT EDUCATION

Hawes acquired human and cultural capital by virtue of her education and job experiences, but she also possessed social capital that was used to help fellow community members. Although Hawes lived in a variety of states, she was always active in those communities. The society section of newspapers such as the *Los Angeles Tribune* and *Atlanta Daily World* was replete with stories of her involvement with her local community (e.g., Lomax, 1959). She had a clear understanding of how things worked, how to get things done, and how to leverage her social capital as a means of reaching her objectives. In 1918, in a letter to W. E. B. DuBois to acknowledge his 50th birthday, she wrote, I "cannot count myself as among your friends" (Hawes, 1918) but by 1933, she had accumulated enough social capital to feel comfortable requesting a meeting with DuBois to discuss a personal problem (Hawes, 1933).

The tentacles of her network were long and reached into many segments of the local as well as national community. Hawes was not a stranger to the elite. *Ebony Magazine* in 1968 reported that "she has known many famous personalities, including Eleanor Roosevelt, James Weldon Johnson and Indian poet Rabindranath Tagore" (Still Hard at Work, p. 66). In spite of her personal associations, which positioned her in the upper echelon of Black social society, Mae was humble, down to earth, and approachable. These traits were critical to her success during the three primary periods she worked as an adult educator.

Mae was never afraid to step out of the comfort zone of the familiar to explore other avenues. By 1922, she had left Georgia, worked as faculty at Tennessee A&T in Nashville, and lived in Washington, DC, while working as a clerk (U.S. Census, 1930). At 36 years of age, she was employed by the Young Woman's Christian Association (YWCA). Like most organizations of the time, the YWCA was segregated and discriminatory. For instance, the YWCA's National Training School (NTS), which provided education for YWCA's professional workers, was started in 1908 but did not admit Black women until 1911 (Robertson, 2007).

It is safe to assume that Hawes was primarily affiliated with the "Colored Branches," as is suggested in the *New York Age* (First Year's Operation of Emma Ransom House, 1927–1928). Mae is listed as the Residential Director of the Emma Ransom House, a YWCA hotel affiliated with the 137th Street Branch in Harlem. During this time, African Americans, especially in professional circles, represented a close-knit national group. Talent was noticed, tapped, and recommended for use in other activities that furthered the cause of racial improvement during a time of intense racial discrimination. As a consequence of her previous achievements at the Ransom House and as National Secretary with the YWCA as well as Dunbar National Bank thrift department head (New Move For, 1931), Hawes was selected to lead an ambitious endeavor to educate African Americans.

The American Association for Adult education (AAAE) sponsored an experiment in Negro Education (Guy, 1996; New Move For, 1931) based in the Atlanta Public Library, Auburn Branch. There was a similar experiment being conducted in Harlem. Hawes returned to the Peach State to assume leadership of the endeavor. It was described in the *Cleveland Plain Dealer* this way: AAAE "for a number of years has been promoting adult education among different groups in America, has just begun its work among Negroes" (New Move For, 1931, p. 2). Because Hawes recognized that "adult education for Negroes ... did not keep pace with adult education for whites" (Rowden, 1934, p. 124), she, along with Alain Locke, would become a strong advocate for Association-sponsored equitable adult learning opportunities for African Americans. As the director of the project from 1931 to 1934, Hawes was integrally involved in the adult education movement and at the forefront of developments in adult education for African Americans. In spite of the success of the "experiment," the program was terminated in 1934.

This appointment allowed Hawes to draw on her innumerable talents, as it required her to collaborate with multiple inter- and intraracial groups such as college presidents, business people, church groups, and women's clubs. She organized programs for African Americans that created greater access to books, study of domestic and international social problems opportunity, and initiatives to decrease the illiteracy rate (Rowden, 1934, p. 126). Hawes also garnered international attention from the World Association for Adult Education in London for her work and reputation for excellence in Atlanta. Her unofficial role as an ambassador of adult education for African Americans culminated in multiple visits to London.

It is not surprising, given her genuine desire to improve conditions for people worldwide, that she joined the London-based Moral Re-Armament Movement. Mrs. Arenia Mallory Belden, assistant to Mary McLeod Bethune, said,

> the principles of the Moral Re-Armament ... when applied to the daily life of my race, or any race, reduce to a minimum all race consciousness, racial antagonism and prejudice; and when these are removed, my people will have freedom to make their full contribution to the national life. (Many Negroes Joining, 1939, p. 1)

Mae C. Hawes made such contributions during her tenure as the Program Director by serving as the Vice-Chairman for the Adult Education Committee of the National Conference on Fundamental Problems in the Education of Negroes in 1934. She reported at a national level on the status of African American adult education to a delegation that included Dr. Ambrose Caliver (Current Events, 1934).

Hawes' contributions to freedom through learning continued even after she retired in 1951. Her postcareer work was perhaps the most rewarding to her. In 1965, at the age of 81, Hawes resumed her role as an educator. After completing training with Volunteers in Service to America (VISTA), she earned the distinction of being the oldest VISTA worker (Still hard at work, 1968). But age was only a number to this humble servant of the people who exchanged a life of privilege for a life of sacrifice. Earning just $50 a month, she lived and worked in the Henry Street Settlement House. In this borough, located in New York's Lower East Side, she was affectionately known as Aunt Mae (Still Hard at Work, 1968).

Her official duty was to tutor community residents, often poor and female. She helped them to learn how to read, learn English, and prepare for job qualification testing and high school equivalency examinations. To assist her adult learners in achieving success, Hawes adhered to culturally responsive adult learning principles by using "a religious song, a soul food recipe, a street sign, just about anything out of students' familiar experiences to teach reading and advance them toward their ultimate goal" (Still Hard at Work, 1968, p. 66). Without question, Hawes was a gifted educator, but her greatest gift was as a mentor known for being a champion for people. The secret to her success lay in developing "other-mothering" relationships with her students (Merriweather, 2011). Other-mothering is a holistic developmentally culturally grounded approach to teaching that promotes well-being through knowledge, guidance, com-passion, encouragement, and consciousness-raising. Othermothers recog-nize that cognitive growth is a shallow victory in the absence of spiritual and emotional growth. One student who could not read or write said Hawes "helped me to accept it and not be ashamed" (Still Hard at Work, 1968). This student talked first about the emotional growth and newfound confidence and then mentioned improvement in literacy skills.

As a community adult educator with a lifetime of experiences with inequality resulting from living through Jim Crow and the tumultuous Civil Rights Movement, Hawes understood the challenges of being Afri-can American in a racialized society. She recognized the power of educa-tion in beating the odds and overcoming hegemonically fueled adversity. She consistently battled the Goliath called White privilege and racial dis-crimination and won with her slingshot of adult learning and stones of persistence. Mae C. Hawes' legacy is characterized by twin pillars of the power of learning and strength of humanity. She spent a lifetime cultivat-ing both and waking up the world.

REFERENCES

Bersch, G. (2011). *Mae C. Hawes: Teacher, leader and lifelong learner.* Unpublished handout presented at the Adult Education Research Conference, Toronto, Canada.

Current events of importance in Negro education. (1934). *The Journal of Negro Education, 3*(4), 648–662.

Dr. Hinton developer of syphilis test dies, Was in-law of locals Canton, Mass. (1959, August 21). *Los Angeles Tribune,* p. 6.

First year's operation of Emma Ransom House. (1927–1928) *The New York Age.* Retrieved from http://fultonhistory.com/Newspaper%2011/New% 20York%20NY%20Age/New%20York%20NY%20Age%201927-1928% 20%20Grayscale/New%20York%20NY%20Age%201927-1928% 20%20Grayscale%20-%200056.pdf

Florida State Census. (1935). *Population census: 1935*. Retrieved from Ancestry.com.

Franklin, J. H. (2013). *Reconstruction after the Civil War* (3rd ed.).Chicago, IL: University of Chicago Press.

Guy, T. (1996). The American Association of Adult Education and the experiments in African American adult education. In E. Peterson (Ed.), *Freedom road: Adult education of African Americans* (pp. 89–108). Malabar, FL: Krieger.

Hawes, M. (1918, February 20). Letter to W. E. B. DuBois. W. E. B. DuBois Papers (MS 312). Special Collections and University Archives, University of Massachusetts Amherst Libraries. Retrieved from http://oubliette.library.umass.edu/view/full/mums312-b011-i347

Hawes, M. (1933, June 20). Letter to W. E. B. DuBois. W. E. B. DuBois Papers (MS 312). Special Collections and University Archives, University of Massachusetts Amherst Libraries. Retrieved from http://oubliette.library.umass.edu/view/full/mums312-b065-i559

Logan, R. (1954). *The Negro in American life and thought: The nadir, 1877–1901*. New York, NY: Dial.

Lomax, M. (February, 1959). Society by Minnie Lomax. *Los Angeles Tribune, 19*(1), 11.

Many Negroes joining moral re-armament movement (December, 1939). *The Negro Star, 32*(35), 1.

Merriweather, L. (2011, November). *Othermothering: The missing ingredient in the recipe for effective mentoring*. Paper presented at the annual meeting of the American Association for Adult and Continuing Education (AAACE), Indianapolis, IN.

New move for education of older people. (November, 1931). *Plaindealer, 33*(44), 2.

Robertson, N. (2007).*Christian sisterhood, race relations, and the YWCA, 1906–46*. Chicago: University of Illinois Press.

Rowden, D. (Ed.). (1934). *Handbook of adult education in the United States*. New York, NY: AAAE.

Still hard at work at 81. (1968). *Ebony, 23*(4), 64–67.

Tennessee Board of Education. (1916). *Bulletin of the Tennessee Agricultural and Industrial State Normal School, Catalogue for 1916, 5*(1), 10.

U.S. Census Bureau. (1900). *Twelfth census of the United States: 1900*. Retrieved from Ancestry.com

U.S. Census Bureau. (1910). *Thirteenth census of the United States: 1910*. Retrieved from Ancestry.com

U.S. Census Bureau. (1930). *Fifteenth census of the United States: 1930*. Retrieved from Ancestry.com

CHAPTER 15

MARIA L. HERNÁNDEZ

An Untiring Fighter

Sylvia Fuentes

Maria Latigo Hernández was born in 1896 in Garza Garcia, a small town outside of Monterrey, Nuevo Leon, Mexico. Her parents were Eduardo Frausto and Francisca Medrano Latigo. Unlike the stereotypical Mexicans of that era, the Latigos were middle class. Maria was one of six siblings and at the age of 15, she graduated from secondary school and taught as a teacher at the school where her father was a superintendent (Villarreal, 2004). Prior to becoming a superintendent, Maria's father was a college professor, solidifying their middle-class status.

The onset of the Mexican Revolution of 1910 eventually forced Maria and her family to come to the state of Texas in 1914 to escape the upheaval in her home country. Before settling in Hebbronville, Texas, the family first arrived in Laredo, Texas, where they were situated on a farm, and it was here where they were first exposed to labor-intensive work: the fields. In 1915, the Latigos' moved to Hebbronville, Texas, and that same year, Maria married Pedro Hernández (Laezman, 2002).

No Small Lives: Handbook of North American Early Women Adult Educators, 1925-1950,
pp. 141–147

BEGINNINGS AS A POLITICAL ACTIVIST

In 1918, Maria and Pedro moved to San Antonio where they owned a very successful grocery store and bakery. It was their prosperous business that allowed Maria to venture out into the political arena on a constant basis. Early on, Pedro supported Maria's political endeavors as he believed in her and realized Maria had a gift for organizing different groups into public movements (Mendez-Morse, 2000). Pedro was acutely aware of Maria's unwavering obligation to bring forth the plight of Mexican Americans and to involve them in politics.

Maria and Pedro's first born was a son whom they named Pedro Hernández Jr. Sadly, he died of typhoid as a child (Villarreal, 2004). They went on to have three other children who also died as babies. However, between 1919 and 1932 Maria successfully gave birth to two sons and four daughters. They later adopted another girl.

Once settled in San Antonio, Maria and her husband began their political involvement around 1924. The pair joined La Orden Hijos De America (the Order of the Children of America). It was the foundation of decades of participation in community activism. It was during this time that the couple challenged the inequalities being confronted by Mexican Americans in San Antonio.

During this time, Maria and Pedro's growing family did not dissuade them from political and economic involvement. Maria and Pedro's flourishing business allowed Maria to become trained as a midwife during the beginning of the 1920s. Shortly thereafter, Maria created La Asociación Protectora de Madres and engaged in fundraising to build a maternity clinic. Maria not only provided free prenatal care and delivered the babies, but she also comprehended the dire economic status of her patients and allowed them to make payments throughout the duration of their pregnancy. If this was not enough, Maria also gave a big discount to pregnant women by only charging them $10 as opposed to doctors who were charging $25. Maria delivered babies for over 25 years (Villarreal, 2004) and also provided health care for the poor.

In 1929, Attorney Santiago Tafolla, along with Maria and Pablo, founded La Ordena De Caballeros de America or the Order of Sons/ Knights of America (OSA). The organization was formed to serve as a public platform in response to discrimination against Mexican Americans (Buitron, 2004). In essence, the OSA was a civil rights organization (Laezman, 2002; Méndez-Morse, 2000; Villarreal, 2004) fashioned in a manner that would help achieve progress in the education and social conditions of Tejanos, a term used to identify a Texan of Mexican descent (Wikipedia, n.d.). For the Hernándezes, this organization became the instrument for a lifetime of activism.

The vision of this organization was to be international. While the focus was to be on Tejanos, Maria believed it was imperative to include Latin Americans, specifically Mexican immigrants. During the Great Depression and using the OSA, Maria helped form the Asociacion Protectora de Madres (the Association for the Protection of Mothers), which afforded pregnant women financial assistance (Orozco, n.d.; Ruiz, 2008). This organization was active until 1939.

Hernández was renowned for her activism. Most of her life was spent calling for civic and social reform, and education (Méndez-Morse, 2000). While most middle-class activists snubbed labor unions, Maria backed the pecan sheller strikers of 1938.

INVOLVEMENT IN EDUCATION

One of Maria and Pablo's main concerns dealt with the disparities in the education of Mexican American children in San Antonio. Hence, in 1934, Maria founded La Liga Por Defensa Escolar en San Antonio (the Scholastic Defense League of San Antonio). The goal of the organization was to close the gap between Mexican American and Anglo students by organizing and assembling groups in response to the appalling environment of the local schools designated for Mexican American children (Hightower-Langston, 2002).

In the same year, Maria became very vocal against racial inequities in the schools. She was a champion for Mexican immigrants and Mexican Americans. At one point, Maria gave a speech in her native Spanish to an audience of 5,000, speaking to them about the importance of La Liga.

La Liga was not interested in integrating Tejano children into Anglo schools. Its primary focus was to improve the Mexican designated schools. On October 24, 1934, over 10,000 people gathered at a rally. The rally was composed of the Tejano leaders of most of the organizations in San Antonio and south Texas (Ruiz, 2008).

Many of the Mexican schools did not have heat, and the teacher-student ratio was absurd. For example, one school was observed having only 1 teacher for 130 students. However, the Anglo schools had better equipment and were certainly better staffed. It is purported that Maria addressed the state school board in an effort to improve the Mexican schools. She pleaded with the board and reminded them that the children were not at fault for their features and that they too were in support of the American flag and what it stood for (Hightower-Langston, 2002).

INVOLVEMENT IN WOMEN'S RIGHTS

Maria was not only an advocate for equal education, but also for women's rights and the promotion of Latino cultural awareness (Laezman, 2002). Moreover, Maria wrote countless articles and continued to make speeches, but specifically in her native language, Spanish. She unremittingly promoted La Liga as a Mexican-oriented organization, evident by the fact that La Liga's constitution, name, and circular were completely in Spanish.

Chicana/Tejana/Mexican's participation in the women's movement in the late 1800s and early 1920s was hindered by the same obstacles as those of other women. The disdain for minorities, socialists, and laborers was prevalent during this era. However, most of these women were supporters and dedicated socialists. Maria was among these women and later became viewed by many as an icon, especially with her work with women (Cotera, 1997).

During this time, another promising organization surfaced, the League of United Latin American Citizens (LULAC). LULAC was an organization that wanted to function as the "umbrella" for all of the Tejano/Mexican American groups. Unfortunately, its policy called for the women members to function in a subsidiary capacity by forming a separate auxiliary. Moreover, many of the LULAC members were assimilated, and the majority of its members spoke English as the primary language. LULAC became known for focusing on assimilation and discarding feminist issues (Laezman, 2002).

Since Maria asserted her energies on women's issues, she would find herself in conflict with other up-and-coming civil rights organizations such as LULAC. In 1935, La Liga became inactive. There had been speculation that the conflicting views on how to continue with the movement contributed to La Liga's demise. Nevertheless, the goal was still to advocate for better educational and social opportunities for Mexican Americans and Mexican immigrants. La Liga was reactivated by a different leadership that fostered a more militant style. Hernández continued her work in Spanish and became a pioneer campaigner of bilingual education (Hightower-Langston, 2002).

In the late 1930s, Curculo Cultural Isabel la Católica surfaced as a women's club in San Antonio. Its purpose was to provide services to women of Mexican origin who were in need. Maria was this organization's first board member (Acosta & Winegarten, 2003). The club existed from the 1930s through the 1940s and was initially called Circulo Social Femenino Mexicana.

OTHER AREAS OF INTEREST

Hernández was a groundbreaker on many levels. Her activism remained unsurpassed. In the 1930s, she was one of the first women to become a radio announcer with a one-hour show called La Voz de las Americas (Voice of the Americas) (Villarreal, 2004).

In the late 1930s, Maria served as a goodwill ambassador to Mexico for the organization that she and Pedro cofounded, La Orden Caballeros de America. While there she met the president of Mexico and she also campaigned for President Franklin Roosevelt (Villarreal, 2004). Maria's activism ultimately transcended borders.

Maria was a big proponent of citizen and familial involvement in the political arena and viewed it as a necessity in order to improve the socioeconomic conditions of Tejanos and Mexican immigrants. In 1945, Maria amplified her beliefs in an essay about the politics and familial relations in Mexico (Buitron, 2004). In the essay, Maria illuminated the function of family and accountability of municipal leaders.

At some point, Maria received correspondence from her oldest son who was overseas and requested that she not continue in her role as a midwife as it had begun to be too dangerous for her to travel by herself (Laezman, 2002). While she did heed his advice and temporarily stopped seeing women for treatment, Maria began to advocate for the women and daughters of the Mexican American soldiers who were fighting in the war and demanding more rights.

After World War II, as a direct result of those who had served in the military, Mexican Americans from San Antonio began to demand equal treatment as Anglos, and most of the leadership identified as middle class (Buitron, 2004). The constant exposure to the Anglo culture caused Tejanos to shift reference points. La Prensa, a Mexican newspaper, declined in circulation and most people opted for the English-language newspapers. While Maria continued her activism, the Mexican ideology did not appeal to supporters until the 1960s.

MARIA'S IMPACT

Maria remained faithful to the United States while never forgetting her motherland country of Mexico. She was a trailblazer and a role model for generations to come. She cofounded many organizations and was relentless in pursing equal rights for Mexican Americans and Mexican immigrants, not only for equal education but also for women's rights.

One of Maria's greatest accomplishments was being one of the first pioneers to promote the causes of citizens on both sides of the Texan/

Mexican border. Hernández was not only one of the first females to host one of San Antonio's Spanish-speaking radio programs, but later went on to host La Hora de la Mujer (the Hour of the Woman), a television program that aired once a week in the 1960s.

Maria and Pedro continued their activism well after they had reached their retirement age. They actively participated in the Chicano movement of the 1960s and 1970s. They were particularly involved with La Raza Unida Party (LRUP; the United Race), which evolved out of Texas in the 70s. In 1972, Maria was asked to be the keynote speaker at La Raza's statewide conference. She and Pedro campaigned throughout the State of Texas for the party's candidates running for office (Laezman, 2002).

Maria fought vigorously for the rights of Latinos for over 60 years. She was an activist, wife, mother, and grandmother and hosted both radio and television programs. Hernández dedicated many decades to activism and service. Because she and Pedro did not have sufficient resources while they worked hard on behalf of the poor and their people, she felt that they could have done more. However, Maria did acknowledge that no amount of money could ever compensate for a person who devoted all of his or her life to the movement.

Pedro Hernández died in 1980 and Maria died in 1986 of pneumonia at the age of 89. She was survived by 5 children, 19 grandchildren, 23 great-grandchildren, and 8 great-great-grandchildren (Laezman, 2002). Many remember her as an advocate for the poor, civic accountability, and equal education.

REFERENCES

Acosta, T., & Winegarten, R. (2003). *Las Tejanas: 300 years of history*. Austin: University of Texas Press.

Buitron, R. (2004). *The quest for Tejano identity in San Antonio, Texas, 1913–2000*. New York, NY: Routledge.

Cotera, M. (1997). Feminism: The Chicana and Anglo versions. In A. M. Garcia (Ed.), *Chicana feminist thought: The basic historical writings* (pp. 223–231). New York, NY: Routledge.

Hightower-Langston, D. (2002). *A to Z of women leaders and activists*. New York, NY: Facts on File.

Laezman, R. (2002). *100 Hispanic-Americans who shaped American history*. San Mateo, CA: Bluewood.

Méndez-Morse, S. (2000). Claiming forgotten leadership. *Urban Education, 35*(5), 584–596.

Orozco, C. (n.d.). Hernandez, Maria L. De. *Handbook of Texas. Texas State Historical Association.* Retrieved from http://tshaonline.org/handbook/online/articles/fhe75

Ruiz, V. (2008). *From out of the shadows: Mexican women in twentieth-century America*. New York, NY: Oxford University Press.

Villarreal, M. A. (2004). Hernandez, Maria Latigo. In S. Ware & S. Braukman (Eds.), *Notable American women: A biographical dictionary, Volume 4*, (pp. 293–294). Cambridge, MA: Belknap.

Wikipedia. (n.d.). *Tejanos*. Retrieved from http://en.wikipedia.org/wiki/Tejano

Dorothy Hewitt
(Photo courtesy of Vassar College Special Collections)

CHAPTER 16

DOROTHY V. HEWITT

Pioneer and Founder of the Boston Center for Adult Education

Mary Alice Wolf

No Small Lives: Handbook of North American Early Women Adult Educators, 1925-1950,
pp. 149–158
Copyright © 2015 by Information Age Publishing
149

Dorothy Vivian Hewitt was born in Buffalo, New York,[1] on September 3, 1897, and died in Northampton, Massachusetts, on May 16, 1987. She was raised in Buffalo and in Worthington, Massachusetts, a rural north-western community where she subsequently retired. Her life was marked with several qualities, not the least of which was her strong capacity for leadership, imagination, and a never-ending love of learning. Mona Sprecker, a relative, commented, "She was interesting, intelligent and led a stimulating active life" (M. Sprecker, personal communication, August 7, 2013). Surely, she was a determined, hard-working, focused woman until the last days of her life: education, she believed was the pivotal feature in all human development and the key to self-determination and a true democracy.

> Of her invention, the Boston Center for Adult Education (BCAE), it was observed:

> > Non-sectarian, removed from politics or religion or class or race, the Center that has grown out of Dorothy Hewitt's idea is compounded of the essence of humanity, is a real dynamic for democracy. Her job, as director of the Center, was literally carved by herself from the raw stuff of opportunity. (Wayman, 1938)

EARLY LIFE

Dorothy's father was Arthur John Hewitt; he was British. Her mother was Abby Corning Otto Hewitt, an American. Neither had attended college. In response to a questionnaire asking for "other nationalities in your ancestry," Dorothy once responded "French, German, Scotch" (Hewitt, 1929, p. 1). She grew up in Buffalo and Worthington, where she attended Lyceum Hall, later graduating from Lady Jane Grey School in Bingham-ton, New York. In 1915 she entered the class of 1919 of Vassar College where she received financial aid and where she was able to combine her interests through an interdisciplinary major in psychology and economics and a minor in mathematics. Always grateful to her alma mater, she remained a supporter, cheerleader, alumna representative, fundraiser, and sharply opinionated voice for educational policy the next 60-some years. Her frequent mantra was that women needed to develop leadership skills, be involved in democracy, social policy, their communities, as well as international affairs. Education, she believed, was the prerequisite for political engagement and ontological development. Sparked by her own experience as a learner, she dedicated herself to the field of adult education.

When asked to evaluate her own higher education before a reunion, Dorothy, age 53, observed,

> I would major in [the] same subjects. My whole experience at V.C. [Vassar College] was highly satisfactory—maybe this isn't sufficiently analytical, but I liked it! V.C. is progressive, democratic, and lays emphasis on social responsibility. Am delighted at increase in number of Negroes at V.C. Keep up the good work with greater numbers of minority groups! (Hewitt, 1950)

Her hope for the future of the college would be "Greater security for faculty with tenure—I know this rests in part on more cash!" (Hewitt, 1950). When asked for her church affiliation, she observed, "member North Presbyterian Church of Buffalo, much more interested in Congregational Church" (Hewitt, 1929). She was, she pronounced, a "progressive." Dorothy never married and lived with Florence D. Chapin (1887–1970) throughout adulthood. She described the burning historical issues of her college day as "World War I, Women's Suffrage, and the election of Woodrow Wilson"; and her answer to "What kept you and your friends talking late into the night?" was "Ideas in the Philosophy courses we took" (Hewitt, 1956). The ideas—and talking about the ideas—was always crucial to Hewitt's educational philosophy.

SEEDS OF EDUCATIONAL THEORY

Dorothy Hewitt had several employment experiences after receiving her AB from Vassar College in 1919. She worked in the psychological clinic of the University of Pennsylvania in Philadelphia (1919); at the Guaranty Trust Company, New York, New York (1919–20); and for the YWCA National Board (1920–23); Harvard Graduate School of Business Administration (1923–25); and the Atwell Company, Boston, Massachusetts (1925–26). These opportunities allowed Dorothy to hone her business and professional persona—an essential trait for an idealist who would later raise money and administer a large organization (Hewitt, 1938).

By 1929, Dorothy Hewitt was living in Cambridge, Massachusetts and was assistant editor of the first volume of Harvard Business Reports. Active in the League of Women Voters, the Association of Vassar College, the Red Cross, and the YWCA, she was the director of the Adult Educational Department of the Boston YWCA. However, "Miss Hewitt's conception of the opportunity for adult education had grown beyond the scope of an organization for young women—it reached out to men and women alike, of all types and ages in our present-day world" (Wayman, 1938).

Hewitt had begun to observe how adults learned, what circumstances and environments provided optimal comfort and stimulation. Her agenda, always, was citizenship—the development of conscientious and responsible adults who would contribute to society. She became involved in the Twentieth Century Club, which was described in the first *Handbook of Adult Education* (Rowden, 1934):

> THE TWENTIETH CENTURY CLUB, Adult Education Center
> 3 Joy St., Boston, Mass.
> Dorothy Hewett, adult ed. exec.
>
> Offers courses under expert leadership four nights a week on Understanding our Present Economic Situation, Psychology in Everyday Life, Keeping Up with Science, Understanding Germany, Modern Poetry, Pleasing Speech, Conversational Italian and French, etc.; all classes limited to 25 people; nominal fee of $4 charged for each course; all classes conducted informally; leaders contribute services; students represent cross section of community; enrollment, 350. (pp. 102–103)

A NOVEL IDEA

Dorothy's concept for a learning community was unique in the United States: it was based on the concept of independent community outreach and focused on philosophical and arts-related programs rather than professional or skill-related topics. Having worked at the Boston Adult Education Department of the YWCA, she knew that an independent organization was preferable to one with a religious or social orientation. *The Boston Center for Adult Education: The First Fifty Years, 1933–1983* describes Hewitt's role in the development of the organization:

> A young woman in her mid-thirties who had previously worked in the finance department of a bank and the Y.W.C.A., Dorothy developed a vision of what she thought an adult education center should be; in "Our Story," she said, "The Center I envisioned was to be a place where small groups of men and women should meet together in a living-room-setting. There, under expert leadership and without regard to credit or any other academic impediment, they could learn, discuss and create for the sheer pleasure of doing so. Their activities might be in the realm of ideas or concrete objects. The sole guide in the choice of courses was to be one's personal desire, nothing more. (McLean, 1992, p. 1)

The Boston Center for Adult Education was a huge success. Spaces were donated (including a downtown mansion), funds were raised, advertising was developed, a board engaged. The first session filled and over 700 men and women were turned away for lack of space. Its philosophy and rubric (people can learn as adults and would choose to study what interested them) were becoming a nationwide trend. BCAE's "philosophy that men and women would not be capable of dealing with rapidly changing social problems unless they added constantly to their knowledge and understanding" (McLean, 1992, p. 1) resonated with the Depression era mentality.

Through the 1930s, Dorothy began to be known as an "incubator" of educational theory and practice; she spoke frequently and began writing about learning and adults. She was active in the new American Association of Adult Education (AAAE) and the National Education Association (NEA). She co-authored *Adult Education: A Dynamic for Democracy* (1937) with Dr. Kirtley F. Mather of Harvard University, focusing on adult education as a means to touch the lives of all people and make them responsible in civic life. Dr. Mather was known for his radical politics and belief in democratic openness. Both Hewitt and Mather believed that people should make their own decisions and that the classroom process should be an open forum for ideas and dissent. "I think the success of the response lies in the fact that instead of laying out courses I think people should have, I am always searching for clews [sic] to what people want themselves" (Hewitt as cited in Wayman, 1938).

Kirtley Mather made an excellent collaborator for Dorothy Hewitt:

Mather was an energetic proponent of readily accessible adult education programs. Although he was associated with an elite university for thirty years, he believed that the interests of democracy were more closely associated with adult literacy and education programs for all citizens. Mather was a highly visible supporter of Dorothy Hewitt and the Boston Center for Adult Education she founded. (Wikipedia, 2013).

Of education, the two concluded, "Above all, there must be an inherent willingness to discover the consequences of social actions of all sorts and a new sense of individual responsibility for the welfare of all members of the human family" (Hewitt & Mather, 1937, p. 2). *Adult Education: A Dynamic for Democracy* was recommended reading by the left-leaning *Commonweal* (Rosten, 1937) and perceived as a "fresh start" in learning theory and practice (Nelson, 2001, p. 397). The implication was that adults could be encouraged to make "a fresh start" and would be empowered in civic affairs.

There was a progressive movement at the time, a growing consciousness of the role that education could play in the lives of working adults, immigrants, minority persons, and others for whom a new ontological development was possible. Discussions and courses could be chosen because of interest, classrooms would be open forums for ideas and information. Imel (2012, p. 7) observed, "Other leaders in adult education during this period expressed similar sentiments about adult education and its relationship to maintaining a democratic society." Dorothy Hewitt, who founded the Boston Center for Adult Education in 1933, wrote that "to strengthen and invigorate the dynamic for democracy is therefore an inescapable part of the task of education in this second third of the twentieth century" (Hewitt & Mather, 1937, p. 3).

Dorothy later reflected on those early, heady days, saying of the Boston Center for Adult Education (BCAE),

> It had absolutely no financial resources, only an idea. This idea was based on the belief that everyone comes into the world with tremendous potentials, most of which were never developed. The purpose of the Center, therefore is to provide the circumstances in which mature men and women can more nearly reach their potential. Here, without regard for background, credits, age, race, or creed and in congenial surroundings, they take part in the most exciting adventure there is—the releasing of latent capacities— spiritual, intellectual, creative.
>
> With the resulting increased enthusiasm and zest for life comes ability to deal more successfully with the questions of the day—anywhere from those occurring in the home and to those on the international scenes. (Hewitt, 1958, p. 1)

Hewitt and Mather's philosophy recommended classroom size, interactions between faculty and learners, and techniques for a forum-style presentation. In democratic situations, they believed, there had to be give and take. The model was specific:

> In 1937, adult educator Dorothy Hewitt and geologist Kirtley F. Mather observed and compared several types of adult group learning. "The Forum" where information is given by the instructor (the expert); then the "thought sequence." The question period "is frequently divided into only two sides, for or against the speaker's position. However, most issues are many-sided, and the dynamic of question and response, regardless of a skilled moderator, does not allow shades of gray. The effective moderator, they conclude, must serve as a kind of orchestra conductor, leading the whole, sometimes drawing out one set of instruments and another, and subduing a third group which may be overbearing. (Meyers, 2012, p. 18)

Hewitt was known for her energy and force. Somewhat of a star, she was advertised as "a well known public speaker whose audience is always assured of an interesting and profitable message" (Local Evening, 1939). Using the headline, "Our Gracious Ladies," the *Boston Traveler* (Gorday, 1944) carried a story about Miss Dorothy Hewitt, accompanied by a photograph of a professional-looking woman adorned by a three-string pearl necklace. The article describes her:

Director and presiding genius of that hive of activity, the Boston Center for Adult Education, which occupies the spacious rooms of the old Baylies residence at 5 Commonwealth Avenue, is Miss Dorothy Hewitt of Cambridge. Tall and slender, with short dark hair and hazel eyes, she has piled up a wealth of experience in many fields, and is now helping others toward the acquisition of useful learning. During the week she devotes 10 to 14 hours a day to the Center, where the enrollment ranges from 800 during the summer, to over 1500 in the winter, with classes every evening and a few during the day (Gorday, 1944).

A SUCCESS STORY

Today's BCAE website includes the following history:

> Founded in 1933, the Boston Center for Adult Education is the oldest, nonprofit adult education center in New England. Its founder, Miss Dorothy Hewitt, envisioned a place where "small groups of men and women would meet together in living room settings to learn, discuss, and create for the sheer pleasure of doing so."
>
> ......
>
> Throughout its history, the BCAE has remained responsive to the demands of a diverse community, as well as to the evolving demands of the individual. Whether serving as a site for volunteer wartime efforts in the 1940s, a haven for social policy debate in the 1960s, or a resource for personal and professional growth as one navigates through the new millennium, the BCAE meets the challenges of a thriving urban community. (Boston Center for Adult Education, 2013, p. 4)

THANK YOU AND GOODBYE: LATER YEARS

Dorothy Hewitt directed the Boston Center for Adult Education for 25 years. In 1958, she and associate director Florence Chapin were asked to take "a leave of absence" and were replaced. "Notwithstanding my refusal to resign, the leaders were either given or sent letters under date of January 27, stating that I had resigned" wrote Hewitt (1958). There are several documents that attest to the negativity of this arrangement, however, her "public persona" did not falter. She began a new enterprise, the Adult Education Institute of New England. Hewitt wrote to a friend:

> I have started a new adventure. In 1958 a group of us founded the Adult Education Institute of NE [New England] for having the assistance of country leaders. As John Ferrell of the Sears Roebuck Foundation put it, "We are

helping people sharpen their tools." We conduct courses at our headquarters in Boston. (Hewitt, 1963)

Here she is explaining the next shift to her Vassar Alumnae friends:

By the time of our reunion, I shall have retired from the Adult Education Institute of New England. At last a successor for me has been found. I shall be a special consultant for one year to be called on when needed. I have been associated with adult education in the Boston area so long, 43 years, that it seems better for me to leave the scene gradually. (Hewitt, n.d.)

In 1970, Dorothy moved permanently to Worthington, Massachusetts, where she cared for a sister with developmental disabilities, continued to correspond with her Vassar counterparts, and dabbled in creating a local adult education organization. She took up gardening, photography, and continued introducing educational meetings for the League of Women Voters and other organizations. She had been developing seminars for many years in the area and was known throughout Massachusetts. In retirement, she could continue this work. "Miss Dorothy Hewitt ... announces a series of seminars for the League of Women Voters of Massachusetts to be financed by the Sears, Roebuck Foundation. The first of the four eight week seminars of 2½ hours each on the subject of 'Leadership' through the discussion method" blared the Hampshire Gazette (Dorothy Hewitt Seminar Leader, 1959).

Dorothy Hewitt died in Northampton, Massachusetts, on May 16, 1987, not far from her "beloved little hill town of Worthington." She was 90 years old (Obituaries, 1987).

CONCLUSION

Dorothy Hewitt claimed that "Adult education is a creative force" to gain in influence, and develop societal goals (Hewitt & Mather, 1937, p. 11). She was cited as an influence on the andragogical theories and practice of Malcolm Knowles (Jarvis, 2001; Smith, 2002). The concept and practice of seeing adult education in light of civic education became central to late 20th century learning theory (Stubblefield, 1976). As she became more active in state and national adult education, Hewitt grew effective at advocating for practical and socially conscious education for adults. Nonetheless, it was clearly a life's work with scant remuneration. In a job application, she described herself in 1938 as

doing pioneer work in adult education since 1933. I do not classify easily. I am one of the two founders of the Boston Center for Adult Education which is in its 5th year. I have been working for very small sums and doing two jobs at once to make both ends meet and not take very much from the Center. (Hewitt, 1938)

The zeal, the independence, the accomplishments of this pioneer of adult education was, indeed, remarkable. Through a foundation of education for empowerment, she certainly empowered thousands of men and women, including herself "in the most exciting adventure there is—the releasing of latent capacities—spiritual, intellectual, creative" (Hewitt, 1958).

NOTE

1. Although Ms Hewitt wrote that she was born in Buffalo, New York, her obituary claims that she was born in Orange, New Jersey, and moved to Buffalo at the age of 2 years (*Berkshire Eagle*, Pittsfield, MA, April 18, 1989).

REFERENCES

Boston Center for Adult Education. (2013). *About us*. Retrieved August 8, 2013, from http://bcae.org

Dorothy Hewitt Seminar Leader. (1959, December 30). *Hampshire Gazette*. AAVC Bio File Hewitt 1919. Poughkeepsie, NY: Vassar College.

Gorday, N. (1944, January 25). Our gracious ladies. *Boston Traveler*. AAVC Bio File Hewitt 1919. Poughkeepsie, NY: Vassar College.

Hewitt, D. (1929). *Biographical records questionnaire*. Alumni Association of Vassar College (AAVC) Bio File Hewitt 1919. Poughkeepsie, NY: Vassar College.

Hewitt, D. (1938). *Resume*. AAVC Bio File Hewitt 1919. Poughkeepsie, NY: Vassar College.

Hewitt, D. (1950). *Associate Alumnae of Vassar College: Biographical Questionnaire*. AAVC Bio File Hewitt 1919. Poughkeepsie, NY: Vassar College.

Hewitt, D. (1956). *100th anniversary questionnaire*. AAVC Bio File Hewitt 1919. Poughkeepsie, NY: Vassar College.

Hewitt, D. (1958). *"As a friend of the Center … "* [Personal correspondence]. AAVC Bio File Hewitt 1919. Poughkeepsie, NY: Vassar College.

Hewitt, D. (1963). *Questionnaire for 1919's forty-fifth reunion bulletin*. AAVE Bio File Hewitt 1919. Poughkeepsie, NY: Vassar College.

Hewitt, D. (n.d.). [Information for AAVC publication.] AAVC Bio File Hewitt 1919. Poughkeepsie, NY: Vassar College.

Hewitt, D., & Mather, K. (1937). *Adult Education: A dynamic for democracy*. East Norwalk, CT: Appleton-Century-Crofts.

Imel, S. (2012). Civic engagement in the United States: Roots and branches. *New Directions for Adult and Continuing Education, 135*, 5–13.

Jarvis, P. (Ed.). (2001). *Twentieth century thinkers in adult and continuing education.* Sterling, VA: Stylus.

Local evening schools will close term coming week. (1939, March 23). *Brookline Chronicle* (Brookline, MA). AAVC Bio File Hewitt 1919. Poughkeepsie, NY: Vassar College.

McLean, H. (1992). *The Boston Center for Adult Education: The first fifty years, 1933–1983.* Boston, MA: Boston Center for Adult Education.

Meyers, A. S. (2012). *Democracy in the making: The open forum lecture movement.* Lanham, MD: University Press of America.

Nelson, A. R. (2001). *Education and democracy: Alexander Meiklejohn, 1872–1964.* Madison: University of Wisconsin Press.

Obituaries. (1987, May 18). Dorothy V. Hewitt. *Berkshire Eagle.* AAVC Bio File Hewitt 1919. Pougheepsie, NY: Vassar College.

Rosten, L. (1937, December 3). Briefer mention [Book review]. *Commonweal,* 167–168.

Rowden, D. (Ed.). (1934). *Handbook of adult education in the United States.* New York, NY: American Association for Adult Education. Retrieved July 1, 2013, from http://archive.org/stream/handbookofadulte009721mbp/ handbookofadulte009721mbp_djvu.txt

Smith, M. K. (2002) Malcolm Knowles, informal adult education, self-direction and andragogy. *The encyclopedia of informal education.* Retrieved from www.infed.org/thinkers/et-knowl.htm.

Stubblefield, H. (1976). Adult education for civic intelligence in the post World War I period. *Adult Education Quarterly, 26*(4), 253–269.

Wayman, D. G. (1938, May 19). Teaching folk to do what they like. *Boston Evening Globe.*

Wikipedia. (2013, August 3). *Kirtley F. Mather.* Retrieved from from http://en.wikipedia.org/w/index.php?title=Kirtley_F._Mather&oldid=566994198

CHAPTER 17

RUTH KOTINSKY

Glancing Back, Reaching Forward

Norma Nerstrom

Ruth Kotinsky (1903–1955) was a major contributor to the developing field of adult education between 1933 and 1955. With her male counterparts such as John Dewey, Malcolm Knowles, and William Kilpatrick, she was a colleague and worthy contender in writing books and articles, serving on high-level committees, and editing publications focused on education. In the years since her death, however, she has rarely been celebrated as a strong influence on adult education. This chapter recognizes Kotinsky as a respected educator whose ideas were years ahead of her time and who remains pertinent today in the still-evolving, sometimes confusing, but very exciting field of adult education.

Kotinsky established herself in adult education at a time when the nation was besieged by the Great Depression and the adult education movement was just beginning to gain momentum. Seemingly unaffected by the Depression, the movement was well funded by the Carnegie Corporation. It was a time of growth in adult education stimulated in part by the concept that adults, like children, were learners.

Kotinsky became involved in adult education via a circuitous route, but one that served the movement well. By 1930, with an undergraduate

No Small Lives: Handbook of North American Early Women Adult Educators, 1925-1950,
pp. 159–165

degree from the University of Wisconsin and enrolled in graduate studies at Columbia University, she was working for the National YMCA, conducting studies, preparing for conferences, and editing research findings. She then became editor of a journal, *Parent Education,* and in 1939 moved into secondary education while working for the Commission on the Secondary School Curriculum. In that capacity she generated publications, some of which earned landmark status, such as her contribution to the 1953 Supreme Court case of Brown v. Board of Education (Nerstrom, 1999). In addition, Kotinsky was an influential contributor to the 1950 Mid-Century White House Conference on Children and Youth. One year after her death, the report, titled *New Perspectives for Research on Juvenile Delinquency* (Whitmer & Kotinsky, 1956), credited her involvement in a spring 1955 conference on juvenile delinquency.

THEORETICAL UNDERPINNINGS

Throughout her relatively short life, Kotinsky maintained that adulthood did not suddenly appear at a certain age but instead was a continuation of experiences from childhood. "Wisdom does not come suddenly to the adult," she wrote. "No more does emotional adequacy, moral insight, or an attitude of responsibility. They must each be practiced during childhood and youth in order to be present during later years" (1933, p. 23). Kotinsky's understanding of adults, then, was that childhood experiences were not isolated from adulthood but were a contributing factor to adult involvement within society. She and others surmised that it was the accumulation of experiences that affected people's thought and behavior. Kotinsky worked under the premise that all of life's experiences added either to the success of society or to the problems plaguing it.

Early in her career, Kotinsky anticipated some of what we understand more readily today. Long before Jack Mezirow (1978) identified perspective transformation, Stephen Brookfield (1995) wrote about challenging the status quo, or John Dirkx (2008) realized the importance of affective learning, Kotinsky recognized and documented these principles as being critical elements in the field of adult education. These observations are strongly demonstrated throughout her work.

INFLUENTIAL CONTRIBUTION:
ADULT EDUCATION AND THE SOCIAL SCENE

Kotinsky's career in adult education was officially launched in 1933 when she completed her PhD at Columbia University. Her doctoral research identified the compelling relationship between societal problems and the educational processes of that time. Kotinsky's dissertation, *Adult Education and the Social Scene* (1933), which was published as a book that same year, concluded that the lack of social progress in the United States was rooted in two realities: that children's education was poorly designed and implemented; and adults were excluded from planning the processes that affected their lives. Her goal became that of educating others to improve these practices. Early on she reiterated the importance of childhood experiences and their contributions to social betterment in adulthood. She also asserted that schools were only partially responsible for improving society's problems. Kotinsky particularly applauded parent groups, stressing that "of all the enumerated programs in adult education, [parent education] comes the closest to dealing educatively and integratively with the serious business of adults" (1933, pp. 129–130).

Kotinsky made numerous contributions in adult education and often challenged the status quo. In her dissertation, she contended that American adult educators were focused more on vocational training and less on improving society; recognized that society caused many of its own problems but then created welfare agencies to rectify them; understood that public consciousness had to be awakened to quality health efforts; acknowledged that churches' role in society was much too authoritative; comprehended that service clubs and patriotic societies of the day fell short in serving the public interest as educational agencies; and argued that the worlds of both work and leisure should offer choice, purpose, and valuable experience (1933).

Although existing problems in these areas were recognized as normal, Kotinsky challenged them for what they really represented—namely, as what Brookfield (1995) later identified as "hegemonic assumptions" (p. 14). As Brookfield defines them, "Hegemonic assumptions are those that we think are in our own best interests but that have actually been designed by more powerful others to work against us in the long term" (1995, pp. 14–15). Through her efforts in adult education, Kotinsky sought to change such hegemonic assumptions. For example, on the topic of leisure she stated,

> If conscious adult education is concerned about the worthy use of leisure, it cannot confine itself to the introduction of decoys away from commercialized amusement. It must see to it that the job agency, which is also teaching the use of time, is so remade as to teach a worthy use. (1933, p. 153)

Influenced by Dewey, Kotinsky advocated that education should be based on democratic principles. Keenly aware that Dewey's thinking had changed the landscape of education, she wrote that "Dewey has ...

insist[ed] that if adult life was to be valuable, then life should be valuable at every stage" (1933, p. 48). Kotinsky affirmed this principle when she argued that the recognition of dangers to children working in factories should apply also to adults working in factories. As a reformer, she believed that such balanced principles would improve society. Kotinsky also contended that adults should have control over their own learning. "It is necessary," she wrote, "to identify adult education with social ferments, dealing with them in such a way as to make the participants intelligent and responsible planners, rather than drifters, sufferers, and undergoers merely, or ruthless schemers for personal advantage" (1933, p. xvi).

OTHER PUBLICATIONS

In addition to *Adult Education and the Social Scene* (1933), Kotinsky authored and edited numerous other publications, five of which are cited here as examples of her broad professional focus: *Reorganizing Secondary Education* (Thayer, Zachery, & Kotinsky, 1939), *Mathematics in General Education* (Commission on Secondary School Curriculum, 1940), *Adult Education Councils* (Kotinsky, 1940), *Elementary Education of Adults: A Critical Interpretation* (Kotinsky, 1941), and *For Every Child—A Fair Chance for a Healthy Personality* (Kotinsky, 1950).

As the secretary of the Commission on Secondary School Curriculum in 1939, Kotinsky collaborated with V. T. Thayer and Caroline B. Zachery on *Reorganizing Secondary Education*, which analyzed the way in which the needs of students in secondary education were relevant to contemporary society. As a member of the Commission's Committee on the Function of Mathematics in General Education, Kotinsky was involved in writing *Mathematics in General Education*, a report that investigated how general education might respond to individuals' needs "in ways that are consistent with and promote social welfare" (Commission on Secondary School Curriculum, 1940, p. 42). The report concluded that

> The newer conception of the individual and the way he learns is particularly important from a social point of view: it gives hope of personalities capable of dealing constructively with ever new environmental conditions—changing them in desirable directions, and being changed themselves in the process. (Commission on Secondary School Curriculum, 1940, p. 9)

Observing the possibility of inner change, Kotinsky, as an adult educator, may have influenced this conclusion and hinted at what Mezirow (1978) later recognized as transformative learning.

Adult Education Councils was instrumental in investigating the value of forming national councils to draw together people with similar interests in adult education. Basing her model on the 1926 formation of the American Association for Adult Education, Kotinsky confirmed that councils could serve as a "powerful potential means for exemplifying the democratic process and focusing the adult education movement upon its major social relevance in furthering widespread realization of democratic values" (1940, p. 167). Current confusion in the field of adult education could be eliminated, she said, when each educator as museum director, librarian, night-school teacher, or home demonstrator could "define just what it is they all have in common" (1940, p. 5) and work toward that end. Kotinsky believed that adult educators could be more successful by collaborating as a group rather than working in isolation.

In *Elementary Education of Adults: A Critical Interpretation* (1941), Kotinsky addressed the educational needs of illiterate immigrants, and even today this book is discussed in the field of literacy (Bersch, 2011). In it she explored

> how the nation shall bestir itself to become universally literate in the fullest sense of the term, which includes primarily social sensitivity, intelligence, and responsibility—the ability to see social problems, the desire to study and understand them, and the creative will to act in accordance with such studied understanding. (pp. 17–18)

In covering topics such as naturalization and Americanization, learner motivation, and teacher training, Kotinsky provided recommendations for how such goals might best be accomplished. One recommendation addressed the new media of film and radio. Kotinsky suggested that, due to time constraints, educators consider using movies and radio in lieu of reading to "demonstrate, explain, and motivate." She recommended that, because the traditional teaching process and the new technology were not "mutually exclusive," both should be utilized "to build a universally literate citizenry" (1941, p. 135).

In her monograph titled *For Every Child—A Fair Chance for a Healthy Personality*, Kotinsky (1950) discussed her involvement with the Mid-Century White House Conference on Children and Youth, which set out to discover how society might develop responsible citizens. Factors similar to those identified by Dirkx (2008) were considered such as democratic practice, spirituality, and individual worthiness. The conference investigated the position that adults may replicate, knowingly or not, children's experiences through hidden motives. Attendees also discussed how the study's results might relate to the work of others such as doctors, social workers, and parents. This monograph was the precursor to the book *Personality in the Making: The Fact-Finding Report of the Mid-Century White House Conference on Children and Youth* (Whitmer & Kotinsky, 1952).

SUMMING UP A LIFE CUT SHORT

In the spring of 1955, Kotinsky continued to contribute to the field of adult education when she accepted a position as director of research for the Family Services Association of America. Her new duties were cut short, however, on November 27, 1955, when she died in an automobile accident. Kotinsky's friends and colleagues honored her 7 years later through a lecture series held in New York in collaboration with the Bank Street College of Education. This memorial was a tribute to Kotinsky's many accomplishments and established a means to further her goals. The lecture series was published as *Integration of Mental Health Concepts with the Human Relations Professions* (1962).

Kotinsky's many accomplishments were built firmly on her heritage. Born in 1903 in Philadelphia, she was an only child of Russian immigrants. In her early years she and her family lived in Woodbine, New Jersey, a strong Jewish community that valued education. Her mother, Sarah, was a public school teacher. Her father, Jacob, was a graduate of Rutgers University and worked as an entomologist for the Department of Agriculture. Kotinsky's positive introduction to education, no doubt, provided the strong foundation for her leadership in the field of adult education.

Kotinsky graduated from Central High School, Washington, DC, in 1919 and was one of 40 students to earn high graduation honors (Washington Times, 1919). She completed her undergraduate studies in 1923 at the University of Wisconsin, Madison, where she was a member of the Phi Beta Kappa society. Her bachelor's degree in letters and science earned her high honors.

In 1926–27 Kotinsky was awarded a National Fellowship in Child Development by the National Research Council in Washington, DC (Bersch, 2011). This award recognized North American women who combined their interest and background in science with child development. Shortly after her father's death in 1928, Kotinsky traveled abroad and by 1930 began work in New York at the YMCA while studying at Columbia University.

An overview of her career indicates that Ruth Kotinsky advocated for the well-being of all using an intergenerational approach to lifelong education informed by democratic principles. Many of the problems she addressed in the first half of the 20th century are still issues we face today. Kotinsky provided an exceptionally solid foundation on which adult educators can continue to build in this still emerging profession.

REFERENCES

Bank Street College of Education. (1962). *Integration of mental health concepts with the human relations professions: Education, medicine, psychology, law, religion, nursing, social work, dentistry.* Proceedings of a lecture series as a Memorial to Ruth Kotinsky. New York, NY: Bank Street College of Education.

Bersch, G. T. (2011, June). *Ruth Kotinsky: Author, editor, sociologist & educator.* Paper presented at the Adult Education Research Conference, Toronto, Canada.

Brookfield, S. D. (1995). *Becoming a critically reflective teacher.* San Francisco, CA: Wiley.

Commission on Secondary School Curriculum, Progressive Education Association. (1940). *Mathematics in general education: A report of the committee on the function of mathematics in general education.* New York, NY: D. Appleton-Century.

Dirkx, J. M. (2008). The meaning and role of emotions in adult learning. In J. M. Dirkx (Ed.), *New directions for adult and continuing education: No. 120. Adult learning and the emotional self* (pp. 7–18). San Francisco, CA: Jossey-Bass.

Kotinsky, R. (1933). *Adult education and the social scene.* New York, NY: D. Appleton-Century.

Kotinsky, R. (1940). *Adult education councils.* New York, NY: American Association for Adult Education.

Kotinsky, R. (1941). *Elementary education of adults: A critical interpretation.* New York, NY: American Association for Adult Education.

Kotinsky, R. (1950). *For every child—A fair chance for a healthy personality.* Washington, DC: Association for Supervision and Curriculum Development.

Mezirow, J. (1978). Perspective transformation. *Adult Education Quarterly, 28*(2), 100–110.

Nerstrom, N. (1999). *Ruth Kotinsky.* Retrieved from http://www.3.nl.edu/acedemics/cas/ace/resources/ruthkotinsky.cfm

Thayer, V. T., Zachery, C. B., & Kotinsky, R. (1939). *Reorganizing secondary education.* York, NY: D. Appleton Century.

Washington Times. (1919, June 27). 16 scholarships to central pupils. *Chronicling America: Historic American Newspapers: Library of Congress.* Retrieved from http://chroniclingamerica.loc.gov/lccn/sn84026749/1919-06-27/ed-1/seq-12/

Whitmer, H., & Kotinsky, R. (Eds.). (1952). *Personality in the making: The fact-finding report of the mid-century White House conference on children and youth.* New York, NY: Harper & Brothers.

Whitmer, H., & Kotinsky, R. (Eds.). (1956). *New perspectives for research on juvenile delinquency.* Washington, DC: U.S. Department of Health, Education, and Welfare, Social Security Administration, Children's Bureau.

Roberta Campbell Lawson
(Photo used with permission of the General Federation of Women's Clubs)

CHAPTER 18

"EDUCATION FOR LIVING"

Roberta Campbell Lawson

Marilyn McKinley Parrish

No Small Lives: Handbook of North American Early Women Adult Educators, 1925-1950,
pp. 167–174
Copyright © 2015 by Information Age Publishing

Women's clubs have become an important social unit in each community through a far reaching interest in education for living.... Upon the American home depends the American nation.... In a word, it means being a good citizen, demanding of yourself, and everybody else, a personal contribution to good government, based on the principles our citizenship binds us to uphold.

—Roberta Campbell Lawson (NBC Radio Broadcast, 1937)

General Federation of Women's Clubs (GFWC) President Roberta Campbell Lawson selected "Education for Living" as the theme for the organization from 1935 to 1938. In her role as president, Lawson promoted the middle-class perspectives of the GFWC during the Great Depression while at the same time celebrating her Native American heritage as the granddaughter of the last chief of the Delaware Indians. This chapter explores Roberta Campbell Lawson's life and practice as an educator and leader of women at the local, state, and national levels.

EARLY LIFE AND EDUCATION

Roberta Campbell Lawson was born in 1878, in Alluwe, Cherokee Nation, Indian Territory. Her father, John Edward Campbell, moved to Indian Territory from Virginia following the Civil War and became a prosperous businessman and cattle rancher. Her mother, Emeline Journeycake, arrived in Indian Territory as a result of the Delaware Indians' forced move from Kansas. As a child, Roberta experienced two competing realities—the privileged world of her wealthy family and the devastation experienced by the Delaware Indians. From her maternal grandfather, Charles Journeycake (the last chief of the Delaware Indians), she learned the stories of hardship experienced in their forced moves from Ohio, to Kansas, and to the Cherokee Nation in Indian Territory over a period of nearly 40 years (Self, 2007). Journeycake was ordained as a Baptist minister at the age of 52 and was instrumental in the development of Bacone College, the first college for Native Americans in the country (Gridley, 1974). He became an inspiration for Roberta's involvement in education and her passion for educating adults about Native American arts and music.

After an early education carried out by a tutor in a schoolhouse on the family property (Peterson, 2006), Roberta went on to study art and music at a private female seminary in Independence, Missouri, and then attended Hardin College and Conservatory of Music in Mexico, Missouri (Rainey, 1939). Her schooling was quite different from that of many Native American children who were forced to leave their home communities to go to boarding schools such as the Carlisle Indian School (Archuleta, Child, & Lomawaima, 2000). The goal of the Indian Schools was to educate, individualize, and Christianize Indian children so that they would leave behind their cultures and take "civilized" knowledge home to their families, becoming assimilated into American culture and ready for citizenship (Adams, 1995).

When Roberta returned home after graduating from Hardin College, she formed a club with three other women, which focused on friendship, culture, and learning (Hardy, 1993). Members of the club travelled to meetings on horseback (Peterson, 2006). This initiative foreshadowed her lifelong commitment to gathering women together to learn.

FAMILY AND COMMUNITY LIFE

In 1901, at the age of 23, Roberta Campbell married Eugene B. Lawson and moved to Nowata, Indian Territory. Their son Edward was born 4 years later. Eugene, an attorney from Kentucky, founded the First National Bank and the Lawson Petroleum Company. Roberta Campbell Lawson's early adult life typifies the involvement of wealthy and middle-class women of the period who actively engaged in community reform initiatives, performing "municipal housekeeping" (Blair, 1980; Jarvis, 2005; Solomon, 1985). Lawson played an active role in the development of the public library, the community park, and the local YWCA. She was founder and president of one of the first women's clubs in Indian Territory, the La-Kee-Kon Club for Nowata women (Gridley, 1974; Peterson, 2006). Lawson later became the State President of the Oklahoma Federation of Women's Clubs (1917–1919), and General Federation Director from 1919 to 1922. During the First World War, she was appointed by Dr. Anna Howard Shaw to serve as the Oklahoma State Chair of the Women's Committee of the National Council of Defense (Rainey, 1939; Sonneborn, 2007).

When her husband's growing oil business caused the family to move to Tulsa in 1927, Lawson continued her involvement in ever-expanding civic and community causes. Lawson served on many boards (sometimes as the only woman), including the Oklahoma Historical Society, the University of Tulsa, the Oklahoma College for Women at Chickasha, and First National Bank (Rainey, 1939).

NATIONAL LEADER

Roberta Campbell Lawson rose to national prominence during the 1920s. Her leadership roles at the national level in the GFWC began with her position as chair of the Music Division from 1926 to 1928, and then as second vice president in 1928. Also active in the Indian Welfare committee of the GFWC, Lawson supported Gertrude Simmons Bonnin in pursuing the rights of Indian families who had been cheated over land or killed in disputes about oil rights (Peterson, 2006; Willard, 1985). While serving as chair of the Music Division, Lawson offered lectures and concerts, teaching adults about the chants and melodies of the Delawares. Lawson published two books for club women: *Indian Music Programs for Clubs and Special Music Days* (1926) and *The Evolution of Indian Music* (1929). Responding to a request from her friend Will Rogers, Lawson also chaired a fund established to benefit states struggling with drought, including Oklahoma (Gridley, 1974).

When Lawson's husband died in 1931, their son Edward, then 26, took over as president of the Lawson Petroleum Company in Tulsa. The following year, Lawson was elected to serve a 3-year term as first vice president of the GFWC. During this time she also participated as a member of the Federation's World Friendship Tour and presented Native American musical programs during the tour's visit to Czechoslovakia in 1933, appearing in a "beaded buckskin Indian costume" (Gridley, 1974, p. 92). In 1934, Lawson agreed to serve on Eleanor Roosevelt's committee for mobilization of human needs and as a delegate to the Woman's Pan-Pacific Association convention in Hawaii.

After a "hotly contested election" in 1935, Roberta Campbell Lawson began her 3-year term as GFWC President (Wells, 1953, p. 106). Club women from Oklahoma had actively campaigned for her candidacy (Rainey, 1939), but the campaign was marred by racist comments by supporters of her opponent, Dr. Josephine Peirce of Ohio. Will Rogers "decried reports that Roberta's Indian heritage would prevent her election" in his radio broadcasts (Peterson, 2006, p. 196).

Lawson moved to the GFWC headquarters mansion at 1734 N Street NW in Washington, DC, soon after the election. Oklahoma newspaper coverage of her early days in Washington, DC, reported that she acclimated well to the energy of the nation's capital. Despite the excitement of beginning a new position, Lawson apparently missed her home in the West. She slept

> in a window recess so that she could watch the sky as dawn broke ... she often stepped out on the balcony of her third floor office "to watch and listen to—nothing—the changing moods of nature ... or the special appeal of twilight." (Peterson, 2006, p. 183)

THE GREAT DEPRESSION

During the middle years of the 1930s, Americans faced the devastating effects of the Great Depression. As New Deal programs began, a network of women leaders emerged in prominent positions within government agencies focused on developing new programs to meet the needs of children and families (Ware, 1981). Alternative perspectives were championed by labor unions, the Communist party, and by groups such as the Catholic Worker movement (Parrish & Taylor, 2007). These alternative voices challenged the socioeconomic status quo, which continued to disenfranchise workers, women, people of color, and the poor.

While women in government agencies created new federal programs (Ware, 1981), and women in the Catholic Worker movement developed a compassionate critical-systemic perspective as they walked alongside the poor and disenfranchised (Parrish & Taylor, 2007), the more than two million women of the General Federation of Women's Clubs under Roberta Campbell Lawson's leadership sought to exercise power within homes and communities to influence local, state, and national political structures. Coming from widely differing philosophical perspectives, women in each of these groups brought belief and practice together to educate and to influence broader society.

EDUCATION FOR LIVING

The General Federation of Women's Clubs had been in existence for 45 years when Roberta Campbell Lawson became president in 1935. Created to bring together women's clubs across the country, the founders sought to create "unity in diversity" as they worked toward "united womanhood throughout the world" (Houde, 1989, p. 27). During Lawson's presidency, there were 14,000 clubs and more than two million members in the United States and abroad (GFWC, 1938a).

Lawson's efforts as president of the GFWC echoed the work of many contemporary initiatives in the education of adults during the Great Depression (Kett, 1994; Stubblefield & Keane, 1994). The focus of growing numbers of study clubs and other adult education initiatives demonstrated a wide array of interests, from economics, literature, and vocational issues to artistic and inspirational topics. The growth of radio also offered new opportunities to reach wide audiences of adults. NBC and CBS took the lead in offering educational programming, including radio book programs during the late 1930s and early 1940s. Community theater groups developed plays created with community members reflecting their concerns. All of these efforts were supported by New Deal initiatives to offer more educational opportunities for adults (Kett, 1994; Ware, 1981).

Throughout its history, the GFWC emphasized mutual development and learning among its millions of members. By 1935, the GFWC had grown to include departments, divisions, and committees at the state and national level that addressed a wide variety of issues of concern to middle class women. GFWC divisions and departments at the time included American Citizenship, American Home, Education, Fine Arts, International Relations, Indian Welfare, Legislation, Conservation, and Public Welfare (GFWC, 1938a).

Women's clubs had long been locations for learning for white middle-class women. Restrictive membership rules led to the development of separate working class, African American, Jewish, Native American, and Mormon women's clubs (Hugo, 2001; Smith, 2010; Tetzloff, 2007). Gathering in members' homes to hear presentations by club members on issues of shared interest, whether about conservation, Italian art, home economics, or Native American culture, refreshments were shared and relationships were forged. Hugo (2001) notes that in white middle-class clubs "people of color or ethnic minorities and their cultures and contributions to American culture, were objects of study ... viewed as the 'other'" (p. 96).

The GFWC educated women to become active citizens during the Great Depression. From positions and programs on Americanization efforts to taxes to conservation and care of the environment, to public libraries and courses in American art, to lobbying for the adoption of driver's licenses, women's clubs took on every issue of importance during the decade. The philosophical perspectives which grounded the programs created by GFWC leaders included self-reliance, patriotism, anti-communism, the value of private property, and active citizenship.

Each division created pamphlet mailers for club members that contained program planning ideas and resource materials for club women to read together. For example, at the Triennial meeting in Kansas City, Missouri, in 1938, the Indian Welfare Division of the Department of Public Welfare of the GFWC created a pamphlet reporting on educational and legislative activities by state, as well as reading list and program ideas (GFWC, 1938b).

Radio broadcasts were initiated during Lawson's presidency and were broadcast monthly by NBC. These half hour broadcasts included music, drama, and speeches by Lawson and other GFWC leaders. The national radio broadcasts allowed Lawson to reach a wide audience with the educational and legislative goals of the GFWC. Lawson sought to engage women in learning about issues that affected their families and communities. Lawson spent much of her time as president meeting with groups across the country, at times driving herself to meetings. The myriad programs initiated during her presidency resonated with women across the country. Lawson advocated for highway safety, cancer research, women's vocational education, and legislation affecting women and families (Peterson, 2006).

When her term as president of the General Federation of Women's Clubs ended in 1938, Roberta Campbell Lawson agreed to take on a leadership role in the Democrats for Wilkie committee. In poor health, she finally returned to Tulsa to spend time with her son and his family. She died of leukemia just 2 years later in December 1940 (Peterson, 2006).

CONCLUSIONS

Several questions emerge from studying the life and work of Roberta Campbell Lawson: How are class, race, and gender issues present in Roberta Campbell Lawson's practice as an adult educator? What opportunities and limitations did women experience through their involvements with GFWC during the 1930s? Was Lawson's celebration of Native American arts an example of education as exoticism or was it a way to rescue and champion the arts and culture of an oppressed group?

Roberta Campbell Lawson's accomplishments were many as she balanced roles in several worlds: family and community life; contributing to the development of the new state of Oklahoma; teaching about and collecting Native American arts, artifacts, and music; developing women's clubs and carrying out social reform; and serving in many roles at the national level of the GFWC and other organizations, including lobbying the President and Congress about issues of importance to women.

REFERENCES

Adams, D. (1995). *Education for extinction: American Indians and the boarding school experience, 1875–1928*. Lawrence, KS: University of Kansas Press.

Archuleta, M. L., Child, B. J., & Lomawaima, T. (2000). *Away from home: American Indian boarding school experiences*. Phoenix, AZ: Heard Museum.

Blair, K. J. (1980). *The clubwoman as feminist: True womanhood redefined, 1869–1910*. New York, NY: Holmes & Meier.

General Federation of Women's Clubs (GFWC). (1938a). *Brief of program and activities of the General Federation of Women's Clubs*. Washington, DC: Author.

General Federation of Women's Clubs (GFWC). (1938b.) *Indian Welfare Division, Department of Public Welfare*. (1938). Washington, DC: Author.

Gridley, M. E. (1974). *American Indian women*. New York, NY: Hawthorn.

Hardy, G. J. (1993). Roberta Campbell Lawson. *American women civil rights activists*. Jefferson, NC: McFarland.

Houde, M. J. (1989). Reaching out: A story of the General Federation of Women's Clubs. Washington, DC: General Federation of Women's Clubs.

Hugo, J. M. (2001). Creating an intellectual basis for friendship: Practice and politics in a white women's study group. In V. Sheared & P. A. Sissel (Eds.), *Mak-

ing space: Merging theory and practice in adult education (pp. 89–108). Westport, CT: Bergin & Garvey.

Jarvis, K. A. (2005). *How did the General Federation of Women's Clubs shape women's involvement in the conservation movement, 1900–1930?* Binghamton: State University of New York at Binghamton.

Kett, J. F. (1994). *The pursuit of knowledge under difficulties: From self-improvement to adult education in America, 1750–1990.* Stanford, CA: Stanford University Press.

Lawson, R. C. (1926). *Indian music programs for clubs and special music days.* Nowata, OK: Author.

Lawson, R. C. (1929). *The evolution of Indian music.* Tulsa, OK: Author.

Lawson, R. C. (1937, October 21). *Government begins at home: Opening program of the Education for Living Series of broadcasts of the General Federation of Women's Clubs.* NBC Blue Network.

Parrish, M. M., & Taylor, E. (2007). Seeking authenticity: Women and learning in the Catholic worker movement. *Adult Education Quarterly, 57*(3), 221–247.

Peterson, N. M. (2006). *Walking in two worlds: Mixed blood Indian women seeking their path.* Caldwell, ID: Caxton.

Rainey, L. (1939). *History of Oklahoma State Federation of Women's Clubs.* Guthrie, OK: Co-operative.

Self, B. E. (2007). Journeycake, Charles, 1817–1894. *Encyclopedia of Oklahoma history & culture.* Oklahoma City: Oklahoma Historical Society. Retrieved from http://digital.library.okstate.edu/encyclopedia/entries/J/JO025.html

Smith, M. J. (2010). The fight to protect race and regional identity within the General Federation of Women's Clubs, 1895–1902. *Georgia Historical Quarterly, 94*, 479–513.

Solomon, B. (1985*). In the company of educated women: A history of women and higher education in America.* New Haven, CT: Yale University Press.

Sonneborn, L. (2007). Lawson, Roberta Campbell (1878–1940) Delaware (Lenni Lenape) civic leader. *A to Z of American Indian Women.* New York, NY: Facts on File.

Stubblefield, H. W., & Keane, P. (1994). *Adult education in the American experience: From the colonial experience to the present.* San Francisco, CA: Jossey-Bass.

Tetzloff, L. M. (2007) "With our own wings we fly": Native American Women Clubs, 1899–1955. *American Educational History Journal, 34*(1), 69–84.

Ware, S. (1981). *Beyond suffrage: Women in the New Deal.* Cambridge, MA: Harvard University Press.

Wells, M. W. (1953). *Unity in diversity: The history of the General Federation of Women's Clubs.* Washington, DC: General Federation of Women's Clubs.

Willard, W. (1985). Zitkala Sa: A woman who would be heard! *Wicazo Sa Review, 1*(1), 11–16.

Florence O'Neill
(Used by permission of Centre for Newfoundland Studies and Archives in the
QEII Library at Memorial University of Newfoundland and Labrador)

CHAPTER 19

FLORENCE MARY O'NEILL

Her Own Path
Through the Newfoundland Wilderness

Katherine McManus

No Small Lives: Handbook of North American Early Women Adult Educators, 1925-1950,
pp. 175–183
Copyright © 2015 by Information Age Publishing

In 1944, Florence Mary O'Neill (1905–1990) left Columbia University in New York with her EdD in adult education. She was in the middle of her own adventure by this time—a 40-year-old woman from the colony of Newfoundland. It is an understatement to say that O'Neill was a "one-of-a-kind" person. The odds against her academic achievement were only overshadowed by the odds against her later achievement as the head of a government department of adult education. None of her achievement came easily, and little of it was recognized as the astonishing feat that it was in either her day or today.

A WOMAN WITH A PLAN

O'Neill became the assistant director of adult education in Newfoundland in 1944, immediately after completing her degree at Columbia (Winter, 1944). She was the first and only woman in a high-level, government, administrative position. Her achievement was due to her passion, persistence, and her supporters. Two high-ranking education department bureaucrats, G. Alain Frecker, the secretary for education, and Vincent Burke, the director of adult education, knew O'Neill and followed her progress through Columbia. A position in adult education was created for O'Neill because Frecker and Burke thought highly of her.

O'Neill gained both men's respect over many years of working as first, an elementary school teacher and later as an adult education fieldworker in a fledgling experiment creating night schools around the island. O'Neill also kept in touch with Frecker throughout her education at Columbia where she had developed a "Plan for the Development of an Adult Education Program for Rural Newfoundland" (O'Neill/Frecker, personal correspondence, 1943).

O'Neill devised her "Plan" based on her experiences as both an elementary and later as an adult education teacher and her exposure to new ideas at Columbia. She knew that problems created by the extreme isolation and poverty of rural communities in Newfoundland could only be surmounted through education and community development—people working together to better their existence. In the 1940s, there were no government services available in all communities, including education (Gorvin, 1938; Handcock, 1977).

O'Neill's experiences working in rural Newfoundland were epitomized in an essay she wrote for a sociology class at Columbia. It became the focus for the development of her "Plan" (O'Neill, 1971). She wrote that while working in the community of Lourdes on the Port-au-Port Peninsula in eastern Newfoundland, she became aware of another community farther along the coast that was nearly impossible to reach because the rutted track to the community was almost impassable. The residents of "Lands End," as O'Neill called it for her essay, were reputed to be the "poorest, most disadvantaged souls in all of Newfoundland." Once she'd heard of the community, she wrote that for "four years I had secretly desired to work in Land's End. To me this settlement connoted all that was hopeless and rotten" (O'Neill, 1971, p. 215).

She travelled to the community with a young, French-speaking girl because the residents of Land's End were French descendants of early settlers of that coast. In Land's End there were 24 families who "endured daily hardship." She wrote, "I must remember that what I saw represented a gradual decay over a long period of years, that extreme isolation and resultant ignorance accounted for the greater part of the present state of affairs" (O'Neill, 1971, p. 220).

O'Neill worked with this community for 3 months to help them learn to grow food, make clothing for themselves by ordering fabric from the co-op store (using her own money) to show the women how to sew clothes for their children and shirts for the men. She also admitted to having to pay her assistant's salary from her own pay because adult education teachers were not given assistants. Her assistant, however, made it possible for her to communicate with the members of the community in their language. She wrote, "I had never started quite so much from scratch before" but she also reported that the 3 months spent in the community were the "most exciting" of her life (Hewson, 1971; O'Neill, 1943).

Working with people to affect lasting change in their lives compelled O'Neill toward a goal of an organized delivery of service island-wide. This was her "Plan." She recognized the difficulty of bringing it to life. She wrote, "Such development is a slow process of evolution plus education" (O'Neill, n.d., p. 5). She knew that it would take time to find and develop leaders, achieve individual community participation, and to coordinate all of the agencies, government-sponsored as well as nonprofit organizations, to work together under one grand organization.

O'Neill (1944) envisioned an interdepartmental committee "whose primary function will be to sit down and look at the whole of Newfoundland, evaluating the actual functioning of the various agencies in light of their particular aims in the light of the vast totality of its [Newfoundland's] needs" (O'Neill, 1944, pp. 62–63). The interdepartmental committee would be composed of the government Departments of Adult Education, Public Health, Rural Reconstruction, and Fisheries, as well as volunteer groups such as the Jubilee Guilds (similar to Women's Institutes) and the Newfoundland Outport Nursing and Industrial Association (an organization that combined health education with craft production). At Columbia, she had learned from Edmund de S. Brunner that effective adult education enlisted those agencies already committed to working in communities in order to maximize the amount of work accomplished (Brunner, 1948; O'Neill, 1944, pp. 58–68)

REALIZING THE PLAN

As soon as she returned to Newfoundland with her new title as assistant director of adult education, she began work to achieve her "Plan." She expected to be able to convince the government to allow her to hire a coordinator and two assistants to oversee regional coordination of resources from a central office. She wrote, "The office would break the geographic area of the island into divisions and oversee multiple small units of field workers in each division distributed across the island." From the central office "two qualified community workers, a man and a woman, permanently employed and suitably remunerated" would ensure that services were provided island wide (O'Neill, 1944, p. 67)

Central office staff members were essentially the life blood, the heart, of the effort. From them, service would flow everywhere in a controlled and effective manner. She knew the central office needed to not only coordinate and organize community field offices but also needed to train adult education fieldworkers as well as develop new programs and approaches through research and professional development. To O'Neill, the quality of the entire enterprise rested on the teaching staff—the fieldworkers.

The Department of Adult Education had, since 1936, been providing some education services to adults. O'Neill's own experience in Lands End came about through her employment as an adult education itinerant teacher. To go to Land's End, however, O'Neill had to petition her department through G. Alain Frecker, because the community itself had not asked for an adult education teacher. The shortcoming of the system was that there was no overall strategy regarding where teachers were sent. The communities with strong leaders requested from the government that their community receive adult education services (NAEA, 1930, 1932). In effect, the stronger communities received more benefits than poorer communities. O'Neill deeply felt the inequity of this system. Her plan was to provide and distribute educational services across the island fairly.

O'Neill began her campaign to convince the people of the island, as well as those in government, that a different approach was necessary to help communities out of poverty. She addressed the Rotary Club in St. John's soon after her appointment as assistant director and warned them against an overemphasis "on the academic side of education" (Key to Better Living, 1945). She proposed, instead, that adult education should provide guidance to communities so that the interests of the people would be developed. She believed that tapping into community-identified needs mobilized the citizens.

By 1946, two years after her return to Newfoundland, a new *Field Workers' Manual* suggests that O'Neill experienced some success in influencing government and her own department. The manual contains a "Tentative Plan for Application and Development of Adult Education Programmes." While the list of "general objectives" focused on objectives for the economic reconstruction of Newfoundland, a favorite preoccupation of the government, it also included language around developing attitudes within communities that promoted action and responsibility. Specific objectives within the "Tentative Plan" included "developing in Newfoundlanders a sense of individual and community interest and responsibility," and "spreading culture and enlightenment and an appreciation of proper standards of living including health, nutrition, prevention and cure of diseases" (NGDE, 1946). These objectives reflect O'Neill's interests as well as her phrasing.

A REVERSAL

Support for O'Neill's "Plan" was strong enough among those in the educational sector of government that there was an interest in publishing her thesis for the purpose of circulating it "amongst the thinking people of the country" (Burke, 1945). A request for the government to bear the cost of publishing O'Neill's thesis was circulated to the six commissioners of the government. Newfoundland at this time was a "dominion" of England, governed by a British appointed commission between 1929 and 1949.

One of the commissioners, H. A. Winter, commissioner for Home Affairs and Education, a lawyer, and a Newfoundlander, viewed O'Neill's dissertation as reckless because, he felt, the document described as typical the human conditions of poverty, ignorance, and isolation. Winter wrote that O'Neill made "damaging statements about this country, it's [*sic*] people, and some of it's [*sic*] institutions" (Winter, 1945). O'Neill wrote not only about poverty and isolation, she also wrote about the church and the merchant's control of people's lives. Winter strongly objected to her views on both of these issues.

O'Neill's observations were not exposing new problems about the educational and economic conditions in Newfoundland, however. The island had lost its sovereignty and economic independence in 1929 due to its inability to control its debt and pay its bills.

Winter warned Vincent Burke, then director of adult education and O'Neill's immediate supervisor, that the thesis should not be printed.

From his tone, Winter seems to have contemplated some sort of censure of O'Neill, or worse, such as demanding her resignation. Winter did neither, but it is easy to imagine the shock O'Neill felt from his response to her work. Until this incident, she had received nothing but praise from those at Columbia and from her immediate supervisors and colleagues in her own department.

CONTINUING THE WORK TO THE END

O'Neill did not let Winter change her mind or her course of action. From 1945 until 1949 she made slow and steady progress. First, she was able to change fieldworker status from government staff to teacher and with that came a requirement that an adult education teacher should possess some university training (Wild, 1945). Secondly, she reorganized the summer school for teachers and brought in Per Stensland, a well-known Danish adult educator, to lead the summer school in 1945 (Stensland, 1946). He brought other experts with him and raised the level of discussion so that participants received some foundation in the sociology of community, agricultural techniques, adult psychology, and group discussion techniques. After this training, the adult education teachers could go into isolated communities with some preparation regarding how to do their work. And finally, she was able to bring together the heads from agriculture, cooperatives, handicrafts, and fisheries into a joint committee in order to develop a routine process for sharing information and resources (McManus, 2000, p. 154).

In 1949, when Newfoundland became a province of Canada, O'Neill became director of adult education (O'Neil, 1949a). She had witnessed growth in her department and was continuing to fight for changes to be made. Within government, education remained highly political and as Newfoundland moved from being a protected colony of Britain to being a province of another country—but with restored democratic elections and the right to make its own decisions—the "winds of change" blew. Her supporters moved on to new positions in government. She did not receive an increase in pay nor was she allowed to hire an assistant, and she continued to have all of her previous responsibilities (O'Neill, 1949b).

As the previous director, C. W. Carter, who had succeeded Burke upon Burke's retirement, was leaving his position as director of adult education, he submitted an article for *Food For Thought* (1949), a Canadian adult education publication, as an introduction to Canada about what was happening in the country's newest province. He described the activities of the department and painted a fairly bleak picture of the accomplishments of adult education to that point. He wrote that the "experiment" that had "been unfolding since 1944 had not worked" and he, as director, had begun to change the plan (Carter, 1949, pp. 10–11). Carter's opinions, aired in a national publication, signaled the thunderclouds and darkness that began to close in on O'Neill.

One serious problem was O'Neill's inability to keep fieldworkers. She created an elaborate educational training program for them and once they were sent out to the small, isolated communities, they would last only a year or sometimes less. She was never able to train and keep enough workers to fulfill her own goal to have two adult educators per site. There was typically one who "manned" a center, alone, and did all of the work (McManus, 2000, pp.149–154).

O'Neill was also frequently in trouble because of her style. She was an active, engaged adult educator. She was not a bureaucrat. Soon after she began working, Frecker, the deputy minister of education, reminded O'Neill in a memo that she had not followed protocol in several instances. O'Neill had violated the hierarchy through which people talked to people. Rather than write to her supervisor, she would send letters, memos, or make telephone calls directly to the top (McManus, 2000, pp. 174–175).

In another instance, O'Neill refused to sign the attendance book that indicated she was at work. Frecker wrote that it was traditional practice to sign the book. O'Neill responded that she had willingly complied until, in 1951, "it was drawn to my attention that four Division Heads with the Department had been exempt." She continued: "I objected in principle as I felt strongly that it was undemocratic and unfair to exempt 4 Division Heads, and discriminate against the fifth" (O'Neill, 1951). The government won this round with O'Neill because they withheld her pay until she again started signing the attendance book (McManus, 2000, pp. 185–186). O'Neill's disinterest in bureaucratic process probably made it easy for enemies of her vision for adult education to, in the end, find a way to silence her.

CONCLUSION

Florence Mary O'Neill, born in 1905, in Witless Bay, Newfoundland, died in Ottawa in 1990. In 1958, the Newfoundland government closed the Department of Adult Education and O'Neill was moved to 4-H Leadership. Her office was a windowless space in the basement of the Colonial building. She was without a staff or a budget (Best, personal communication, May 18, 1999).

O'Neill passionately embraced adult education as a career. She worked tirelessly to bring opportunities to people who had none. Along the way, she frustrated and angered those who were in a position to aid her efforts because she was blunt and sometimes rude—but always committed. The effects of her work can be seen on the island in remnants of programs originally created by her.

REFERENCES

Brunner, E. de S. (1948). The Cooperative Extension Service of the United States Department of Agriculture. In M. L. Ely (Ed.), *Handbook of adult education in the United States* (pp. 96–100). New York, NY: Teachers College, Columbia University.

Burke, V. (1945, March 23). Secretary for Education, St. John's, to Morse A. Cartwright, Columbia University. CNSA, QEII, MUN (collection 212).

Carter, C. W. (1949). Adult education in Newfoundland. *Food for Thought, 9*, 10-14; 20.

Gorvin, J. H. (1938). Papers relating to a long range reconstruction policy in Newfoundland: 1939–1953. CURBM. file: Newfoundland Department of Education.

Handcock, W. G. (1977). English migration to Newfoundland. In J. J. Mannion (Ed.), *The peopling of Newfoundland* (pp. 15–48). St. John's: Institute for Social and Economic Research, Memorial University of Newfoundland.

Hewson, J. (1971). Transcribed interview between John Hewson and Florence O'Neill. CNS, QEII, MUN (collection 212).

Key to better living. (1944, December 18). *Daily News* (St. John's, Newfoundland).

McManus, K. (2000). *Florence O'Neill, A Newfoundland adult educator: Alone in the wilderness.* (Unpublished doctoral dissertation). University of British Columbia, British Columbia, Canada.

Newfoundland Adult Education Association (NAEA). (1930). *What is it? What are its aims?* [pamphlet]. St John's, Newfoundland: Advocate.

Newfoundland Adult Education Association (NAEA). (1932).*The Opportunity Schools of the N.A.E.A.* [newsletter]. St. John's, Newfoundland.

Newfoundland Government Department of Education (NGDE). (1946). *A tentative plan for application and development of adult education programmes.* Division of Adult and Visual Education.

O'Neill, F. (1943, December 3). [Letter to G. A. Frecker]. Centre for Newfoundland Studies (CNS), QEII Library (QEII), Memorial University of Newfoundland and Labrador (MUN) (collection 212).

O'Neill, F. (1944). *A plan for the development of an adult education program for rural Newfoundland* (Unpublished doctoral dissertation). Columbia University, New York, NY.

O'Neill, F. (1949a, May 31). [Letter to G.A. Frecker]. CNSA, QEII, MUN (collection 212).

O'Neill, F. (1949b, Sept. 6). [Memo to G.A. Frecker, St. John's]. Provincial Archives of Newfoundland and Labrador (file #7/02, Vol. III).

O'Neill, F. (1951). [Memo to S.J. Hefferton – Minister of Education] CNSA, QEII, MUN, (collection 212).

O'Neill, F. (1971). Thou beside me in the wilderness. In J. A. Draper (Ed.), *Citizen Participation: Canada* (pp. 215–225). Toronto, Canada: New Press.

O'Neill, F. (n.d.). *How a course in rural sociology has helped prepare me to do a better job in Newfoundland.* (Unpublished Essay) CNS, QEII, MUN (collection 212).

Stensland, Per G. (1946). New plans for Newfoundland. *Food for Thought,* (6) 4–9, 47–49.

Wild, I. (1945). Commissioner for Finance, Commission of Government, Newfoundland to H.A. Winter [Memo]. Provincial Archives of Newfoundland and Labrador (PANL) (folder H.A.E., 1945).

Winter, H. A. (1944). Proposed appointment of assistant director of adult education. PANL, H.A.E. 61—'44.

Winter, H. A. (1945, December 6). Commissioner of Home Affairs and Education to Vincent Burke, Secretary for Education. Government correspondence: Winter's response regarding G.A. Frecker's interest in having O'Neill's thesis published CNS, QEII, MUN (collection 212).

Bonaro Wilkinson Overstreet
(Photo from the Rappaport personal photo collection was taken by Yvonne Rappaport)

CHAPTER 20

BONARO WILKINSON OVERSTREET

Adult Education for an Educated Citizenry

Yvonne K. Rappaport and Marcie Boucouvalas

Bonaro Wilkinson Overstreet functioned both individually and collectively as a team with her husband, Harry Allen Overstreet (1875–1970),
well known in the field of adult education for his influential book *The
Mature Mind*[1] (1949). Educating the mass populace, they reasoned, was a

No Small Lives: Handbook of North American Early Women Adult Educators, 1925-1950,
pp. 185–192

challenge that necessitated our learning from all disciplines that informed the human phenomenon.

Rappaport's research[2] (1998) depicted them as "missionaries" deeply concerned with the crucial contribution of adult education to the health of democracy. Their work underscored the value and importance of adults continuing to learn throughout life both for fulfillment as well as to lead mature responsible lives and improve social conditions. According to the Overstreets, educators had a responsibility to encourage adults to address and solve social problems, to help them understand that they had capability in that regard, and to provide education toward that end. They spent 40 plus years working together to achieve that goal.

Abraham Maslow, with whom they were good colleagues, seems to have been influenced by the Overstreets. Not only had he cited many quotes from *The Mature Mind* (1949) in his book *Motivation and Personality* (1954), but he also wrote a handwritten inscription on their personal copy of his article on "Science and Self-Actualization" (Maslow, 1965), which read, "To the Overstreets with all my admiration."

Malcolm Knowles also heralded the Overstreets as a great influence and inspiration to him, as noted in his autobiography, *The Making of an Adult Educator* (1989). Harry Overstreet wrote the introductory preface to Knowles' first book entitled *Informal Adult Education* (1950). In the Overstreets' personal copy of the book, Knowles wrote the following inscription: "To Harry Allen Overstreet, whose life and works have chiefly inspired this book and whose grand foreword gives it a real send-off." Moreover, in an inscription to his book, *The Adult Education Movement in the United States* (1962), Knowles wrote to Harry and Bonaro "with deep gratitude for the contributions you have made to this movement and to my understanding of it." Later, with the publication of *The Modern Practice of Adult Education* (1970), Knowles wrote to Bonaro, "With gratitude and thanks for the great contributions you and Harry have made to my maturing as a person and as an adult educator." Not long after Bonaro's death, Knowles shared with the author that he thought their influence was inestimable because of the thousands of people they had reached and helped. He added that the Overstreets had a marked impact on him and many others, not only because of their teachings and the example they set but also because they gave to those who worked in adult education a very real sense of pride and worth. Pioneer adult educator James Robbins (Roby) Kidd also held the Overstreets in high regard as evidenced by his personal inscriptions written in their copies of his books and the manner in which he quoted from their works in his classic book *How Adults Learn* (Kidd, 1959).

Bonaro, however, had already begun to distinguish herself even before the partnership with Harry Overstreet and carried on after his passing in

1970 as well. This chapter illuminates her life and contributions both as a member of the team as well as an independent force in her own right.

BONARO WILKINSON OVERSTREET: A FORCE IN HER OWN RIGHT

Early Life and Influences

Bonaro Wilkinson Overstreet was born on October 30, 1902, to a family of modest means in Geyserville, California, a rural area where her parents had a small fruit farm. The youngest of three children, her brother, Clarendon, was 5 years older and sister, Muriel, 3 years older. While all three children worked on the farm, education was a top priority in the household with daily read-alouds of the Bible, classical literature, the US Constitution, and poetry (Y. Rappaport, personal communication, 2013).

In this setting, Bonaro began writing and keeping a daily diary even before starting her formal schooling. Poetry was her special love and several of her pieces at an early age were published in local newspapers.

The importance of education to the Wilkinsons extended beyond the immediate household in that her father's efforts, along with neighbors, led to building Geyserville Union High School from which Bonaro graduated in 1920 as the valedictorian of her class. This feat of establishing the school resulted from the organization of town meetings that led to the passage of a local levy. Interestingly, the first book co-authored with Harry Overstreet was entitled *Town Meeting Comes to Town* (Overstreet & Overstreet, 1938).

Graduation from high school was followed by college graduation from UC Berkeley and a job teaching high school English and Spanish from September 1926 to June 1929, after which she headed to Columbia University (New York) for her master's degree in psychology, studying with William Kilpatrick, who was also publishing in the *Journal of Adult Education* at that time. Returning to California after graduation, Bonaro taught another 2 years in California, at a junior college.

It was during the summer of 1928 while attending a lecture at UC Berkeley that she met visiting professor from New York, Harry Overstreet. It was a friendship that continued during her years at Columbia. In the summer of 1929, she participated in an innovative 6-week residential summer training session for educators of adults directed by Harry Overstreet at UC Berkeley. The experience resulted in a published article (Wilkinson, 1930), and her developing friendship with Overstreet would culminate in marriage during 1932.

Although her poetry had already been published in various sources while a student, her first book of poetry (*The Poetic Way of Release*) was published in 1931 when she was 29 (Wilkinson, 1931), with a forward written by Harry Overstreet. David L. MacKaye, director of the Tulare, California, Evening and Weekend School, read this book and invited her to speak there, resulting in her first public lecture. During her teaching years, her interest in adult education was developing, and after her marriage to Harry Overstreet in August of 1932, adult education and the mental health movement became her major concerns. She continued to write, lecture, and teach even after Harry's death in 1970; her last lectures and classes were with the University of Virginia's Division of Continuing Education in the fall of 1984, just prior to her passing in 1985.

Professional Contributions

From 1930 to 1984, a year prior to her passing, Bonaro published extensively, sometimes producing five to six publications a year. During this 50-plus-year span, her works were read and applied both by educators of adults as well as the mass populace. In fact, several of her books are still on the market today. A quick perusal of a site such as Amazon.com will yield an array of her publications for sale. Like her first (Wilkinson, 1931), her last book (Overstreet, 1984) published one year prior to her death, was a book of poetry.

Both Dorman (1990) and her doctoral advisor Ron Newsom (1997, 1998) recognized the value of her many books and the lessons bequeathed to contemporary times. Michael Day's dissertation (Day, 1981), which analyzed articles submitted to the then *Journal of Adult Education*, 1929–1941, recognized Bonaro as one of the largest contributors of articles, and in June 1980 at a reception for the Board of the International Council for Adult Education, in Washington, DC, Roby Kidd introduced her as the "first lady of adult education."

COLLABORATING WITH HARRY OVERSTREET

Bonaro and Harry's written publications, public appearances, lectures, and presentations were a collaborative effort. As Norman Cousins remarked, they "functioned synergistically," and their commitment to each other and their greater aims reached popular magazines such as *McCall's* (Overstreet & Overstreet, 1957) and *Good Housekeeping* (Overstreet & Overstreet, 1960). Individually and collectively, they made sure that their work was based on sound science, engaging in extensive research to gain the most recent valid data on whatever topic on which they wrote or spoke, and then were able to make it accessible to professionals in many fields as well as to the lay public.

Their first written collaboration focused on the town hall meeting as a format for adult audiences (Overstreet & Overstreet, 1938), followed by *Leaders for Adult Education* (Overstreet & Overstreet, 1940), which was the result of a comprehensive study commissioned by the American Association for Adult Education (AAAE). Subjects of the study included people from all walks of life functioning as education leaders in the field and as continuous learners throughout life. Among those recognizing the importance of this publication were Roby Kidd, Cyril Houle, and Harold Stubblefield. Harry's year as president of AAAE that followed found the Overstreets stressing the role of adult education in community consciousness and civil rights.

During the years of World War II, the Overstreets created an innovation in their lecture method which they termed a *colloquy*. The two would have a dialogue on the topic before welcoming questions from the audience. The flexibility of the colloquy fit two professionals who had mutual respect for each other and were comfortable with an informal method. The colloquy became a trademark for them. During this period, Bonaro also forged forward, independently writing five books between 1941 and 1945 and numerous articles. She also wrote a newspaper column each week, often a long narrative poem that was like a letter from home. Many poems became radio dramatizations throughout the country; some were reprinted by Armed Services organizations for distribution in the United States and abroad, along with requests from universities and associations for permission to reprint for distribution.

Increasingly, the team became firmly entrenched in the adult education movement as they traveled throughout the world. As Rappaport (1998) aptly articulated, "The whole world was their classroom." During post–World War II, their efforts regained focus on parent education, an area in which Bonaro retained involvement long after Harry's passing. In addition, while Harry's publication of *The Mature Mind* (1949) was gathering accolades, Bonaro was excelling in her own right with books such as *How To Think About Ourselves* (1948), reissued as well 30 years later, and *Understanding Fear* (1951), in print for more than 30 years, and considered one of the best books on fear. Many other publications followed, educating the public about mental health matters as well as democratic principles and adult civic education, including a confrontation with communist ideology. One such well-researched and written book, *What We Must Know about Communism* (Overstreet & Overstreet, 1958), was read by many, including then Secretary of State John Foster Dulles, who gave a copy to President Eisenhower, catapulting the Overstreets' presence worldwide, especially when the media captured a photo of Eisenhower carrying it. Other books and lectures followed on communism as well as extremism. Their last co-authored publication was published in 1969: *The FBI in an Open Society*. In August of 1970, Harry A. Overstreet died, just prior to his 95th birthday, his last words, spoken to Bonaro being, "It's been wonderful, hasn't it?" (Rappaport, 1998, p. 175).

ONWARD: AFTER HARRY OVERSTREET'S PASSING

Even during their collaborative efforts, Bonaro wrote and published articles independently, so after Harry's passing in 1970, she continued her writing as well as speaking engagements. She was recognized with numerous awards during this period, including in 1973, from the Adult Education Association of Virginia: Kurt A. Schneider Award "For outstanding service to adult education"; in 1974, the Pioneer Award from the Adult Education Association of the USA "For her dedicated commitment to the cause of adult education and her untiring efforts in behalf of increased participation by all citizens in the democratic process"; and the Social Justice Award from National Association for Public, Continuing, and Adult Education (NAPCAE) (Rappaport, 1998, p. 176).

She took on assignments overseas for the United States Information Agency, with a 3-month around-the-world speaking tour in 1973; lectured each year for the Menninger Foundation in Topeka, Kansas; and spent 2 weeks each year speaking at Berry College in Georgia. There, she was invited to sit in on classes in every discipline and then speak to each class about relating what they were learning to the world in which they lived. She spoke often at state and national adult education conferences and had speaking engagements on mental health, citizen responsibility, and poetry. During 1978, she published another book of new and selected poems.

Bonaro continued contributing to the growth of adult education throughout the world via her involvement with the International Council for Adult Education. In the spring of 1985, despite the fact that the United States had temporarily withdrawn from UNESCO, she joined the delegation to the UNESCO Fourth International Conference on Adult Education in Paris, where she was a speaker and co-leader of a workshop on "Identifying and Developing Leaders in a Community." During 1983 and 1984, she continued participation in adult education conferences and lecturing at the Menninger Clinic and Berry College, and occasional lectures elsewhere if they did not require too much travel. She had received a heart pacemaker and had been advised by her cardiologist to cut down on travel and limit it to the same time zone. On September 3, 1985, Bonaro died, having lived and contributed a very full life to the adult education movement.

Active until the end of her life, Bonaro's final speaking engagement was with the University of Virginia's Northern Virginia Center, of which the first author was director and in the same building where the second author was working as faculty since 1980 with Virginia Tech's Northern Virginia Graduate Center. Rappaport and her family became close friends with Bonaro and could often be seen traveling together to conferences and maintaining a friendship, which still carries warm memories and huge respect for this early pioneer.

NOTES

1. In addition to his widely read and influential volume (*The Mature Mind*), Overstreet's publications were prolific over his lifetime. Since this chapter focuses on Bonaro, however, only references where Bonaro was sole author or where the couple were joint authors are included. Due to space constraints, only selected publications are included. A more complete bibliography is available from the authors, and archival materials are available from the Lilly Library of Indiana University, Bloomington, Indiana.

2. Boucouvalas served on the dissertation committee of Rappaport, but would like to also acknowledge Harold Stubblefield, Professor Emeritus, Virginia Tech, for his role as advisor and chair.

REFERENCES

Day, M. J. (1981). *Adult education as a new educational frontier: Review of the Journal of Adult Education 1929–1941* (Unpublished doctoral dissertation). Ann Arbor: University of Michigan.

Dorman, B. B. (1990). *Bonaro Wilkinson Overstreet: Her significance in adult education* (Unpublished doctoral dissertation). University of North Texas, Denton.

Kidd, J. R. (1959). *How adults learn.* New York, NY: Association.

Knowles, M. S. (1950). *Informal adult education.* New York, NY: Association.

Knowles, M. S. (1962). *The adult education movement in the United States.* New York, NY: Holt, Rinehart & Winston.

Knowles, M. S. (1970). *The modern practice of adult education: Andragogy versus pedagogy.* New York, NY: Association.

Knowles, M. S. (1989). *The making of an adult educator: An autobiographical journey.* San Francisco, CA: Jossey-Bass.

Maslow, A. H. (1954). *Motivation and personality.* New York, NY: Harper & Brothers.

Maslow, A. H. (1965, 28 July). Science and self-actualization. *MANA, 18*(30), 1–14.

Newsom, R. (1997). Bonaro Overstreet as adult educator: An interpretation from her writings. *Mountain Plains Journal of Adult Education, 25*(1), 27–38.

Newsom, R. (1998). Living by the principles of adult education: What can we learn from Bonaro Wilkinson Overstreet. *Adult Learning, 9*(3), 26–17.

Overstreet, B.W. (1948). *How to think about ourselves.* New York, NY: Harper.

Overstreet, B. W. (1951). *Understanding fear: In ourselves and others.* New York, NY: Harper.

Overstreet, B. W. (1978). *Signature: New and selected poems.* New York, NY: W. W. Norton.

Overstreet, B. W. (1984). *Footsteps on the earth.* New York, NY: Knopf.

Overstreet, H. A. (1949). *The mature mind.* New York, NY: W. W. Norton.

Overstreet, H. A., & Overstreet, B. W. (1938). *Town meeting comes to town.* New York, NY: Harper.

Overstreet, H. A., & Overstreet, B. W. (1940). *Leaders for adult education.* New York, NY: American Association for Adult Education.

Overstreet, H. A., & Overstreet, B. W. (1957, May). What togetherness means to us. *McCall's, 84*(8), 2.

Overstreet, H. A., & Overstreet, B. W. (1958). *What we must know about communism.* New York, NY: W. W. Norton.

Overstreet, H. A., & Overstreet, B. W. (1960, May). Love is their reason. *Good Housekeeping, 150*(5), 71–73.

Overstreet, H. A., & Overstreet, B. W. (1969). *The FBI in our open society.* New York: W. W. Norton.

Rappaport, Y. K. (1998). *The whole world was their classroom: The contributions of Harry and Bonaro Overstreet to the field of adult education* (Unpublished doctoral dissertation). Virginia Tech/National Capital Region, Falls Church, VA.

Wilkinson, B. (1930, January). Teaching teachers in a new way: An experiment in adult education at the California Summer Session of 1929. *Journal of Adult Education, 2,* 67–74.

Wilkinson, B. (1931). *The poetic way of release.* New York, NY: Knopf.

Elizabeth Peratrovich
(Photo used with the permission of Alaska State Library Historical Digital Archive
Collection, Alaska State Library Photograph Collection, P01-3294)

CHAPTER 21

ELIZABETH PERATROVICH

The Right to Education

Diane E. Benson (Lxeis')

No Small Lives: Handbook of North American Early Women Adult Educators, 1925-1950,
pp. 193–200
Copyright © 2015 by Information Age Publishing

A 26-year-old Martin Luther King Jr. spoke in Tennessee in 1956 and a 45-year-old Tlingit Indian woman in the audience was validated by his words. Elizabeth Peratrovich from the (then) Territory of Alaska, living in Oklahoma, was in Nashville attending a conference on adult Indian education. Prior to this conference, her life had taken her well away from her youthful desire to teach and instead segued onto a path of civil rights leadership. She wanted the dignity of good education for her children and others, but she found she had to first fight for equal rights for Alaska's indigenous people.

ELIZABETH'S EARLY LIFE

In the tiny towns and villages dotting the rain forested islands and coastline of Southeast Alaska in the early 20th century lived the Tlingit and Haida peoples, adjusting to increased missionary and military presence. Tlingit and Haida people had retained their own language and culture while living side by side for decades with Russians; many never had contact with non-Indians at all. The United States purchase of Alaska and the large migrations of gold seekers, loggers, and settlers throughout the southeast changed that, with devastating results for Alaska's first peoples. Within this climate, Elizabeth was born July 4, 1911, and was adopted by the Wanamakers, a Tlingit missionary couple. Unlike many others, she was raised with the appreciation and benefits of both Tlingit and Western education.

Elizabeth's early education meant leaving home, and she attended school in Petersburg and in Sitka, towns dominated by non-Natives but with schools that allowed certain Alaskan Native enrollment. The system for the education of Native people in Alaska has been a convoluted one. For the first 17 years after the purchase of Alaska, no provision was made for education in the territory (Case, 1984). Presbyterian, Moravian, and other churches maintained missions in Alaska that educated Native children. However, the effort was primarily one of acculturation and often required rejection of cultural and familial ties. To further this arrangement, acts were passed to freely provide 640-acre grants to missionary stations. When the Nelson Act was passed in 1905 creating what became known as a "dual system of education," the federal government, the missions, and the Territory shared responsibility. Which school an Alaska Native might attend however, weighed primarily on blood quantum. Mixed blooded Natives who could prove they were "civilized" were allowed to go to public schools. Other Natives were placed in schools operated by the federal government or by missions. The Territory of

Alaska avoided the financial burden or responsibility of educating Alaska's first peoples.

For the first 13 years of Elizabeth's life, she was not an American citizen, but she was the daughter of missionaries and therefore had access to education. She attended Ketchikan High School, a public school, where she met the captain of the basketball team, Roy Peratrovich, a young man from the Southeast village of Klawock, on Prince of Wales Island.

Roy and Elizabeth graduated in 1931 from Ketchikan High School and were married that December in Bellingham following their first semester in college. Elizabeth and Roy had decided to be teachers, so Elizabeth attended Bellingham Normal (now Western Washington College of Education). They both worked to pay their way. Life has a way of affecting the best-laid plans, and children and financial realities sent them back to Alaska (R. Peratrovich Jr., personal communication, 2012). Roy immediately found supervisory work on Prince of Wales Island and for the next 10 years Elizabeth focused on her children while Roy moved up the ladder, becoming Mayor of Klawock. But times were tough; tuberculosis had taken its toll on Native communities, discrimination was blatant across Alaska, and the threat of war on the homefront prompted more and more Alaska Native young men and women to join the Armed Forces.

FIGHTING FOR SOCIAL CHANGE

Although Alaska Native peoples were not provided citizenship until Congress passed a bill in 1924 granting citizenship to all Native Americans, the rights known to most Americans remained elusive for Native people. In 1912 and 1915, respectively, the Alaska Native Brotherhood (ANB) and the Alaska Native Sisterhood (ANS) formed to fight for citizenship, fishing rights, and equality (R. Petratrovich et al., n.d.). These organizations became the catalyst for important social change, and Elizabeth would be at the heart of it.

Roy and Elizabeth were both very active in the ANB and ANS. Many communities in Alaska had a chapter or camp, and these were governed by the Grand Camp. In 1940, Roy became the ANB Grand Camp president and in 1941 Elizabeth was elected ANS Grand Camp president.

The ANS and ANB were growing more incensed by blatant signs and attitudes that denied Alaska Native people access to most establishments and schools. The Snyder Act of 1921 had turned the administrative authority of Native education over to the Bureau of Indian Affairs (BIA). But when the Territory was permitted the transfer of Indian schools, it didn't really want it. Case (1984) reported that the Territory transferred 19 "all-Native" schools back to the BIA. The reported treatment, segregation, and unhappiness of Native children were not things Elizabeth wanted for her own children.

In 1941, Elizabeth and Roy made the decision to move their family to Alaska's capitol where they could better fight for equality and for an anti-discrimination bill. Travel during these days was no trivial matter, but they made the difficult move from Ketchikan, and Elizabeth and her family settled into the modest city life of Juneau.

Elizabeth and Roy set out to find a suitable home to raise the family and to be near the capitol building. They found a home, but when the owners learned that they were Indian, they said no. People described Elizabeth as lovely, poised, well-dressed and dignified. To walk through town and have others look away as you try to greet them, seeing signs in restaurants that deny your patronage, and hotels and renters rejecting your interest, were more than Elizabeth could bear.

In December 1941, the Japanese attacked Pearl Harbor in the Hawaiian Islands and Alaska went on alert. Windows were covered with tin foil or other means for blackouts in Juneau and other coastal communities. Mail and magazines were censored, eliminating any information about Alaska's geography for fear it might inform the enemy. The war did land on Alaska's Aleutian Islands and a 2,000-mile war ensued. Native people from all regions responded; even 12-year-old Native boys were serving as Territorial Guard (Gruening, 1973). Yet Alaskan Native men serving in the Armed Forces were not allowed to be seen socializing with Native women. Elizabeth and Roy took action. Together, they crafted letters to military officials, politicians, and newspapers. They wrote eloquently against these discriminatory practices, as in this letter to the Governor regarding a "No Natives Allowed" sign at a restaurant,

> In view of the present emergency, when unity is being stressed don't you think that it is very Un-American? We have always contended that we are entitled to every benefit that is accorded our so-called White Brothers. We pay the required taxes, taxes in some instances that we feel are unjust, such as the School tax. Our Native people pay the School tax each year to educate the White children, yet they try to exclude our children from these schools.
>
> The proprietor of "Douglas Inn" does not seem to realize that our Native boys are just as willing as the White boys to lay down their lives to protect the freedom that he enjoys. Instead he shows his appreciation by having a "No Natives Allowed" on his door.
>
> We were shocked when the Jews were discriminated against in Germany. Stories were told of public places having signs, "No Jews Allowed." All Freedom loving people in our country were horrified at these reports yet it is being practiced in our country. (Peratrovich & Peratrovich, 1941)

The letter was published in the newspapers as well.

Although it would often appear, by the mere fact that the many letters written were almost always signed by Roy, that Elizabeth played the usual role of the times as supportive wife; in reality, she was quite active and visionary. Roy said about Elizabeth, "She got me started and suggested we move where we could be of more use. She was the manager. She saw the possibilities. She never once stepped out in front … [But] made it look as if I made my own way" (Koester, 1988, p. 39).

PAVING THE WAY FOR AN ANTI-DISCRIMINATION BILL

The governor of the Territory of Alaska was Ernest Gruening, a Jewish man from New York who was keenly aware of the irony that Native soldiers were fighting in Europe against racially motivated tyranny, while Native people in Alaska were segregated and ostracized, often by immigrant shop owners. His impassioned efforts to end discrimination and advance an anti-discrimination bill in Alaska were thwarted and needed a boost. It came with the tenacious efforts of the ANS and ANB, led by Elizabeth and Roy.

The letters written by Roy and Elizabeth likely contributed to the growing interest in the anti-discrimination bill, as well as their actions. Cecilia Kunz shared the story of how Elizabeth and other Alaska Native Sisterhood members moved a sign from a restaurant that read, "No Natives Allowed." They placed the sign in front of the Armed Forces recruitment station (C. Kunz, personal interview, 1991).

Elizabeth's Key Role

Throughout the duration of the war, the ANB and ANS were diligent in their pursuit of an anti-discrimination bill. Elizabeth made frequent trips to the capitol building, lobbying legislators and rallying the people. Some Territorial senate members, like Whaley and Shattuck, were skilled at killing bills, such as the seemingly innocuous bill to provide benefits to returning veterans (Gruening, 1973). It appeared unlikely, especially after the failure of previous similar legislation, that an anti-discrimination bill would have any chance with this group.

In 1945, the anti-discrimination bill went before the senate. No other state had as sweeping a policy to end discrimination, and now it was on the table. Senator Shattuck was vehemently opposed to the bill. "Who are these people, barely out of savagery, who want to associate with us whites with five thousand years of recorded civilization behind us?" (Gruening,

1973, p. 329). Following heated debate and Roy's testimony, Elizabeth raised her hand to speak. It was not usual for polite women to make such a move, but then women filled many roles while men had been away at war. Native women speaking before a white male senate was not imagined. The 34-year-old Elizabeth was acknowledged.

"I would not have expected that I, who am barely out of savagery, would have to remind gentlemen with 5,000 years of recorded civilization behind them, of our bill of rights," she stated in response (Gruening, 1973, p. 330). Elizabeth went on to give a careful and passionate picture of discrimination, providing personal experiences including their humiliation in finding a home in Juneau and being rejected. It was effective. "Opposition that had appeared to speak in a strong voice was forced to a defensive whisper" (Super Race Theory Hit in Hearing, 1945, p. 8).

A burst of applause followed Elizabeth's testimony and the bill passed 11 to 5. Governor Gruening attributes much of the success to Elizabeth, and the *Daily Alaska Empire* newspaper wrote, "It was the neatest performance of any witness yet to appear before this session, and there were a few red senatorial ears as she regally left the chamber" (Gruening, 1973, p. 330). That evening, Roy and Elizabeth danced in the ballroom at the Baranof Hotel, where only hours before they would have been denied access (Silverman, 2009).

ELIZABETH'S ONGOING WORK IN CIVIL RIGHTS

The year 1945 was one of great hope and change as the war ended. Alaska could lay claim to passing the first comprehensive anti-discrimination bill in the United States, nearly 20 years before the Civil Rights Act. Elizabeth's advocacy did not wane with this new bright future. She volunteered and promoted the Red Cross, primarily in their support of the troops. She sought funding for nursery schools from the Federal Works Agency traveling throughout Southeast at her own expense (Koester, 1988). At home she read classics to her son and "a group of teenage boys every day after school" (B. Peratrovich, 2011, p. 3). In all things she continued to push education. In 1955, she was elected to the Executive Council of the National Council of American Indians (NCAI) during the annual convention in Spokane, Washington (Hall, 2011). Her efforts there made it possible for Alaskan Natives to become members. She remained active with the Presbyterian Church, worked for the legislature, was a member of the Juneau Business and Professional Women's Club, and was employed in the office of the Territorial Vocational Rehabilitation Director.

Known for her passion for education, Elizabeth was invited to Washington, DC, for a conference on Indian adult education programs, something she was helping to build (B. Peratrovich, 2011). It was this dedicated interest that took her to Fisk University in Nashville Tennessee in 1956 (Kiffer, 2010). It may not have been known by attendees that more than one civil rights activist was in the room when Martin Luther King spoke during his speaking tour on *Brown v. the Board of Education* (Martin Luther King Research & Education Institute, n.d.).

Elizabeth was a quiet and graceful woman who was simply compelled to get the school doors opened to all people regardless of race and to advance equality and opportunity for Native peoples. She was never able to realize her dream to teach as advocacy continued to be her calling until her life was cut short by cancer. Elizabeth Peratrovich died December 1, 1958, at the age of 47, one month before Alaska became a state.

In 1988, Governor Cowper signed a bill making February 16 Elizabeth Peratrovich Day (Bohi, 1988). Elizabeth Wanamaker Peratrovich was inducted into the Alaska Women's Hall of Fame in 1989 (Elizabeth Peratrovich Named to Women's Hall of Fame, 1989). She continues to be celebrated in the State of Alaska.

NOTE

1. Personal information and details about Elizabeth and Roy Peratrovich were obtained through numerous visits and communications with Roy Peratrovich Jr. and Betsy Peratrovich and others in support of my portrayal of Elizabeth, and for the writing of the play, *My Spirit Raised its Hands: The Story of Elizabeth Peratrovich and Alaskan Civil Rights* and for my research for the film *For the Rights of All: Ending Jim Crow in Alaska*.

REFERENCES

Bohi, H. (1988, June 20). Feb 16: Elizabeth Peratrovich day. *Tundra Times*, pp 5–6.

Case, D. S. (1984). *Alaska Natives and Native American laws*. Fairbanks: University of Alaska Press.

Elizabeth Peratrovich named to women's hall of fame. (1989, December 14). *Seward Phoenix LOG*, p. 6.

Gruening, E. (1973). *Many battles: The autobiography of Ernest Gruening*. New York, NY: Liveright.

Hall, T. (2011, July 4). A lifetime of fighting for rights. *Alaska Newspapers Inc.*

Kiffer, D. (2010, February 18). *Alaska celebrates civil rights pioneer: Peratrovich's efforts pre-dated Martin Luther King*. Retrieved from http://www.sitnews.us/Kiffer/Peratrovich/021808_e_peratrovich.html.

Koester, S. H. (1988). *Western speakers: Voices of the American dream*. Manhattan, KS: Sunflower University Press.

Martin Luther King Research and Education Institute. (n.d.). Retrieved from http://mlk-kpp01.stanford.edu/index.php/encyclopedia/chronologyentry/1956_02_19/

Peratrovich, B. (2011, July 4). Why my grandmother was so loved. *Alaska Newspapers: Special Section Commemorating Elizabeth Peratrovich*, p 3.

Peratrovich, E., & Peratrovich R. (1941, December 30). Letter to Governor Gruening on behalf of the Alaska Native Brotherhood. *Roy Peratrovich Jr. collection*.

Peratrovich, R. Jr. et al. (n.d.). A recollection of civil rights leader Elizabeth Peratrovich: 1911–1958. *Alaskool.org*. Retrieved from http://www.alaskool.org/projects/native_gov/recollections/peratrovich/elizabeth_1.htm

Silverman, J. L. (Producer/Director). (2009). *For the rights of all: Ending Jim Crow in Alaska* [Film]. Blueberry Productions: Native American Public Telecommunications.

Super race theory hit in hearing: Native sisterhood president hits at "rights" bill opposition. (1945, February 6). *Daily Alaska Empire (Juneau Empire)*, p. 8.

CHAPTER 22

VIRGINIA ESTELLE RANDOLPH AND THE JEANES TEACHERS

Bernadine S. Chapman

So it happened that the aged Quaker lady of Philadelphia (Anna Thomas Jeanes) and the humble Negro teacher (Virginia Estelle Randolph) in a rural district in Virginia contributed each in her own way to one of the most fruitful undertakings that has touched the life of the Blacks in the South. The Jeanes Board simply adopted Virginia Randolph's plan by placing supervising teachers similar to her throughout the South and so brought the schools to bear upon the life of the communities in a practical way (Dabney, 1969, p. 447).

The Jeanes Movement covered the countryside with teachers and brought help and hope to many rural schools. In times both of prosperity and adversity, the Jeanes Movement "provided a channel through which the better elements of both races were able to find expression in co-operative effort for the common good" (Jones, 1937, pp. xv–xvi). Initially, the Jeanes Industrial Supervisor Teachers were Black female educators who indeed exerted a powerful influence upon the education of southern African Americans of all ages. Their work, which began in 1908 and lasted almost through six decades, has gone virtually unrecognized (NASC, 1979). Jeanes Industrial Supervisor Teachers taught children, teachers, and adults how to improve themselves, their schools, their communities by becoming better educated and active citizens. These educators took

No Small Lives: Handbook of North American Early Women Adult Educators, 1925-1950,
pp. 201–209
Copyright © 2015 by Information Age Publishing

their charge as "educational ambassadors" very seriously. As their educational support increased throughout the South and internationally, they became known only as Jeanes Teachers or Jeanes Supervisors.

Educational, political, and economic gains acquired by African Americans during Reconstruction (1867–1877) were rescinded, and political participation and advancement were legally curtailed and in some instances, totally prohibited (Alexander 1943; Buni, 1967; Chapman, 1990). In the 1890s and the early 1900s, a series of state constitutional conventions and revised election codes effectively disenfranchised most Blacks in the South (Ragsdale & Treese, 1990). *Plessey v. Ferguson* (1896), "separate but equal" doctrine was thoroughly enforced at all levels, state and federal, and it framed the White supremacist or "Jim Crow" social order that pervaded Virginia and the entire South. However, by the turn of the 20th century, many noticeable and significant changes began to occur in schools, as various philanthropic organizations (e.g., Carnegie, General Education Board, Phelps-Stokes, Julius Rosenwald and Anna T. Jeanes Fund) began to support and improve public education for Black and White Americans. These foundations were established between the years of 1902 and 1917, and collaborated in their efforts to provide monetary subsidies to those schools, primarily Hampton and Tuskegee, teaching Black industrial training skills (Anderson, 1988; Curti & Nash, 1965). In May 1905, a campaign involving representatives from these major philanthropic funds, coupled with educational reformers to improve schools and educational opportunities, sparked an educational renaissance that started in Virginia and moved throughout the South. The campaign contributed immensely to the educational improvement of Blacks and Whites in rural Southern areas; however, African American one-room schools and colleges in the South were specifically targeted. Therefore, when Anna Thomas Jeanes, a wealthy Philadelphia Quaker, contributed $1 million for the sole purpose of "rudimentary education" in small rural African American southern schools and communities, she paved the way for White superintendents to request funds to assist those schools and their teachers. Because Anna T. Jeanes became the major sponsor for the industrial training of undereducated rural teachers and the teacher supervisors who taught them, a model evolved and became known as the "Henrico Plan" (Chapman, 1990; Davis, 1935; Wright & Redcay, 1933).

The Jeanes movement took place during a very repressive and segregated era of our history, but throughout the southern states, the Jeanes Teachers were successful in improving the preparation of teachers who possessed limited schooling, while also developing the surrounding school communities. Therefore, this chapter will concentrate on the adult learning activities emanating from the work beginning with Virginia Estelle Randolph and her desire to "teach the teacher" while simultaneously engaging the immediate community. Consequently, the adult education focus is on teacher training and community development that were both instrumental in bringing about a real transformation for the educational advancement of African American adults in Virginia and other participating Southern states.

VIRGINIA ESTELLE RANDOLPH

Virginia Estelle Randolph was born in Richmond, Virginia, on June 8, 1874. She was the second of four children born to the marriage of Sarah Elizabeth Carter and Edward Nelson Randolph. Randolph and her siblings were primarily reared by their religious mother, who was widowed when her youngest child was only 1 month old. Randolph was greatly influenced to pursue teaching by her mother, who worked as a domestic for a professor who taught at the University of Richmond. She graduated from Armstrong High School in 1890, and attended Virginia State College in Petersburg 2 years before entering the teaching profession. In fact, due to her successful passing of the Henrico Teachers placement examination for rural schools, she began teaching at the unofficial age of 16 in Goochland County, before moving to the impoverished one-room school in Henrico County, Virginia (Alpha Kappa Alpha Sorority, 1982).

In the autumn of 1905, while working in a one-room school, "Striving with patience, tact, and resourcefulness to make her school a centre of community life," (Jones, 1937, p. xi), Virginia Estelle Randolph was discovered by Jackson Davis, another Virginian and educational reformer. Davis met Virginia Randolph and observed her teaching activities after being appointed as the superintendent of Henrico County Schools. Randolph's ideas were practical, simple, and reflective of the needs of an agrarian rural community; she believed in the holistic development of the child. Randolph taught basic reading, writing, and arithmetic skills. She also taught girls to cook and sew and boys to make useful handicrafts from honeysuckle vines, hickory, and other materials. Hampton Institute's industrial training philosophy, which taught manual skills as well as religious and moral precepts, undoubtedly influenced Randolph's belief in the importance of using one's hands above the use of one's mind. Davis's industrial educational beliefs were also reinforced while visiting Hampton Institute. Randolph's teaching methods convinced Davis to seek support from the Anna Thomas Jeanes Fund to instruct other African American teachers in one-room rural schools throughout the state and region using Randolph's practices (Chapman, 1993; McKinney, Miller, & Boyd, 2009). Subsequently, in 1908, the appointment of Virginia Estelle Randolph as the first Jeanes Industrial Supervisor Teacher, at the Old Mountain

School, commenced a most significant epoch in the development and expansion of educational opportunities for African Americans in Virginia and throughout the southern states (Alexander, 1943).

Quite early, Randolph demonstrated how encompassing not only the children but their families in the educational process positively affected the entire community and elevated the role of the school as a means for social progress. For example, she united the school and community by creating parent organizations such as "Willing Workers Clubs and a Patrons Improvement League" to support school programs. With the support of the Patrons' Improvement League, on March 30, 1908, Randolph purchased 12 sycamore trees for the school grounds. Each tree was named after a disciple; this planting activity resulted in Randolph being known as the first individual in Virginia to celebrate Arbor Day (Chapman, 1993; McKinney et al., 2009). Patrons, fathers, and mothers collaborated with the school by raising funds and providing individual assistance to improve the school grounds, buildings, and other resources they were able to secure (Jones, 1937).

Randolph visited many rural schools within the state; she traveled to North Carolina and Georgia to provide professional development on the Jeanes model for one-room schoolteachers and advocated for the teaching of practical skills and vocational education. Because of her extensive educational contributions, Randolph received many honors and accolades. In 1915, the Virginia Randolph Training School was named for her, and in 1926 she was the first African American to receive the prestigious Harmon Award for meritorious achievement in education from the Harmon Foundation. On this auspicious occasion, she received multiple gifts from the Richmond Community Fund, the Virginia Randolph County Training School, and the Negro Teachers of Henrico County. In 1934, Sidney E. Dickinson painted a lovely portrait of Randolph, which hangs at the Hampton Institute Library. Just 4 years later, Randolph was awarded a certificate of meritorious service by Virginia State College and was appointed to the Industrial School Board for Colored Children. In 1940, the first accredited African American high school in the state was named in her honor (Chapman, 1993; McKinney et al., 2009).

JEANES TEACHERS AND COMMUNITY DEVELOPMENT

Over a period of 6 decades (1908–1968), Virginia E. Randolph and the Jeanes Teachers implemented processes to develop the school as a center for improving community living. In an effort to improve themselves and their communities, specific goals were established. The goals of the Jeanes Teachers were reflected, but not fully captured in the paper presented in 1938 by Zehmer, "Rural Adult Education for the Negro," at Hampton's Conference on Adult Education and the Negro. Zehmer's goals accentuated a positive and inclusive approach for reaching all of the people, but did not include basic community literacy.

1. Rural adult education should inspire the people to a better life. Not necessity, but the desire to overcome difficulties is the mother of invention. Adult education should give them the vision.

2. Rural adult education should help the people in formulating in clear and workable terms their ideals of the good life—their hopes, aspirations, and what they want to become. It should help them to clarify their ideas.

3. Rural adult education should help the people to discover and teach the ways by which the ideals can be translated into everyday life. This will involve, in all probability, a study of the ways and means to better themselves (Zehmer, 1938).

Because the Jeanes Teachers were immediately confronted with rampant illiteracy in African American communities, they collaborated with agencies such as the Works Projects Administration (WPA), the National Youth Administration, the Farm Society Administration, and many others, both public and private organizations, to significantly raise literacy rates for African Americans. This coordinated effort, by various agencies and the Jeanes Teachers, served to establish and administer programs of primary education for illiterate youth and adults that spoke to Zehmer's goals and the practical needs of the African American masses (Alexander, 1943; Chapman, 1990).

Jeanes Teachers, in collaboration with other agencies, also assisted in the formation of various clubs within the rural communities. For instance, vocational clubs, 4-H, Farmers of America, and "Negro Home Economics Clubs" were organized with parent teacher associations and patron leagues started earlier by Randolph. The patron leagues became instantly popular and cooperated with the Jeanes Teachers to implement a variety of activities (e.g. securing school transportation, extending school term, promoting health care, etc.) that eventually became a part of the school's overall program. The Jeanes Teachers covered numerous and diverse concerns, but the greatest community effort was directed toward health care. In cooperation with community health and welfare agencies, they promoted health clinics, fairs, and hot lunch programs. These multiple coalitions also encouraged sanitation within the school and home (Alexander, 1943).

Programs specifically for the education and development of African American adults continued in the early 1940s. One very popular activity was the discussion forums organized to address a variety of community interests. The Jeanes Teachers were most often at the forefront for the organization of these study groups or discussion forums. In attendance were laymen, college faculty, school officials, and teachers. These individuals met on a regular basis to discuss and reexamine, based on their experience and research, the philosophies, purposes, and procedures that were characteristic of educational programs for African Americans. Topics under study included growing professionally, solving community problems cooperatively, developing worthy home and school interrelationships, developing a personal philosophy of education, organizing instruction in one-teacher schools, and civic participation (Chapman, 1990; Richardson, 1976).

As adult education maintained its growing momentum during the decade of the '40s, the Jeanes Teachers developed specific objectives;

1. Investigate educational conditions in local communities;
2. Provide educational information on African American history;
3. Improve facilities and local instructional programs through efforts of community groups and local officials. (Richardson, 1976, pp. 53–54)

The mid 1940s also concentrated on more frequent regional conferences, which were designed to strengthen educational programs to meet the academic and social needs of pupils and adults in the school community. Home economics, vocational agriculture, trade and industrial, as well as distributive education, were addressed at these regular sessions. The Department of Education also sponsored a study conference to tackle broader concerns like the training of prospective teachers and the improvement of school and community relationships (Chapman, 1990; Richardson, 1976).

JEANES TEACHERS AND TEACHER TRAINING

At the beginning of the movement, the Jeanes Teachers traveled to one-room schools to assist rural underprepared teachers; however, as time progressed and standards improved, more formalized institutional training was provided. During the summer of 1917, the Whittier Practice School at Hampton Institute was established to address the training of teachers for the public sector, and the preparation of the Jeanes Teachers for rural schools (Chapman, 1990; Davis, 1931).

The Jeanes Movement underwent several changes due to state certification teacher-training requirements. In 1926, education emphasized subject-matter competence. As a result, Jeanes Teachers had to incorporate content-centered courses into their already rigorous curriculum, which included industrial work, school supervision, health, school organization, and the teaching of reading (Chapman, 1990).

In the 1930s, Shellie T. Northcutt, an experienced Jeanes Supervisor Teacher, developed a course that dealt specifically with teacher in-service training. The training covered topics such as integrated program development, student performance assessments, industrial arts, and community development. For enrichment and leisure, the Jeanes Teachers visited historical and educational centers; attended social and cultural activities; and were exposed to outstanding speakers, such as Professor Mabel Carney of Teachers College and Ambrose Caliver, adult educator and specialist for the United States Office of Education (Chapman, 1990; NASC, 1979). In 1940, Jeanes Teachers expanded beyond teacher certification to concentrate on supervisory and management skills and the pursuit of graduate study. Consequently, the 1940s dictated a more pronounced and organized focus not only for teacher vocational activities, but for more advanced academic degrees as well.

The Jeanes Teachers experienced the greatest change in their professional careers during the 1950s, when once again the social order was changing. The 1954 *Brown v. Board of Education* decision, which reversed the long-standing *Plessey v. Ferguson 1896* ruling, impacted the educational, political, and economic landscape for African Americans. The policies enacted from *Brown v. Board* directly affected the Jeanes Movement by diminishing the roles and influence of Jeanes Teachers (Chapman, 1990; NASC, 1979). Segregation had provided them with the opportunity to teach and lead, but integration reversed the prospect for a continued impact from Jeanes Teachers. In the late 1960s, schools took on new organizational patterns, causing the role and influence of the Jeanes Teachers to degenerate. Even so, as one Jeanes Teacher spoke, while some doors were closing, others were opening (NASC, 1979), and the new educational improvements helped them cope with their losses and changing roles.

CONCLUSION

After 57 years of a rich and rewarding career, Randolph retired in 1949 as supervisor of Negro education. She never married but provided shelter, over the years, to approximately 59 children. Randolph was not selective in her support of others; she assisted the juvenile youth, the handicapped, and the rural poor (Chapman, 1993; Schools Days, 1975).

Virginia E. Randolph died March 16, 1958, but her memory and contributions to society remain. In 1960, the Virginia Randolph Elementary School was built. A museum, which holds many documents, personal items, letters, and artifacts connected with her life's work, was dedicated in her memory 10 years later. Her body is interred on the site and in 1976, the Virginia Historic Land Marks Commission recognized the museum as a National Historic Landmark, and registered the site as a Virginia Historic Landmark, along with the Twelve Sycamore trees, by the Virginia Historic Landmarks Commission (H. J. Cosby, personal communication, February 21–22, 2013).

The legacy of Virginia E. Randolph was recounted most vividly at her funeral by her friend D. Tennant Bryan when he stated,

> Virginia Randolph's greatness is not to be measured in the honors that came to her during her life, but rather it is to be found in … men and women who, thanks to her interest and leadership, have attained the better life she, almost alone in her time, foresaw for them. (Cosby, n.d.)

REFERENCES

Alexander, F. M. (1943). *Education for the needs of the Negro in Virginia*. Washington, DC: Southern Education Foundation.

Alpha Kappa Alpha Sorority. (1982). *Black women and Richmond: Sketches for heritage I*. Richmond, VA: Upsilon Omega, Alpha Kappa Alpha.

Anderson, J. D. (1988). *The education of Blacks in the South, 1860–1935*. Chapel Hill: University of North Carolina Press.

Buni, A. (1967). *The Negro in Virginia politics 1902–1965*. Charlottesville: University Press of Virginia.

Chapman, B. S. (1990). *Northern philanthropy and African-American adult education in the rural South: Hegemony and resistance in the Jeanes Movement* (Doctoral dissertation). Available from UMI Dissertation Abstracts database. (UMI No. 9110735)

Chapman, B. S. (1993). Randolph, Virginia Estelle (1874–1958). In D. C. Hines (Ed.), *Black women in America: An historical encyclopedia*. Brooklyn, NY: Carlsonc.

Cosby, H. J. (n.d.). *Virginia Estelle Randolph*. [Biographical sketch]. Glen Ellen, VA: Randolph Museum

Curti, M., & Nash, R. (1965). *Philadelphia in the shaping of American higher education*. New Brunswick, NJ: Rutgers University Press.

Dabney, C. W. (1969). *Universal education in the South. Vol. II: American education— Its men, ideas and institutions* (Reprint ed.). New York, NY: Arno Press & The New York Times.

Davis J. (1931, June). The Phoenix School. *The Southern Workman, 50*, 264–268.

Davis, J. (1935, May 27). *The Jeanes visiting teacher*. Address presented at the Inter-Territorial Jeanes Conference. Salisbury, Southern Rhodesia: Carnegie Corporation of New York.

Jones, L. (1937). *The Jeanes in the United States, 1908–1933*. Chapel Hill: University of North Carolina Press.

McKinney, T. (Producer), Miller, D., (Producer), & Boyd, S. L. (Producer/Director). (2009). *Virginia Estelle Randolph: Pioneer educator, 1974–1958*. [DVD]. Henrico County, VA: Relations & Media Services.

NASC Interim History Writing Committee. (1979). *The Jeanes story, A chapter in the history of American education 1908 –1968*. Jackson, MS: Southern Education Foundation.

Ragsdale, B. A., & Treese, J. C. (1990). *Black Americans in Congress, 1870 –1989*. Washington, DC: U.S. Government Printing Office.

Richardson, A. G. (1976). *Development of Negro education in Virginia 1831–1970*. Richmond, VA: Phi Delta Kappa.

School Days. (1975, December). *8*(1).

Wright, A. D., & Redcay, E. E. (1933). *The Negro Rural School Fund, Inc.* Washington, DC: Negro Rural School Fund.

Zehmer, B. (1938, October 20). *Rural adult education for the Negro*. Paper presented at Conference on Adult Education and the Negro, Hampton Institute, VA.

Harriett Rouillard

(Photo is used with the permission of John Riddle, Harriett Rouillard's grandson.)

CHAPTER 23

HARRIET ROUILLARD

"The Stamp of Its Editor" on the CAAE's Food for Thought

Leona M. English

No Small Lives: Handbook of North American Early Women Adult Educators, 1925-1950,
pp. 211–218
Copyright © 2015 by Information Age Publishing
All rights of reproduction in any form reserved.

The contributions of women writers and editors to the Canadian Association for Adult Education (CAAE; formed in 1935) has basically been unknown or, in some cases, given cursory attention, even though women such as Harriet Page Lane Rouillard (1904–1987), Jean Hunter Morrison, Ruth McKenzie, and Isabel Wilson ran radio programs such as *Citizen's Forum* and *Farm Forum*, wrote and edited books, journal and magazine articles, and produced pamphlets. Their educational levels were high and their political leanings were often socialist, yet their particular influence on the field of adult education is largely undocumented.

Harriet Rouillard was editor of the CAAE's journal, *Food for Thought*, between 1947 and 1953 (volumes 8–13). During those years she led the publication and wrote editorials that influenced, and were influenced by, the policies of the CAAE. However, apart from a book she edited for the CAAE, *Pioneers in Adult Education in Canada* (H. Rouillard, 1952), which consisted of a collection of biographical articles from *Food for Thought*, her influence on the field has been largely forgotten. In contrast, the male leaders whom she worked alongside, such as Ned Corbett (1886–1964) and Roby Kidd (1915–1982), were to go on to very distinguished careers in adult education. Kidd, for instance, was arguably the best-known Canadian adult educator in the 20th century, both as director of the CAAE and as founder of graduate degrees and professor of adult education at the Ontario Institute for Studies in Education. As a way of ensuring that her contributions are known, this chapter provides some background on Harriet's early life and then focuses on her specific contributions to adult education literature.

HARRIET'S EARLY YEARS

Harriet was one of three children born to Susan Foster Lauriat Lane and Alfred Church Lane, a geologist and professor at Harvard and Tufts College, Boston (Marquis Who's Who, 2009a). Alfred was a graduate of Harvard and Susan a graduate of Smith College, one of the group of seven women's colleges in the northeast of the United States. Of her two brothers, Frederic and Lauriat, more is known of Frederic (1900–1984), who graduated from Harvard and went on to a distinguished career as a professor of medieval history at Johns Hopkins University (Marquis Who's Who, 2009b).

Harriet, a tall and confident young woman, attended Smith in 1921 and graduated in 1925 with a BA. A collection of her weekly letters home during these years shows that Harriet was a curious young woman (Lane, 1921–1925). In a letter addressed to her father, she discussed what she wanted out of life: "I hate the philanthropic societies—women's clubs, church societies and such. I hate to give up time to them. I want a real job with intellectual stimulus and I want to do things for people I love" (February 15, 1924). Her zeal to be intellectually stimulated is reflected in the activities she involved herself in at the college. According to her yearbook, she was the music critic for the *Smith College Weekly*, involved in the Press Board club, and member of the Blue Pencil Club. She also sang in the choir and was a member of the Granddaughters Club. Her days were abuzz with stories of friends, lunches, and sororities such as Alpha and Phi Delta Kappa societies (see Smith College Class Book, 1925).

Harriet married Clarence Dana Rouillard (1904–1991) in 1928, after which she completed her MA at Smith, graduating in 1935 with a thesis on Henry James and Art. She did this degree while he was teaching at Amherst College and completing his doctoral studies at Harvard. After Dana graduated with a PhD in 1936 in French literature, they moved to Toronto where he was an important figure in the development of the University of Toronto's French Department. He taught there for the remainder of his career, with a brief 2-year interlude in Ottawa during World War II (1943–1945), during which Harriet took political science courses. In Toronto, Harriet and Dana lived in the upper-class neighborhood of Rosedale, and they became an integral part of the intellectual life of the city and the University, entertaining CAAE director Roby Kidd, international literary critic Northrup Frye, and many of the University faculty. They were lifelong friends of Kay Dobson Riddell (1906–2006) and her husband Robert Gerald Riddell, a history professor who became Canada's ambassador to the United Nations. Although Gerry died suddenly in 1951, Kay was to have a distinguished career as director of International Students' Centre at University of Toronto; following Harriet's death in January, 1987, she and Dana married and spent their few remaining years together (D. Rouillard, 1928–1982).

Much of what is known of Harriet's personal and professional life in Toronto can be gleaned from Dana's diaries (1928–1982), which are housed, along with his other papers and effects, in the archives at the University of Toronto. Dana wrote every day a veritable list of activities that both he and Harriet (called Happy by Kay and Gerry's daughter Susan Riddell Stylianos) were involved in. These diaries resemble calendars more than personal journals or reflections, yet their detailed listing of events is insightful and reflective of a remarkable partnership between them. Harriet had a full life as a volunteer, editor, and leader in many organizations such as the YWCA, for which she wrote for the YWCA *Quarterly*, served on committees, and researched their history. The diaries reveal an active social life; it is a rare day that they do not have lunch or dinner with another couple or colleague, either at their home or at the University, or during one of their many European trips. A typical day traveling would be Friday, August 13, 1937, when they were summering in Europe: Dana and "H. go off on an excursion. Bus to Monte Carlo, an hour at the Casino ... Climb to old villages ... wonderful lunch." They were quite a team: on occasion, Dana typed for Harriet (D. Rouillard, August 19, 1951) and helped her make marmalade (September 19, 1962), and she entertained and supported his career. Testimonials from some of the 300 people who attended her funeral indicate that she was an integral part of the building of the Department of French and the University in the major expansion of the 1960s. Yet she remained a loyal American, true to her New England intellectual roots and did not take out Canadian citizenship until late in life (J. Riddell, personal correspondence, February 1, 2013).

Harriet also took an active role in St. Andrew's United Church, participated in the University Women's Club for which she co-wrote a history, and pursued her lifelong interest in learning (see McCool, Pratt, & Rouillard, 1978). She became a teaching assistant for Instructor Chase at Smith College from 1932 to 1937; attended classes at Cambridge 1935 to 1937, and joined numerous study groups in Toronto on topics such as Germany, Russia, the American constitution, and Brazil. Over the years, she took lessons in Italian, dance, and spinet; sang in choirs; and spent her summers with Dana in their rustic cottage called *Heyday* in a remote part of Georgian Bay, Ontario, Canada (J. Riddell, personal correspondence, February 1, 2013).

Following their sojourn in Ottawa during the war, Harriet became chair of the Public Affairs Committee for the YWCA, which led to co-organizing a major conference with the CAAE in Toronto in 1947. Here she likely drew the attention of Roby Kidd who was looking for an editor for the journal *Food for Thought*. Harriet became the editor that year and continued this work until 1953.

HARRIET ROUILLARD'S EDITORIALS (1947–1953)[1]

When Harriet began working for the CAAE, it was still a relatively young organization. It had been formed in 1935, under the directorship of Ned Corbett, and when his tenure was complete, Roby Kidd became the director. The influence of an editor is not always known in academic circles, yet it is the editor who chooses the articles, solicits contributions, sets the general tone of the discussion, and writes the editorials. She is the one who sets the agenda, and in the absence of specific policies, the one who establishes them. In short, she has a great influence on what was said and how it was said. As the CAAE director, it was Ned Corbett who welcomed her onboard *Food for Thought* in the opening Opinion column in October

1947. Harriet's first meeting of the editorial board was held in September of 1947 at her home at 8 p.m., presumably a dinner meeting (Minutes of the Board Meeting, September 15, 1947). She wrote her first editorial in November of that year (Volume 8, no. 2) in a special issue on cooperative housing. Her editorial argued for a Canadian Commission for UNESCO, especially since the government seemed all too quick to prioritize having a place at the Security Council of the UN rather than supporting education at UNESCO. In this editorial, she drew attention to gaps in public policy and spending, and pointed out that Canada was not adequately represented on the world stage; her next editorial in December expressed great concern over increased militarism (p. 4). In short order, she established herself as an editor with strongly held and well informed arguments.

Like Ned Corbett and Roby Kidd, her vision for adult education was concerned with all matters in civil society—use of school buildings, housing, immigration policy, consumer spending, voluntary organizations, mental health, culture, aboriginal rights, responsibilities of the press, and the United Nations. In contrast to the somewhat myopic interests of adult educators in the 21st century, Harriet's vision seems global, broad, and forward-thinking by comparison. When it came to women and their rights, she was most assertive, dismissing patriarchal comments of a certain Professor McHenry of the Ontario Educational Association, who argued for the place of women in the home. She abhorred essentialism, patriarchy, idealization, and tokenism of women. Presumably in defense of her own role and keeper of house and part-time employee, she said, "Good cooking and a sense of social responsibility are not mutually exclusive" (Volume 8, no. 8, 1948, p. 4). Following a leave from *Food for Thought* for an extended European tour in 1951, she came back to the issue of women, this time their virtual absence from public office: "In this respect Canada is one of the world's most backward nations" (Volume 11, no. 5, 1951, p. 3). At times in these editorials, Harriet could seem a bit preachy. In her January 1948 (Volume 8, no. 4) editorial, for instance, she spent considerable time telling readers what it meant to be a good citizen and what their civic duties were. Indeed, in one of the tributes at her memorial service, a friend noted that she could be somewhat blunt.

True to her intellectual roots, she opposed the introduction of television (Volume 9, no. 4, January, 1949) and quoted routinely from the *New Yorker*, *Saturday Night*, and *Atlantic Monthly*. Along with being the editor (helped by an assistant editor), Harriet was involved in an intercultural relations subcommittee of *Food for Thought*, as well as participated in later years in an Indian-Eskimo association. Not surprisingly, the theme of race surfaced in a progressive editorial on race relations (Volume 8, no. 4, January, 1948, p. 4). While these are liberal, not radical views, they are certainly reflective of a keen mind, and great sociocultural understanding. The editorial board minutes show that the *Food for Thought* tried to avoid party politics, but Harriet's editorials were very political (Minutes of the Editorial Board, April 11, 1946).

The CAAE directors were most appreciative of her editorials. When she retired from the *Food for Thought* in March 1953, Roby Kidd was effusive in his praise. He said,

> For more than a year we have been trying to brace ourselves for the shock, but it is still very upsetting. HR has left the editor's chair which she inherited back in 1947.... This journal is the product of many minds and hands, in the best sense a cooperative project, but it has always displayed the stamp of its editor. Like her it cared for things: for people and causes, for ideas and principles, and for a good English sentence. Its editorials were clear and vigorous but never did they rant. Few journals with a comparatively tiny circulation enjoy the respect that this holds in many parts of the world. (Volume 13, no. 6, p. 1)

Harriet was involved in shaping the field of adult education at an early time in its history. Under her leadership, the field of adult education made clear policy pronouncements, called government to task, and rallied for human rights. It was current in its issues and adamant in its causes, standing up for reform and justice.

EDITOR AND CO-WRITERS OF BOOKS

One of Harriet's greatest contributions to *Food for Thought* was promoting the development of personal profiles of eminent adult educators. These biographies are reminiscent of her graduate thesis on Henry James, and they culminate in an edited volume, *Pioneers in Adult Education in Canada* (H. Rouillard, 1952). While the editorials are largely discussions of public policy, the profiles are a significant means of talking about leaders in educational circles. The book was one of the 11 books funded by the Ford Foundation (Fund for Adult Education) and became an important means of documenting adult education in Canada in that time period. Pioneers included were Alphonse Dejardins, founder of the cooperative movement; Jimmy Tompkins and Moses Coady of the Antigonish Movement (both written by fellow Nova Scotian Ned Corbett). Harriet was also willing to stretch the boundaries by including essays on artists such as Arthur Lismer, written by Helen Frye (wife of literary theorist Northrup Frye). Harriet's interest in this artist was likely heightened by the fact that her close friend Kay Riddell had worked as Lismer's assistant while she was a university student, and Helen Frye who also knew him, was a friend of the Rouillards. Intellectual circles in the city of Toronto in the 1950s were tight and Harriet was deeply ensconced in them. The selection of writers and topics was reflective of Harriet's social circles. She invited seven women and four men to contribute essays to the journal. Although only two of the final 16 essays focused on women (Adelaide Hoodless and Helen Gordon Stewart), *Pioneers* remains one of the few records we have of women in the field of Canadian adult education.

Shortly after *Pioneers* came out, Harriet resigned as editor of *Food For Thought*. In the minutes of several meetings prior to her resignation, she complained of the terrible amount of work she had to do, so when she stepped down there was likely no surprise. She resigned and became a member, and then chair, of the board until 1957, when Miss Charity Grant replaced her.

CONCLUSIONS

Harriet's contributions to adult education were typical of the world in which she was reared and lived—a prosperous intellectual elite—and she had a vision of making the world a bit more literate, literary, and civilized. Although it is unlikely that Harriet thought of herself as adult educator, she was both polished and scholarly, and contributed a great deal to establishing the field in Canada. She displayed the finest adult education trait possible: she was fully aware of her responsibility as a citizen of this nation and supporter of lifelong education.

When Harriet died in 1987, her CAAE colleague Clare Clark spoke of her abilities, "Harriet had the instincts of an investigative reporter heightened by her human and intellectual qualities. She finessed the role of colleague and wife." Her good friend, Kay Riddell, remembered her in a similar way at the funeral:

> Harriet took such a scholarly approach to being a housewife. She was a Mary and a Martha all in one. Each home that she and Dana created became a hub of cultural interests—music, art, literature, current affairs. Whenever friends gather there was bound to be good talk around the Rouillard table. (Harriet Page Rouillard Files, January 24, 1987)

As editor of *Food for Thought*, Harriet showed herself to be a progressive woman for her time. She put her partnership with Dana at the center of her life, and she contributed greatly to many causes, including the Canadian Association for Adult Education.

ACKNOWLEDGMENTS

The author would like to acknowledge the financial support of the Social Sciences and Humanities Council of Canada (grant number 430-2012-0056); research support from Smith College Archives, University of Toronto Archives, Archives of Ontario; helpful assistance from Kay Dobson Riddell's children, John Riddell and Susan Harriet Riddell Stylianos, also Harriet's goddaughter; and archival research by Marilyn Nazar at the University of Toronto Archives.

NOTE

1. This section references editorials in *Food For Thought*. Volume and issue number are given for each.

REFERENCES

Food For Thought. (1947–1953). Canadian Association for Adult Education. Volumes 8–13.

Harriet Page Rouillard Files. (n.d.). Smith Alumni and Sophia Smith Collection, Smith College, Northampton, MA.

Lane, H. P. (1921–1925). Correspondence. Series of weekly letters home to Professor and Mrs. Alfred C. Lane. Deposited by Harriet Rouillard in Sophia Smith Collection, Smith College, Northampton, MA.

Marquis Who's Who. (2009a). Lane, Alfred Church. In *Who was Who in America 1607–1984*. Marquis Who's Who LLC.

Marquis Who's Who. (2009b). Lane, Frederic Chapin. In *Marquis. Who was Who in America 1607–1984*. Marquis Who's Who LLC.

McCool, K., Pratt, P., & Rouillard, H. (1978). *75 years in retrospect; University Women's Club of Toronto 1903–1978*. Toronto, Canada: Hunter Rose.

Minutes of Editorial Board Meetings. (1945–1954). *Food for thought*. Canadian Association for Adult Education, F-1205 series C-III. Archives of Ontario, Toronto.

Rouillard, D. (1928–1982). Personal diaries. University of Toronto Archives. Rouillard Family Fonds, Accession B1997-0045, correspondence files and diaries.

Rouillard, H. (Ed.). (1952). *Pioneers in adult education in Canada* (Learning for Living Series, Canadian Association for Adult Education). Toronto, Canada: Nelson.

Smith College Class Book. (1925). Sophia Smith Collection: Women's History Archives at Smith College Northampton, MA. Retrieved from http://archive.org/details/class1925smit

Amy Paddon Row passport picture May 2, 1962
(Photo courtesy of Schlesinger Library, Radcliffe Institute, Harvard University.)

CHAPTER 24

"WHISTLING IN THE DARK"

The Adult Education Work
of Prison Arts Teacher Amy Paddon Row

Dominique T. Chlup

What mostly thrills me when I enter the Art Centre is the classroom. Chairs and tables like in a real classroom, and it makes me feel like truly going ahead to accomplish something worthwhile.

—(Virginia [pseudonym],
one of Amy Paddon Row's student inmates, March 23, 1937)

No Small Lives: Handbook of North American Early Women Adult Educators, 1925-1950,
pp. 219–225
Copyright © 2015 by Information Age Publishing
All rights of reproduction in any form reserved.

Near the end of her 92-year life, Amy Paddon Row (1884–1977) won-
dered if there were any virtues in growing older. In her journal, she wit-
tingly quipped: "I feel as did the writer Somerset Maugham—'There are
many virtues in growing old,' but I, too, 'am still just trying to think what
they are.'" In the journal lines that followed, instead of being haunted by
nostalgia, Row initiated a contemplative life review. Rather than longing
for her childhood or reminiscing her lost youth, Row personally favored
to

> never think of age or of growing old. It is like whistling in the dark, and I
> prefer whistling or singing in the light out in the open fields or climbing
> mountains. That is, if I have any breath left for voice effect on a windy day.
> It all depends on one's pace.

Viewing her life as a sustained journey, she composed, "Alas! All my life
has been one long quick pace, catching up, but never slowing down, and
with no time to think of age or ailments" (Row, 1977).

Feeling it captured her life's spirit, Row's friends and family distributed
this journal entry at her funeral. This optimistic outlook, one of gratitude
and preferring to whistle in the light, must have served Row well over the
course of her life. In particular, her optimism would have benefited her
during the Great Depression, when she worked for 9 years (1931–1940) as
an arts teacher at the Massachusetts Reformatory for Women at Framingham. For Row, it was about teaching her students how to "whistle in the
dark," so one day after their prison sentence was behind them they would
have breath left to whistle in the light (Row, 1977).

Amy Paddon Row was not an active member of the adult education
profession; rather she worked in corrections education. Additionally, Row
experienced life not only as a teacher of adults but as a visual artist,
archaeologist, ornithologist, botanist, entomologist, personal acquaintance of Gandhi, nanny to President Woodrow Wilson's grandchildren,
aspiring novelist, and founder of the Massachusetts Reformatory for
Women's *Art Centre*. By sharing Amy Paddon Row's history, I emphasize
the particular, the local, and provide a counternarrative to the sweeping
prison histories, the ones devoid of personal histories, aimed at re-creat-
ing a so-called objective historical record rather than accurately capturing
the nuances and details of the lived experiences of the past.

As Heilbrun (1988) proposed, there are many women in history for
whom, "The narrative she lived is not yet textually embodied" (p. 38). I
would argue Row is one of these women. This is the story of a woman
whose mark was not left in the annals of historical record but rather Row
left her mark in the classroom. Therefore, I situate Row's history within
the context of her historical era and ask, How does Amy Paddon Row's

story fit with what we know about women's work in adult education during the national period of the Great Depression, particularly in a correctional institution? The answer: Her work with women inmates was directly tied to the mission of both adult education—preparing citizens—and correctional education—reforming citizens.

EARLY INFLUENCES: "FROM BULLFIGHTS AND EARTHQUAKES TO CHATS WITH CANNIBALS AND GANDHI"

Born on March 7, 1884, in Cornwall, England, to John H. Row and Hephzibar A. Paddon, Row had one brother, Arthur, and a sister named Edith. Formally educated at Bella Vista College, at the age of 23, Row left a nursing position at the East London Children's Hospital to travel the world. A journalist for the *Boston Transcript* once described Row's "extraordinary experiences in odd corners of the world, ranging from bullfights and earthquakes to chats with cannibals and Mahatma Gandhi" (From Bullfights, 1931). For 5 years, Row traveled through Norway, Belgium, South Africa, Australia, Tasmania, Canada, and New Zealand. Under the direction of Reverend Fred H. Spencer of the British and Foreign Bible Society, she spent 2 years engaged in missionary work and teaching among the Maori tribe in Wanganui and Wharerata, New Zealand.

Row came to the United States in 1914, at the age of 30, as a nanny for Jessie Woodrow Wilson Sayre's children. Sayre also happened to be the daughter of United States President Woodrow Wilson, who was president from 1913 to 1921 (Gove, 1988). Row seemed to possess an inimitable knack for befriending the "famous," as prior to moving to the United States she also made an acquaintance with Mahatma Gandhi. Row met Gandhi through her friend Muriel Lester, founder of the London settlement house, Kingsley Hall. Gandhi was very interested in the work Row's sea captain father undertook in founding the Home for Indian Seamen, which was located near the British India docks in London and served as a haven for the "untouchables," India's lowest caste (From Bullfights, 1931). Row maintained a friendship with Gandhi and was known to sketch him during their visits.

It appears Row's work as a teacher of adults developed due to her interest in international students and their studies. Row founded the International House in Cambridge, Massachusetts, which she headed for 1 year. Additionally, Row was appointed to work as a "friend and counselor" to the students at MIT—Massachusetts Institute of Technology (From Bullfights, 1931).

Row carried these distinctive experiences with her on the day in October 1931 when she entered the Massachusetts Reformatory for the first time. Row remained an unpaid volunteer for 16 months before being made a full-time paid staff member. At 49 years old, and a wiry, blue-eyed, diminutive woman with wisps of white hair, Row commanded an unlikely presence as a prison staff member.

EDUCATING WOMEN INMATES

From the beginning of her career at the reformatory in 1931 until she was forced to leave in 1940 due to funding cuts, Row believed in the women she was teaching. Row held broad aspirations for her work with her students. She sought to inspire them, acquaint them with all that was beautiful in the natural world, give them artistic skills, model for them good behavior, provide for them a sanctuary on the prison grounds, and uplift their spirits so it would be impossible for them not to recognize their own self-worth. Row described her work with her students as "opening fresh channels of creative living" (Row, n.d., p. 2). She arranged exhibits for over 40 student inmates' work at the Grand Central Art Gallery in New York and at the Boston Art Museum (Prisoners, 1934). The press in both Boston and New York commented widely and positively on her students' art shows (Encouraging, n.d.)

Row clearly did not designate her Art Centre as a place where only art would be studied. Her teacher notes indicated that she valued trips outside of her classroom, for instance, to the research library and on nature walks, where it can be assumed students collected samples to display in the Museum. The Museum opened in 1936, the same year the Art Centre officially opened (Row, 1936). Row's own handwritten notes detailed her expectations of her students in the scientific fields of ornithology, botany, and entomology (1937a).

Row rejoiced in Framingham's philosophy of an "unwalled" reformatory, one in which the community should come into and one in which the students should be allowed outside of. Row employed a "hands-on learning" philosophy with an "open-air classroom" to give her students the opportunity to learn outside the classroom. She adhered closely to Assistant Director of Prisons and Founder of the Correctional Education Association (CEA) Austin H. MacCormick's belief that prison education programs should not simply be giving juvenile instruction to adult inmates. Rather, he stressed the programs should be of the same type and quality found in adult education programs operating outside of prisons (MacCormick, 1931).

Row's belief in the axioms of adult education could be seen in the questions she asked students the first day they entered the Art Centre:

In your own experiences, can you recall any artwork in your elementary or high school years that had genuine interest for you? Any that was imposed on you in spite of your lack of interest? What differences were there in the results in your learning? In the attitudes and satisfactions you acquired? (Row, 1937b)

Row demonstrated her genuine interest in her students when she questioned them in this way. She was a concerned teacher who recognized the value of students sharing their experiences. In her own teaching, Row echoed MacCormick's sentiments, who "felt education would enrich the lives of prisoners allowing them to return to society as more productive, responsible, involved citizens" and that "the most successful prison education programs operated under a premise of teaching inmates subjects out of interest rather than compulsion" (Chlup, 2006, pp. 168–169). Row shared the beliefs of the earliest members of the Correctional Education Association, who believed inmates should be encouraged to pursue education not just for practical purposes but for intellectual and esthetic value (Hunsinger, 1987).

Row was not only a well-known, respected community artist, but she was also a prolific writer. While many of her manuscripts would remain unpublished, including her book-length fictional account of prison life, *Clipped Wings*, her writings were varied and included essays on several topics such as "Channels of Creative Living or A Search for Beauty"; "Ellen Shillingham" (re: women at the Framingham Reformatory for Women); "The Greatest Good" (re: health care in England); "Why Mr. Gandhi Went to Kingsley Hall" (re: Gandhi's visit); "Maternity and Child Welfare" (re: 1948 visit to nursery in Westminster); "The Head and the Hand in the Gift of Painless Surgery" (re: anesthesia) (Gove, 1988).

Row's close connection to her students did not end once they left the reformatory. Correspondence from her students, after their release, indicated her far-reaching influence: "The Art Centre meant so much to me while at Framingham—my happiest hours were spent there with you" (Sardello, n.d.).

Row's students remembered their time fondly in her Art Centre and described it as a "sanctuary" within the reformatory walls; a sanctuary where they were absorbed in the "rehabilitative outlet" of creating art (Dotty K., 1941). This was one of Row's goals—to provide a haven for students within the walls of the reformatory. While reformatory-prisons are often deemed to have remained prisons at heart, Amy Paddon Row's classroom was a space where inmates could "forget lock and key" and operate as students rather than inmates (Chlup, 2004).

THE END OF ROW'S TENURE

Unfortunately, Row's good work was forced to cease in 1940 when Governor Leverett Saltonstall transferred funding from the art program to the girls on parole program (Sayward, 1940). Several of Row's associates wrote letters on her behalf. Ashton Sanborn, the secretary of the Museum of Fine Arts Boston, wrote the governor, extolling the value of Row's fine work. "The psychologically remedial value of this work is unquestionable" (Sanborn, 1940).

After her dismissal from the reformatory, there is little account of what happened to Row. During the 1970s, she did have a showing of her landscape portraits at the Concord Library (Brooks, 1992). Row managed to sell several paintings in her later life and procured an agent (Brooks, 1992). Row died at the age of 92 on January 6, 1977, of heart failure (Death Certificate, 1977).

I return now to the single-page leaflet distributed by Row's friends and family at her funeral, which quoted her as saying she preferred not to whistle in the dark, but instead, "I prefer whistling or singing in the light out in the open fields or climbing mountains" (Row, 1977). Considering the work Miss Row undertook at the prison, the image of her preferring to whistle, not in the dark but rather in the light feels like the most appropriate image to represent her educational work. Row aspired to teach her students how to "whistle in the dark," so in the future, after their time in prison was done, they would have breath left to whistle in the light.

REFERENCES

Brooks, J. M. (1992, July 27). To Eva S. Moseley. In Amy Paddon Row Papers. Schlesinger Library, Radcliffe Institute, Harvard University. Cambridge, MA.

Chlup, D. T. (2004). *Educative justice: The history of the educational programs and practices at the Massachusetts Reformatory for Women, 1930–1960*. Unpublished dissertation, Harvard University.

Chlup, D. T. (2006). The legacy of Miriam Van Waters: The warden who would be their teacher first. *The Journal of Correctional Education, 57*(2), 158–187.

Death Certificate of Amy Paddon Row. (1977). In Amy Paddon Row Papers. Schlesinger Library, Radcliffe Institute, Harvard University. Cambridge, MA.

Dotty K. (pseudonym). (1941, May 10). To Amy Paddon Row. In Amy Paddon Row Papers. Schlesinger Library, Radcliffe Institute, Harvard University. Cambridge, MA.

Encouraging the mind to leap o'er confining walls. (n.d.). [Newspaper clipping]. In Amy Paddon Row Papers. Schlesinger Library, Radcliffe Institute, Harvard University. Cambridge, MA.

From bullfights and earthquakes to chats with cannibals and Gandhi. (1931, November 4). *Boston Transcript*. In Amy Paddon Row Papers. Schlesinger Library, Radcliffe Institute, Harvard University. Cambridge, MA.

Gove, K. (1988, April). Inventory for Amy Paddon Row Papers. In Amy Paddon Row Papers. Schlesinger Library, Radcliffe Institute, Harvard University. Cambridge, MA.

Heilbrun, C. G. (1988). *Writing a woman's life*. New York, NY: Ballantine.

Hunsinger, I. (1987). Austin MacCormic [*sic*] and the education of adult prisoners: Still relevant today. *The Journal of Correctional Education, 48*(4), 160–165.

MacCormick, A. (1931). *The education of adult prisoners: A survey and a program*. New York, NY: The National Society for Penal Information.

Prisoners and physicians. (1934, April 9). *New York Times*. In Miriam Van Waters Papers. Schlesinger Library, Radcliffe Institute, Harvard University. Cambridge, MA.

Row, A. P. (n.d.). *Channels of creative living or a search for beauty*. In Amy Paddon Row Papers. Schlesinger Library, Radcliffe Institute, Harvard University. Cambridge, MA.

Row, A. P. (1936). Art Centre 1933–1935. In Amy Paddon Row Papers. Schlesinger Library, Radcliffe Institute, Harvard University. Cambridge, MA.

Row, A. P. (1937a). *Ornithology, botany, and entomology*. In Amy Paddon Row Papers. Schlesinger Library, Radcliffe Institute, Harvard University. Cambridge, MA.

Row, A. P. (1937b). [Loose leaf paper contained in blue notebook]. In Amy Paddon Row Papers. Schlesinger Library, Radcliffe Institute, Harvard University. Cambridge, MA.

Row, A. P. (1977, January). [Single-page leaflet distributed at Amy Paddon Row's funeral]. In Amy Paddon Row Papers. Schlesinger Library, Radcliffe Institute, Harvard University. Cambridge, MA.

Sanborn, A. (1940, October 28). To Honorable Leverett Saltonstall. In Amy Paddon Row Papers. Schlesinger Library, Radcliffe Institute, Harvard University. Cambridge, MA.

Sardello, K. (n.d.). To Amy Paddon Row. In Amy Paddon Row Papers. Schlesinger Library, Radcliffe Institute, Harvard University. Cambridge, MA.

Sayward, M. P. (1940, May 19). To Honorable Leverrett Saltonstall. In Amy Paddon Row Papers. Schlesinger Library, Radcliffe Institute, Harvard University. Cambridge, MA.

Virginia (pseudonym). (1937, March 23). *A view point of the art centre*. In Amy Paddon Row Papers. Schlesinger Library, Radcliffe Institute, Harvard University. Cambridge, MA.

CHAPTER 25

DOROTHY ROWDEN

Tireless Editor, Writer, and Advocate

Lisa M. Baumgartner

Although the names of men involved in adult education efforts of the 1920s through the 1950s are known, such as Lyman Bryson and Morse A. Cartwright, women's contributions to adult education efforts during that time remain in the shadows. This chapter will discuss the contributions of Dorothy Rowden to adult education efforts from the 1920s forward. She was an integral part of the achievements of the American Association of Adult Education (AAAE), the National Advisory Council on Radio in Education (NACRE), and the John and Mary R. Markle Foundation.

DOROTHY ROWDEN'S EARLY DAYS

Dorothy was born on February 17, 1901 (Social Security Death Index, 2011), in Haverhill, New Hampshire, to Canadian-English parents, Thomas and Lillian Rowden. Known as "Annie D," she was the second of five children. She had one brother 2 years her senior (Henry), one younger brother (Martin), and two younger sisters (Margarete and Muriel) (U. S. Federal Census, 1910).

No Small Lives: Handbook of North American Early Women Adult Educators, 1925-1950, pp. 227–234
Copyright © 2015 by Information Age Publishing

A 1918 Woodsville High School, Woodsville, New Hampshire graduate (Woodsville High School, 2012), Dorothy subsequently enrolled at Simmons College in Boston, Massachusetts, and studied library science (Simmons College Twentieth Annual Catalogue, 1921–1922). Simmons College, a "Vocational College for women" (p. 22), was composed of various schools, including Household Economics, Secretarial Studies, Library Science, General Science, Social Work, Education for Store Service and Public Health Nursing. The 4-year students received a liberal arts education with training in a particular area (Simmons College Twentieth Annual Catalogue, 1921–1922). Dorothy completed a 2-week library practica in outside libraries at Worcester Public Library (Howe, 1922) and graduated with her library science degree in 1922 (Simmons College Twenty-First Annual Catalogue, 1922–1923)

In *The Microcosm* (1922), which was the Simmons College Annual, Dorothy appeared to be an energetic, active student. She was named "Best Sport" and "Best Natured." and was described as follows:

> A blonde whirlwind typifying jubilant enthusiasm bursts in upon our calm philosophical reveries. She throws herself on our carefully made beds and says something like this: "Hello, kids! By chowder, I'm tired. Listen, let me tell you, I've met a new man and—say, can you sit at the Hall Table to-morrow fourth hour and take pledges for Endowment? Got anything to eat? Honest, we've got to make a better showing for Endowment. By chowder, this is good cake!" (p. 79)

Between the time she graduated from college and married Elmer Loemker in the late 1920s (U. S. Federal Census, 1930), Dorothy discontinued the use of "Annie" and was known as Dorothy. However, she continued to use her maiden name professionally. By July of 1922, she had been appointed as a children's librarian at a public library in Englewood, New Jersey (Donnelly, 1922). By March of 1924, she was listed as "with the Western Electric Company in NY" (Anonymous, 1924, p. 67).

INVOLVEMENT IN ADULT EDUCATION EFFORTS

By 1927, Dorothy and her husband, Elmer Loemker, were living in Chicago, where Elmer was working for what would become the McGraw-Hill Company (Reminiscences, 1967, p. 3). Dorothy was employed at the American Library Association headquarters and was "editing the bulletin" and "doing the publicity" at the time (Reminiscences, 1967, p. 2). That year, Dorothy met Morse Cartwright, executive director of the American Association of Adult Education (AAAE) and Bob Lester, future secretary of the Carnegie Corporation, at an American Library Association meeting in

Toronto, Ontario, Canada. Mr. Cartwright expressed interest in hiring Dorothy if she ever came to New York (Reminiscences, 1967, p. 3).

In 1929, Elmer and Dorothy moved to New York and Dorothy began working for the American Association for Adult Education (AAAE), where she was told to "Do something about adult education" (Reminiscences, 1967, p. 3). Dorothy proofed reports and did the publicity. She resigned in July of 1930 as she was pregnant and had twins in September (Loemker, 2000; Reminiscences, 1967, p. 5). In November of 1930, Bob Lester asked her to return to work and she worked for AAAE and the National Advisory Council on Radio in Education (NACRE) (Reminiscences, 1967, p. 5).

Founded in 1926, the AAAE received financial support from the Carnegie Corporation (Keith, 2007). The Carnegie Corporation turned its attention to adult education while under the direction of President Fredrick P. Keppel. Keppel decided that the Carnegie Corporation would support the continuing education done by adults in their "leisure time" (Keith, 2007, p. 274).

The "AAAE existed mainly to distribute [Carnegie Corporation of New York] money for adult education projects" (Keith, 2007, p. 274). In 1929, the organization began publication of the *Journal of Adult Education*, which disseminated information about the results of these projects. From 1926 to 1936, the AAAE awarded almost $3 million to adult education projects (Keith, 2007).

As part of her duties for the AAAE, Dorothy recruited more members when membership was between 1,200 and 1,500 (Reminiscences, 1967, p. 31). She noted that gaining new members was "an impossible thing, because we had sold practically all the people in the country who were professionally interested in adult education. It was a pretty hopeless job. There was great celebration when we'd get as many as two members a day" (p. 31).

In addition, Dorothy edited the 1934 and 1936 *Handbook of Adult Education in the United States* (Rowden, 1934, 1936). Morse A. Cartwright, the director of the American Association for Adult Education, acknowledged Dorothy's contributions to the 1934 *Handbook of Adult Education in the United States*, saying,

> No preface to the first edition of this handbook would be complete without a tribute to the devotion and care that have gone into these compilations on the part of the editor Miss Dorothy Rowden. Almost a year and a half of painstaking effort is represented in these pages—a bit of educational pioneering worthy of admiration and respect. (Rowden, 1934, p. x)

The AAAE shifted its focus from funding community adult education projects to providing money for booklets that detailed the settings in which adult education occurred (Carnegie Corporation, 1937; Reminiscences, p. 33). The change caused some consternation amongst some AAAE members at the time (Reminiscences, 1967, p. 33). Perhaps this shift favored the predilections of Morse Cartwright, AAAE's executive director, who had been the associate director of the University of California Press prior to his association with the Carnegie Corporation (Keith, 2007).

One booklet that documented adult education efforts, *Enlightened Self-Interest: A Study of Education Programs of Trade Associations*, was produced by Dorothy (Rowden, 1937). To satisfy what she considered to be her two main audiences—vocational educators who she believed knew something about trade associations and general adult educators who were perhaps less familiar with trade associations—she consulted about 100 trade union executives and roughly 50 educators (Rowden, 1937). In addition to consulting individuals, she read "books and pamphlets" (Rowden, 1937, p. vi), and sent questionnaires and letters to individuals. The book included a definition and a brief history of trade associations in the United States, their purposes, and narrative accounts of four trade associations, including the Laundry Owners National Association; American Institute of Banking; American Bakers Association; and Heating, Piping and Air Conditioning Contractors National Association (Rowden, 1937).

As part of this accounting for what kind of adult education was occurring in the United States, Dorothy also wrote "Four Rural Counties" (Rowden, 1938). She reported the results of surveys conducted in four counties in Ohio. The survey asked what schools, libraries, churches, and organizations in rural communities were doing and what should be done in education and allied activities for adults. Some 10 librarians, 54 churches, and 103 organizations responded. Rowden concluded that community organizations were "more sensitive to community needs than either the church or the school" (Rowden, 1938, p. 75). Respondents desired better recreation facilities, better libraries, and more adult education (Rowden, 1938).

In addition to working for AAAE, Dorothy also worked for the National Advisory Council on Radio in Education (NACRE). NACRE was founded in 1930 and was funded by the Carnegie and Rockefeller Foundations (Saettler, 2004). Dorothy recalled that educational radio programs were constructed around a subject. A series of talks would be developed, and Dorothy worked on the pamphlets associated with the radio program (Reminiscences, 1967, p. 18). She stated, "The programs were awfully amateurish because none of these people, except for Judith Waller, for example, knew anything about how to approach the public on radio" (Reminiscences, 1967, p. 18). This approach, in addition to program schedule changes, meant programs were less effective (Reminiscences, 1967, p. 19). Educational program series included such subjects as vocational guidance, the government, and the economy (Leach, 1983/1999). A series of programs titled *You and Your Government*, sponsored in conjunction with NBC, was particularly well received (Saettler, 2004). Radio broadcasters believed that working with the NACRE organization was a way to satisfy Federal Communications Commission (FCC) requirements for educational programming before broadcasting companies had their own education departments (Reminiscences, 1967, p. 23).

During the 1940s, Dorothy's contributions to adult education via radio continued. In 1945, Dorothy Rowden and Mildred Game edited the *Calendar Manual* for the American School of the Air, CBS Education Division (Rowden & Game, 1945). By that time, she was on the staff of the Institute for Adult Education at Teachers College Columbia and she also worked with Lyman Bryson, director of education, at Columbia Broadcasting System. The *Calendar Manual* contents included information about the five areas of programs including the Story of America, Gateways to Music, Science, This Living World, and Tales from Far and Near (Children's Books). Each program description was followed by questions about that program's content.

Dorothy and Lyman Bryson also coauthored *Radio as an Agency of National Unity*, where they discussed ethics, program standards, and the problems of balancing the demand for popular radio shows with educational programming (Bryson & Rowden, 1946). They noted that radio was easily accessed by millions of individuals. Hence, radio must provide programs that appeal to and educate the public. They discussed the importance of promoting tolerance in radio programs and conceded that "there are many successful programs, measured by audience, that are built around stereotypes. Their popularity proves that they meet a public demand. And until the public refuses to listen to such programs, they will hear [these stereotypes]" (Bryson & Rowden, 1946, p. 143).

Dorothy ended her career as an assistant secretary and director for the John and Mary R. Markle Foundation (Loemker, 2000). The Markle Foundation, established in 1927 to promote "the advancement and dissemination of knowledge and for the good of mankind" (Markle Foundation, n.d., para. 1), turned its attention to funding medical doctors who remained in academic medicine or research (Anlyan, 2004). President John Russell spearheaded the Markle Scholar Program in 1946. Medical schools nominated one candidate who was moving from "their residency training to careers in academic medicine" (Anlyan, 2004, p. 43). The rigorous selection process yielded approximately 25 Markle Scholars annually (Markle Foundation, n.d.). Dorothy was Russell's assistant and was considered a "mother figure" by some of the scholars. They asked her for advice about potential employment possibilities and other matters (Anlyan, 2004, p. 45).

Dorothy died in Bridgeport, Fairfield, Connecticut, at age 99 on August 10, 2000, (Connecticut Death Index, 2011) leaving twin children, 6 grandchildren, and 10 great grandchildren (Loemker, 2000). Like many women of her era, she worked largely behind the scenes, supporting national adult education efforts through her tireless promotion, writing, and editing activities.

REFERENCES

Anlyan, W. G. (2004). *Metamorphoses: Memoirs of a life in medicine.* Durham, NC: Duke University Press.

Anonymous. (1924). Personal. *Special Libraries, 15,*(3), 66–67.

Bryson, L., & Rowden D. (1946, March). Radio as an agency of national unity. *The Annals of the American Academy of Political and Social Science, 244,* 137–143. doi:10.1177/000271624624400118

Carnegie Corporation of New York. (1937). *Annual report 1936–1937.* Retrieved from http://www.accesspadr.org/cdm4/document.php?CISOROOT=/acamu-acarc&CISOPTR=8405&REC=5

Connecticut Death Index 1949–2001. (2011). [online database]. Provo, UT: Ancestry.com   Retrieved   from   http://search.ancestry.com/cgi-bin/sse.dll?rank=1&new=1&MSAV=0&msT=1&gss=angs-c&gsfn=Dorothy&gsln=Loemker&msbdy=1901&msddy=2000&uidh=bd1&msbdd=17&msbdm=2&pcat=34&h=1365296&recoff=7+8&db=ct1949-96&indiv=1

Donnelly, J. R. (1922, July). Simmons College. *Public Libraries: A Monthly Review of Library Matters and Methods, 27*(7), 451. Retrieved from https://play.google.com/books/reader?id=vbQUAAAAYAAJ&printsec=frontcover&output=reader&authuser=0&hl=en&pg=GBS.PA451

Howe, H. E. (1922, April). Simmons College. *Public Libraries: Monthly Review of Library Matters and Methods, 27*(4), 250–251. Retrieved from https://play.google.com/books/reader?id=vbQUAAAAYAAJ&printsec=frontcover&output=reader&authuser=0&hl=en&pg=GBS.PA251

Keith, W. M. (2007). *Democracy as discussion: Civic education and the American forum movement.* Lanham, MD: Lexington. Retrieved from https://play.google.com/books/reader?id=j_3inshlj2EC&printsec=frontcover&output=reader&authuser=0&hl=en&pg=GBS.PA6.w.1.1.61.0.1

Leach, E. (1983/1999). *Turning out education: The cooperation doctrine in education.* Retrieved from http://www.current.org/wp-content/themes/current/archive-site/coop/coop5.shtml

Loemker, D. (2000, August 20). Obituary. *New York Times.* Retrieved from http://www.nytimes.com/2000/08/20/classified/paid-notice-deaths-loemker-dorothy-rowden.html

Markle Foundation Records. (n.d.). About Markle. *Markle.* Retrieved from http://www.markle.org/about-markle

Microcosm: The Simmons College Annual (Vol. 13). (1922). Boston, MA: Simmons College. Retrieved from http://archive.org/details/microcosm1922simm

Reminisces of Dorothy Rowden Loemker. (1967 June 28). Interview with Isabel S. Grossner [transcript]. In the Columbia Center for Oral History Collection, Carnegie Corporation Project. Columbia University, Oral History Office, New York, NY.

Rowden, D. (Ed.). (1934). *Handbook of adult education in the United States.* New York, NY: American Association of Adult Education.

Rowden, D. (Ed.). (1936). *Handbook of adult education in the United States.* New York, NY: American Association of Adult Education.

Rowden, D. (1937). *Enlightened self-interest: A study of education programs of trade associations.* Studies in the Social Significance of Adult Education in the US. New York, NY: AAAE.

Rowden, D. (1938, January). Four rural counties. *Journal of Adult Education, 10*(1), 74–75.

Rowden, D., & Game, M. (Eds.). (1945). *CBS American school of the air.* New York, NY: Columbia Broadcasting System, Education Division.

Saettler, P. (2004). *The evolution of American educational technology* (2nd ed). Charlotte, NC: Information Age.

Simmons College Twentieth Annual Catalogue. (1921–1922). *Part 1 General Information.* Boston, MA: Merrymount. Retrieved from https://play.google.com/books/reader?id=-H7OAAAAMAAJ&printsec=frontcover&output=reader&authuser=0&hl=en

Simmons College Twenty-first Annual Catalogue. (1922–1923). *Part 4.* Boston, MA: Merrymount. Retrieved from http://books.google.com/books?id=-H7OAAAAMAAJ&pg=RA2-PA77&lpg=RA2-PA77&dq=Simmons+College+Twenty-first+Annual+Catalogue,+1922-1923%29&source=bl&ots=pLNLZI-kRgd&sig=ZKFm6dt_xX212oT3_BlQahoeCEY&hl=en&sa=X&ei=1pGzUZvUOYivqAG-yIHwAg&ved=0CC0Q6AEwAA#v=onepage&q=Simmons%20College%20Twenty-first%20Annual%20Catalogue%2C%201922-1923%29&f=false

Social Security Death Index. (2011). [online database]. Provo, UT: Ancestry.com. Retrieved from http://search.ancestry.com/cgi-bin/sse.dll?rank=1&new=1&MSAV=0&msT=1&gss=angs-c&gsfn=Dorothy&gsln=Loemker&msbdy=1901&uidh=bd1&msbdd=17&msbdm=2&pcat=34&h=37191793&recoff=13+14&db=ssdi&indiv=1 Examined for any reference to Dorothy Loemker accessed on June 7, 2013. Original data: Social Security Administration. *Social Security Death Index, Master File.* Social Security Administration. Number 104-20-6820; Issue State: New York; Issue Date: Before 1951.

U. S. Federal Census. (1910). [online database]. Provo, UT: Ancestry.com. Retrieved from http://search.ancestry.com/cgi-bin/sse.dll?rank=1&new=1&MSAV=0&msT=1&gss=angs-c&gsfn=Dorothy&gsln=Rowden&msbdy=1901&msrpn__ftp=Haverhill+New+Hampshire&uidh=bd1&pcat=35&h=161263868&db=1910USCenIndex&indiv=1&hovR=1

U. S. Federal Census. (1930). [online database]. Provo, UT: Ancestry.com. Retrieved from http://search.ancestry.com/cgi-bin/sse.dll?rank= 1&new=1&MSAV=0&msT=1&gss=angs-c&gsln=Loemker&msbdy= 1897&msbpn__ftp=South+Dakota&msrpn__ftp=Manhattan%2c+ New+York%2c+New+York%2c+USA&msrpn=11127&msrpn_PInfo=8- |0|1652393|0|2|3244|35|1652382|2162|11127|0|&uidh=bd1&_8300400 3-n_xcl=f&pcat=35&h=42139622&db=1930usfedcen&indiv=1

Woodsville High School Alumni Class Lists. (2012). *Commencement Exercises of the Woodsville High School*. Retrieved from: http://search.ancestry.com/cgi-bin/ sse.dll?rank=1&new=1&MSAV=0&msT=1&gss=angs-c&gsfn= Dorothy&gsln=Rowden&msbdy=1901&msrpn__ftp=Haverhill+New+ Hampshire&uidh=bd1&pcat=35&h=161263868&db= 1910USCenIndex&indiv=1&hovR=1

Hilda Worthington Smith
(Photo courtesy of School of Management and Labor Relations, Rutgers University)

CHAPTER 26

HILDA "JANE" WORTHINGTON SMITH

Pioneer in Women Workers Education

Gretchen T. Bersch

No Small Lives: Handbook of North American Early Women Adult Educators, 1925-1950,
pp. 235–243
Copyright © 2015 by Information Age Publishing

Hilda Worthington Smith was an educator, activist, poet, and labor leader who was a pioneer before her time. She believed in progressive education, in self-government, and in the freedom of expression. She dedicated her life to her belief that education had the power to transform lives, and most of her work transformed the lives of countless people, especially women workers.

BACKGROUND

From the 1880s, efforts for women's suffrage and rights grew. The vote for women was approved state by state, with states in the West the earliest to approve the vote. Nationally, the 19th Amendment to the US Constitution was approved in 1920. In addition, there were other forces that contributed to the changing role of women. They included the greater public roles of women seeking education beyond domesticity and involvement in social causes, the impact of the first graduates of women's colleges, and labor reforms generally (Heller, 1986). There was a vision of education as a tool for improving society that was promoted by progressive educators. Into this mix, the adult education movement was birthed.

From early college, Hilda Worthington Smith worked with women's suffrage and social work. In 1921, 5 years before the American Association for Adult Education (AAAE) began, Bryn Mawr opened the Summer School for Women Workers in Industry with Hilda as director. It drew women workers from a wide range of ethnicities, occupations, and locations. The programs were liberal, nonvocational, and worker-student self-governed. Hilda believed this education could be a nonviolent path to social change (Heller, 1986). She worked tirelessly for decades as educator, activist, and lobbyist for workers education for women. So, who was she?

HILDA "JANE" WORTHINGTON SMITH

In her autobiography, Hilda Worthington Smith gives insight into her early life (Smith, 1978). She was born June 1888 in New York City as the oldest of three children to John Jewell and Mary Helen (Hall) Smith. Her father had done very well as president of a steam-heating business, her mother was the daughter of a New York City lawyer. She grew up near Central Park and with her family, spent summers at the family home at West Park, New York. Her beloved father died in 1901. Her mother was demanding and quite critical of Hilda, and though she and her mother were close, Hilda struggled to measure up. Her younger sister, Helen Hall

Smith, devoted her life to working in settlement houses for women workers.

After graduating from the Veltin School, Hilda was escorted in 1906 to Bryn Mawr College by her strong mother. Hilda's friend Lyn Goldfarb wrote in Hilda's *Selected Poems* about how Hilda came to be known as Jane to her friends.

> She arrived on the campus of Bryn Mawr to start college—accompanied by her mother, which restricted considerably her ability to get acquainted with the other students. Looking at this young woman with her pigtail still down her back in the fashion that Mama thought appropriate, her roommate sized her up at a glance and said, "You don't look like a Hilda, you look like a Jane." Jane it was. (Smith, 1977, p. xiv)

From then on, she was known to her friends as Jane.

Hilda graduated from Bryn Mawr in 1910. While most women in the early 20th century, even college graduates, were expected to go home, marry, and settle down to a life of domestic activities, Hilda couldn't see herself doing that. She went on to earn her MA in ethics and psychology at Bryn Mawr and then a degree in social work from the New York School of Philanthropy. She remained single all her life, and the unorthodox path she took seemed to unfold almost accidently. In her wonderful autobiography, Hilda talks about her early work (Smith, 1978). Her earliest work after college was involved with community work. After graduating with her social work degree, she went to the community of her childhood summers on the Hudson River. A blue-collar community, the Smith summer home had always been an informal gathering place. Hilda decided to organize a neighborhood association; neighbors joined together to perform a pageant on the town's history. While it had a bumpy beginning, it ended up bringing the whole community together. In the fall, still in need of a job, she began to volunteer at a children's orphanage, beginning to create activities for the children there, but the changes threatened the board and administration.

Susan M. Kingsbury, energetic and strong-willed, became director of the Department of Social Economy and Social Research at Bryn Mawr in 1916. Kingbsury decided creating a community center would help the less fortunate Bryn Mawr residents and at the same time be a fertile ground to offer practical experience for her graduate students. Hilda took the center's director job. Hilda writes about the adventure of setting up a program for disadvantaged kids in the back of the public school (Smith, 1978). Everyone believed the kids would just ruin any center facilities. Hilda insisted it be a democratically run center and, under her innovative guidance, it flourished and grew. A playground and library emerged; hot meals for hungry children and then night school classes for underprivileged men taught by college student volunteers followed. She drew in tough gang boys, and eventually a small kindergarten allowed women to attend classes. It was a unique experiment in its time and gave Hilda rich experiences and insight she drew on for the rest of her life, especially in her years with labor schools for women workers. Through Kingsbury, she met many famous people who were involved in settlements and community work.

In 1917, Hilda was made dean at Bryn Mawr, a job she did well but for which she didn't have passion. M. Carey Thomas was the president of Bryn Mawr at that time; raised a Quaker, Thomas was a feminist, a visionary, and revolutionary. Thomas visited British labor schools and then with her cousin Alys Russell, wife of philosopher Bertrand Russell, traveled to Egypt. While riding on camels there, Thomas had a vision of opening Bryn Mawr College in summers to educate blue-collar women workers (Smith, 1978).

Thomas chose Hilda to direct this new program. This became Hilda's life work and great passion; she went on to direct it for 13 of its 17 years, during which time she created the Affiliated Schools for Women Workers. When the Bryn Mawr program closed in 1938, Hilda managed to create and open the Hudson Shore Labor School for both men and women at her Hudson River family home (Smith, 1978).

BRYN MAWR SUMMER SCHOOL
FOR WOMEN WORKERS IN INDUSTRY

In 1921, Bryn Mawr College opened the Summer School for Women Workers in Industry—82 blue-collar women workers were chosen for the residential program. It was liberal arts study at the elite Bryn Mawr college, not vocational training. The women came from 22 states, 49 trades, and 25 nationalities. Examples of their trades included shirtmaker, button-hole maker, shoe worker, and milliner (Factory girls, 1931; Heller, 1986; Schugurensky, n.d.).

The goal of the summer school was to offer women in industry a chance to study liberal subjects and to gain insight into economic problems with the belief that they might become change agents. Information about the program was sent through the YWCA, unions, and churches. Women who were accepted ranged in age from 20 to 35 years, had finished elementary school, and had 2 years of industrial experience; they represented a mix of races, religions, and ethnicities. Money from large industrialists of the day provided scholarships for the women who attended. From the beginning, the summer faculty came from outside Bryn Mawr from a wide variety of colleges and universities such as Smith,

Vassar, and Wellesley. Bryn Mawr became the model program in labor education. In 17 summers, some 1,600 factory women were educated. Hilda went against M. Carey Thomas' wishes and integrated the summer school in 1926, accepting five Black women. Each summer, faculty and students became a close-knit learning community, with innovative teaching techniques including drama and role-play, poetry, science experience, and physical education. Those who had been at the school reported they became more curious, socially aware, and that their self-image improved. Many went on to further schooling; others became leaders in their unions. "Smith took the factory women totally by surprise as they had not encountered anyone like her before. They were unaccustomed to being taken seriously, let alone by an imposing, genteel, upper class, social reformer-poet" (Heller, 1986, p. 63).

From the outside, we see an accomplished, brilliant woman. From her autobiography, Hilda confides her lack of confidence and her struggles to find direction and meaningful work (Smith, 1978). Hilda believed in the democratic process; she used it with delinquent teenage boys, poor children, inexperienced young college girls, uneducated immigrants, and women workers. All around her, people in authority said it wouldn't work, but time and again, it not only worked but brought out eagerness, leadership, and enthusiasm that changed people for the rest of their lives. She was a starter—she drew people together, got them involved, and delegated tasks to others so people felt a part. She was an outstanding mediator. She collaboratively created democratic policies for operating, and then when the operation was a success and others had been mentored into leadership roles, she moved on. Her brilliance lay in her ability as a great negotiator, bridging social and cultural classes and groups, resulting in admiration from all ends of the spectrum. She was a skilled administrator. While her autobiography shows she disliked raising funds, she was extremely effective at it. Her calm but surprising suggestions at just the perfect moment solved many problems time and again. Her autobiography is wonderfully readable and poetic; she humbly relates her years of experiences as they unfolded over 6 decades. Carolyn Ware wrote,

> She is a unique combination of the visionary, the realistic activist, and the pioneer, guided always by an unshakeable common sense which never permits her to substitute ideology, conventional wisdom or lofty principle for the direct approach to meeting a clearly perceived human need. Above all, she brings out the best in other people through her genuine warmth of feeling, her imaginative insight into their potentialities, her belief and trust in them, and her sense of the wholeness and richness of life which has made her insist that poetry and astronomy are as relevant to workers' education as are economics and public speaking. (Fitzpatrick, n.d.)

While Hilda was working in Washington, DC, in the 1930s, the Bryn Mawr summer school had several tumultuous years and eventually closed. Hilda didn't waste any time establishing the Hudson Shore Labor School at her lovely home in West Park, New York, in 1939. The press release read,

> The Hudson Shore Labor School's ... first session [is] to be held in the new year-round home of the school at West Park, New York. Here, two hours from New York City, in a delightful rural setting on an old estate overlooking the picturesque and historic Hudson River, 60 women workers will enjoy healthful outdoor living combined with opportunities for study and discussion of problems of labor and industry. (Hudson Shore Labor School, 1939).

Like the Bryn Mawr program, the program included recreation, leadership training, planning activities for labor women and children, analyzing labor issues, and regular classes. It operated successfully, with Hilda acting as founder and serving on the board of directors. It became co-educational, offering programs for both men and women (Fitzpatrick, n.d.). The program was eventually transferred to Rutgers University in 1951.

AMERICAN ASSOCIATION FOR ADULT EDUCATION

Hilda's Bryn Mawr Summer School had already been operating for 3 or 4 years before the new American Adult Association for Education was created. Hilda was already known as a pioneer in educating women workers; she was involved in the adult education movement and the Association from the beginning. By 1929, Hilda was on the executive board of the Association and served for over a decade. She also served on the AAAE Council (AAAE *Journal* issues, listing of boards and committees).

In collaboration with AAAE, Hilda published *Women Workers at the Bryn Mawr Summer School* (1929), and, between 1929 and 1940, contributed many articles to the *Journal of Adult Education* such as "Chapter Thirteen of the Bryn Mawr Story" (1933) and "New Directions for Workers' Education" (1940). She contributed a chapter, "Schools for Women Workers in Industry," to the 1934 *Handbook of Adult Education in the U.S.* (Rowden, 1934). Her contributions to *Adult Education in Action* (Ely, 1936) were two chapters entitled, "Emergency Education for Industrial Workers" (pp. 112–114) and "Bryn Mawr Summer School Students" (pp. 340–344). She continually advocated for advancing the opportunities for women workers.

When the AAAE ended in the late 1940s, Hilda was involved in the founding of the new association, Adult Education Association of USA. As part of its formation, an important retreat was held in August 1950, and

Hilda, then chair of the Committee for the Labor Extension Act in Washington, DC, was one of only four women who attended this retreat. Old timers like Hilda, Eleanor Coit, and Eduard Lindeman were there, as well as newer adult educators like Howard McClusky and Malcolm Knowles (Hiemstra, 2003).

FEDERAL LABOR WORK

Hilda became involved in wider circles than the Bryn Mawr programs. By 1927, she created and directed the Affiliated Schools for Workers, drawing in many labor schools, which was later changed to the American Labor Education Service (Hilda W. Smith, 95, Educator, 1984). Hilda already knew Eleanor Roosevelt from her many years at West Park, New York. Eleanor was a great supporter of Hilda and her work and had visited her summer labor programs (Smith, 1978).

When the Bryn Mawr Summer School came to a close in 1938, Hilda went to Washington, DC, to see if she could find funds to continue. Instead, Hilda was tapped by President Roosevelt's advisor Harry Hopkins. Harry was head of the WPA (Works Progress Administration) and asked Hilda to set up educational programs for what was called the Federal Emergency Relief Administration, which later became the WPA's Workers Education Service. She passed her responsibilities for the Affiliated Schools for Workers off to Eleanor Coit and went to work for the government. Hilda supervised a variety of programs, including a program to train 2,000 out-of-work teachers. Another program she directed provided housing and education for unemployed women, nicknamed the She-She-She Camps after the CCC Camps for men. During World War II, she coordinated a Community Services for War Housing program. In 1952, she set up programs for the elderly (Hilda W. Smith, 95, Educator, 1984; Smith, 1978).

In 1965, at age 76, Hilda was hired by Sargent Shriver at the new Office of Equal Opportunity (OEO). She worked and advised many projects. She worked for OEO until President Nixon eliminated the program. Hilda retired in 1972 at age 83 and at last had time to write about her 6 decades of work in her autobiography, *Opening Vistas in Workers' Education* (Hilda W. Smith, 95, Educator, 1984; Smith, 1978).

OTHER ACTIVITIES IN HILDA'S LIFE

Hilda/Jane was a lifelong poet. Her first book, *Castle of Dream*, was published in 1910, the year she graduated from Bryn Mawr; two other poetry books were published later. A colleague, Lawrence Rogin, wrote in the forward to her *Selected Poems*,

> Jane has many causes; education and workers, but mostly I think it was women. When it was less popular than today, she never let me forget that our society was sexist, although she didn't use that term; and that unions and education were among the sinners. (Smith, 1977, p. xiii)

She remained active well into old age, and her connection to poetry never left her. When she was interviewed at age 95, she recited one of her poems, "Freedom Train," from memory. She died at age 95 in March 1984 (Hilda W. Smith, 95, Educator, 1984). The impact of her work and her influence on thousands of people, particularly women, lives on.

REFERENCES

American Association for Adult Education. (1929–1941). *Journal of Adult Education*. New York, NY: AAAE.

Ely, M. (1936). *Adult education in action*. New York, NY: American Association for Adult Education.

Factory girls take liberal arts work. (1931, July 5). *The New York Times*, p. 39. Retrieved from http://search.proquest.com.proxy.consortiumlibrary.org/docview/99333380/pageviewPDF/1430C7E01CD2079F936/4?accountid=14473

Fitzpatrick, K. M. (n.d.). *A home, a school, a dream: Hilda Worthington Smith and the Hudson Shore Labor School*. Retrieved from http://www.rci.rutgers.edu/~smlr/library/Digilib/album2.htm.

Heller, R. R, (1986). *The women of summer: The Bryn Mawr summer school for women workers: 1921–1938*. New Brunswick, NJ: Rutgers University.

Hiemstra, R. (2003, March 7). *Founding of the AEA of USA, 1949–1955*. Presentation at 2003 International Adult & Continuing Education Hall of Fame conference.

Hilda W. Smith, 95, Educator. (1984, March 14). *The New York Times*, p. B10. Retrieved from http://search.proquest.com.proxy.consortiumlibrary.org/docview/122344330/1430C8F51AC15D8ABA3/1?accountid=14473

Hudson Shore Labor School. (1939, March 29). *Summer school office in New York City* [Press release].

Rowden, D. (1934). *Handbook of adult education*. New York, NY: American Association for Adult Education.

Schugurensky, D. (n.d.). 1921—The Bryn Mawr summer school for women workers opens its doors. *History of Education: Selected Moments of the 20th Century*. Retrieved from http://fcis.oise.utoronto.ca/~daniel_schugurensky/assignment1/1921brynmawr.html

Smith, H. W. (1910). *Castle of dream*. Bryn Mawr, PA: Bryn Mawr College.

Smith, H. W. (1929). Women workers at the Bryn Mawr Summer School. New York, NY: *Affiliated Summer Schools for Women Workers in Industry and American Association for Adult Education.* Retrieved from http://nrs.harvard.edu/urn-3:RAD.SCHL:415746

Smith, H. W. (1933). Chapter thirteen of the Bryn Mawr story. *Journal of Adult Education, 5,* 425–427. New York, NY: American Association for Adult Education.

Smith, H. W. (1934). Schools for women workers in industry. In D. Rowden (Ed.), *Handbook of adult education in the United States.* New York, NY: American Association for Adult Education.

Smith, H. W. (1940). New directions for workers' education. *Journal of Adult Education, 12,* 162–166. New York, NY: American Association for Adult Education.

Smith, H. W. (1977). *Selected poems.* New York, NY: Institute for Education and Research on Women and Work, New York State School of Industrial and Labor Relations, Cornell University.

Smith, H. W. (1978). *Opening vistas in worker's education.* Washington, DC: Privately printed.

Women from Local 22 Picketing Reynolds Tobacco
(Photo courtesy of Forsyth County Public Library Photograph Collection,
Winston-Salem, NC)

CHAPTER 27

MORANDA SMITH

From Tobacco Plant Worker, to Local Union Educator, to First African American Woman to Head a Southern Regional Union

Jovita M. Ross-Gordon and Geleana Drew Alston

No Small Lives: Handbook of North American Early Women Adult Educators, 1925-1950,
pp. 245–251
Copyright © 2015 by Information Age Publishing

This chapter tells the story of Moranda Smith, an African American woman who, during her short life ending in 1950, made remarkable contributions to adult education history, most notably as a union educator and leader. Ms. Smith's personal story begins with her birth in Dunbar, North Carolina, in 1915 (Korstad, 2003, p. 232). Her family's move to Winston-Salem North Carolina, when she was 5 years old would lead her to employment at the Reynolds Tobacco Factory there at the age of 18. It was as an employee of Reynolds that she became drawn into a larger struggle for worker's rights. But first it is important to set the stage for understanding the place of Black workers, male and female, in the pre–Civil Rights era.

BACKGROUND

According to Marshall (1976, p. 6), "In the early 20th century labor leaders were unabashed about their racist sentiments. Many unions excluded blacks outright or placed them in segregated locals, with the express approval of the American Federation of Labor." Similarly, in a special issue on adult education of the "Negro" in the *Journal of Negro Education*, Hall (1945) described a wide array of adult education programs offered by the Workers Education Bureau, formed by the American Federation of Labor in 1921, but added, "All of the data relating to Negro membership in the national and international organizations affiliated to the A F of L indicate that both by constitutional provisions and ritualistic restrictions, Negroes were very effectively debarred from the majority of the organizations" (p. 407). This effectively excluded them from union-sponsored educational activities. Hall suggests the most significant event for Blacks in the history of organized labor was when 10 unions affiliated with the Committee for Industrial Organization were expelled from the AF of L in 1936, marking the formation of the separate Congress of Industrial Organizations (CIO), which welcomed Blacks into its activities and programs, opening up participation in union-based adult education to Blacks for the first time. This paved the way for the role Moranda Smith would come to play as a local and national leader of the CIO during the 1940s. Giddings (1980) notes, "It is no wonder that with the birth of the CIO in 1935—the first union to encourage large numbers of blacks to join its ranks—black women were often found in the forefront of organizing locals" (p. 544). According to Lerner (1992), "As late as 1944, low wage-scales prevailed: white women earned 57¢ an hour, black women 44¢ an hour. There were other patterns of race discrimination which worked to the disadvantage of black workers" (pp. 265–266).

CIO LOCAL 22—WINSTON-SALEM, NORTH CAROLINA

It was in this context that Moranda Smith was transformed from a tobacco factory worker, said to be initially reluctant to join a work stoppage, to a local and later national union leader and educator, a local Communist Party leader, and an advocate for Black voting rights years before the Voting Rights Act of 1965 (Adams, 1998; French & Atwood, 2008; Giddings, 1980; Korstad, 2003). Fed up with mistreatment and low wages, the turning point for Black women working in the stemmery at Reynolds Tobacco came on a Thursday in June 1943, when a widow and mother of five was fired after becoming too ill to keep up with her work. Women workers, led by Theodosia Simpson and joined by Smith, decided to turn their backs to their machines and stop work (Korstad, 2003). When one of the men, who stood to speak in support of their work stoppage dropped dead, an immediate sit-down quickly morphed into an organized strike of more than 10,000 workers, who spilled into the streets by the weekend. The strike ended 6 days later, but in the interim, Local 22 of the CIO was born. That same month, an article appearing in the *Winston-Salem Journal* speculated that the organization of labor could help bring a bigger and better Winston-Salem, fostering a better understanding between "white and colored people" of Winston-Salem (On Your Radio, 1943, p. 9).

Local Union 22 of the CIO soon became a fulcrum for change in Winston-Salem, and an incubator for leadership development of Black and White, male and female leaders, including Moranda Smith. Smith is said to have been mentored by Eleanore Hoagland, Local 22's first education director, who mentioned how Smith "came by every day after work to talk and read" (Korstad, 2003, p. 233). Under Hoagland, the education department offered classes on labor history, Black history, and current events; maintained a union library that housed labor newspapers and pamphlets on political and international affairs; worked with the Hampton Institute and the Southern School for Workers to develop literacy programs for Black workers; and used media such as the local radio and a self-published newspaper called *The Worker's Voice* to promote democratic participation in local issues beyond union affairs. Local 22 activities attracted notable visitors, including Zilphia Horton from the Highlander Center, Pete Seeger, and Paul Robeson (Korstad, 2003). Local 22's educational efforts were not limited to its own members. For instance, a flyer distributed in 1948 carried the header "To the Community ... Take a Step Forward With Us," and reported that North Carolina was 6th from the bottom in adult education and 43rd in income payments to individuals at $689 a year, compared to a national average of $1,082 (Local 22, n.d.).

MORANDA SMITH—FROM LOCAL 22 TO NATIONAL LEADER

According to Korstad (2003), Local 22's education department quickly became the center of women's activities in the union. Those activities, in turn, often became the springboard by which women emerged as rank-and-file leaders and as the union's most effective political educators. Moranda Smith, one of Local 22's most eloquent and beloved representatives, was a case in point. Smith went on to become the director of the education department. In 1944, the local served as the hub for a 1-week summer school offered by Southern School for Workers under the auspices of the CIO, reported to be attended by 41 workers from six southern states (Hall, 1945). With other Local 22 leaders, including Theodosia Simpson, who initiated the Reynolds strike in 1943, Smith became a force in the city's political life through Local 22's Political Action Committee. In 1947, she went on to become the first African American woman to serve on the executive committee of the Food and Tobacco Worker's Union (Korstad, 2003).

Unfortunately, Smith's election to this position had limited impact on the willingness of the tobacco magnates to negotiate with workers. Following the 1943 strike that led to the birth of Local 22, the next several years were marked by continuous strife between the union and the Reynolds company, reflected by negotiations, lawsuits, and strikes seeking better working conditions (Local 22, n.d.). The constant efforts of the union leaders did result over time in some improvements in wages and working conditions, but were also met typically by company resistance and intermittently by harsh police actions. In one instance, a Black union leader was even falsely accused of assaulting a White woman (Local 22, n.d.). The downward turn in the Local 22's struggle for workers rights and local democracy seems to have come with a strike starting in spring of 1947. Lerner (1992, p. 266) remarks, "The R. J. Reynolds Company 'Camel' strike was marked by violence, the eviction of strikers, some Communist influence, the intervention of the House Un-American Activities Committee and a militant rank-and-file movement of black women." In the midst of this strike, Reynolds suddenly refused to negotiate due to the enactment of the Labor Management Relations Act of 1947, better known as the Taft-Hartley Act. The local newspaper, the *Winston-Salem Journal*, began printing articles insinuating that the Communist Party had captured Local 22 and other union leaders (Reds Dominate, 1947). Eugene Pratt told the *Journal* he joined Local 22 to clean out its communist influence. He persuaded Anne Matthews to speak with a reporter for the *Journal*. During her conversation with the reporter she named names of communists among Local 22 leadership, including Moranda Smith (Korstad, 1987).

During the same year, Smith captured attention nationally with a moving speech she gave at the CIO's national convention in Boston in 1947 (Taylor, 2008). She rose to speak with the aim to motivate her audience to continue the crusade against the forces wishing to undo the efforts of her union:

> We want people to walk the picket lines free and unafraid and know that they are working for their freedom and their liberty. When you speak about this protection of democracy, it is more than just words.... Ask the people who are suffering, and together you will come out with a good program where civil rights will be something to be proud of. (Smith, 1947, para. 7)

Encouraging favorable consideration of a CIO resolution in response to the Taft-Hartley Act, she spoke passionately to convention attendees:

> You talk about political action and you talk about politics. How can there be any action when the Negroes in the South are not allowed to vote? Too long have the workers in the South stopped and looked to Congress for protection. We no longer look to the government in Washington for protection. It has failed. Today we are looking for an organization that says they are organized to fight for the freedom of all men regardless of race, creed or color, and that is the CIO. (Smith, 1947, para. 5)

She ended her fiery speech with a call to action for all present:

> When the civil liberties of Negroes in the South are interfered with [and] you do nothing about it, I say to you, you are untrue to the traditions of America. You have got to get up and do something in action, as I have said before and not by mere words. (Smith, 1947, para. 10)

In 1948, Smith went on to become the first regional director for an international union in the south, a role noted to be a dangerous one in an era of Klan activism (Adams, 1998; French & Atwood, 2008). Even in this role, she apparently made efforts to support the work of Local 22. A 1948 flyer asking for community support reported that Local 22 leaders met with Moranda Smith—serving as assistant director of the South Atlantic Region—and other national leaders of the FTA-CIO in Washington, to discuss Reynolds Tobacco Company efforts to destroy Local 22 "and get complete control over the workers and the community" (Local 22, n.d.). Serving in the position of regional director no doubt added tremendously to the stress she experienced, and along with R. J. Reynolds' continued refusal to negotiate with Local 22, probably contributed to her untimely death in 1950 at the age of 34 (Davis, 1950). Her death was due to a stroke that occurred in the middle of a meeting of union and party activists at her home (Korstad, 2003). In the words of Adams (1998, p. 171),

"She had literally worked herself to death for the cause." On March 23, 1950, R. J. Reynolds held elections wherein workers voted whether to keep the union. Local 22 lost the election to "no union" by 66 votes (Korstad, 2003). The nearly decade-long struggle came to a halt.

CONNECTIONS TO KNOWN HISTORIES OF THE FIELD

The labor educational activities of Moranda Smith and Local 22 are similar to that of Myles Horton and Highlander Folk School, Hilda Smith and the Bryn Mawr Summer School for Women Workers, and Sarah G. Bagley and the Lowell Experiment (Stubblefield & Keane, 1994). However, Smith and Local 22 specifically focused on Black women workers because during this time "White society did not extend its 'true womanhood' philosophy to include black women, and the 'race uplift' philosophy did not distinguish between the education of black men and women" (Stubblefield & Keane, 1994, p. 124). The efforts of Smith and her colleagues to expand voting rights for Blacks can also be seen as precursors to similar efforts intensified during the civil rights era. Hence, their efforts can be viewed within the vein of civil rights in addition to labor education and worker rights. Nevertheless, stories of crusaders like Moranda Smith are often not within the dialogue of "organized labor's response to adult education" (Stubblefield & Keane, p. xiv), nor have their early interactions with the Highlander Center been chronicled. Although her contributions as a labor educator and civil rights activist seem to have escaped notice of historians of adult labor education, Moranda Smith's legacy for workers has not been entirely forgotten. In 1951, on her posthumous 36th birthday, thousands of workers stopped work to honor her memory (Adams, 1998). And on April 20, 2013, local activists and Winston-Salem community members celebrated the 70th anniversary of the historic strike and unveiled a commemorative state marker in the honor of Moranda Smith and Local 22 (Cox, 2013).

REFERENCES

Adams, J. (1998). *Freedom days: 365 inspired moments in civil rights history* [NetLibrary electronic reproduction]. New York, NY: John Wiley & Sons.

Cox, W. (2013, February 21). *Marker to celebrate tobacco unionizing in Winston-Salem* [Press release]. Retrieved from http://www.local22nc.com/uploads/Press_Release_2.pdf

Davis, L. (1950, April 14). Activities of colored people. *Winston-Salem Journal*, p. 13.

French, M., & Atwood, M. (2008). *From eve to dawn: A history of women, Volume IV: Revolutions and struggles for justice in the 20th century.* New York, NY: Feminist Press at the City University of New York.

Giddings, P. (1980, December). Mrs. Bethune: Spingarn Medalist. *The Crisis,* 543–544. Retrieved from http://books.google.com/books?id=PSoEAAAAM-BAJ&pg=PA572&dq=the+crisis+December+1980&hl=en&sa=X&ei=UL2LUbyRG7LJ4AOhyYHABQ&sqi=2&ved=0CC4Q6AEwAA#v=onepage&q=the%20crisis%20December%201980&f=false

Hall, W. A. (1945). Adult education programs of labor unions and other worker groups.*The Journal of Negro Education, 14*(3), 407–411.

Korstad, R. R. (1987). *Daybreak of freedom: Tobacco workers and the CIO, Winston-Salem, North Carolina, 1943–1950* (Unpublished doctoral dissertation). Chapel Hill: University of North Carolina at Chapel Hill.

Korstad, R. R. (2003). *Civil rights unionism: Tobacco workers and the struggle for democracy in the mid-twentieth-century South* [NetLibrary electronic reproduction]. Chapel Hill: University of North Carolina Press.

Lerner, G. (1992). *Black women in White America: A documentary history.* New York, NY: Vintage.

Local 22. (n.d.). (Folder 3: Tobacco Workers Union: Broadsides, 1944–1950, Scan 1-Scan 46). In the Myron Howard Ross Papers, #4079, Southern Historical Collection, The Wilson Library, University of North Carolina at Chapel Hill. Retrieved from http://dc.lib.unc.edu/cdm/search/collection/ead/searchterm/04079/field/descri/mode/exact/conn/and/cosuppress/

Marshall, R. (1976, December 20). Organizing women, Blacks: Labor's come a long way. *In These Times,* 6–7. Retrieved from http://www.unz.org/Pub/InTheseTimes-1976dec20-00006a02?View=PDF

On your radio tonight! (1943, June 30). [Graphic announcement]. *Winston-Salem Journal,* p. 9.

Reds dominate tobacco union, house group told. (1947, August 2). *Afro American,* p. 3. Retrieved from http://news.google.com/newspapers?nid=2211&dat=19470802&id=jx0mAAAAIBAJ&sjid=y_0FAAAAIBAJ&pg=2916,6539972

Smith, M. (1947, October 15). *Moranda Smith addresses the Congress of Industrial Organizations annual convention.* Final Proceedings of the 9th Constitutional Convention of the CIO, Boston, MA. Retrieved from http://www.blackpast.org/1947-moranda-smith-addresses-congress-industrial-organizations-annual-convention-boston

Stubblefield, H. W., & Keane, P. (1994). *Adult education in the American experience: From the colonial period to the present.* San Francisco, CA: Jossey-Bass.

Taylor, Q. (2008). *From Timbuktu to Katrina: Sources in African American history.* Boston, MA: Thomson Higher Education.

Isabel Wilson
(Photo courtesy of Cynthia Flood, Isabel Wilson's niece.)

CHAPTER 28

THE VISION AND PEDAGOGICAL SENSIBILITY OF ISABEL WILSON

Giving Credit Where Credit is Due

Shauna Butterwick and Jonathan B. Fisher

No Small Lives: Handbook of North American Early Women Adult Educators, 1925-1950,
pp. 253–259
Copyright © 2015 by Information Age Publishing

This chapter reviews the indispensable contribution of Isabel Creigh-ton Wilson to the Canadian Association for Adult Education (CAAE), especially her work as national secretary of the popular CBC (Canadian Broadcasting Corporation) radio program *Citizens' Forum* (*CF*) that involved the researching and editing of over 300 listening group pamphlets.[1] *CF* ran for 20 years and was one of the CAAE's highest profile and most ambitious projects, regarded as a key contributor to the creation of the postwar ideal of a unified Canada. Research into the primary documents shows that while Wilson and her colleagues (men and women alike) at the CAAE valued Wilson's contribution to adult education very highly, the specific nature of her work, which involved responsibility for editing of hundreds of study pamphlets, allowed it to go unrecognized outside of the leadership of her organization despite her work having touched the lives of many thousands of Canadians. The goal of this chapter is to give credit where credit is due; to appreciate the enormous work undertaken by Isabel Wilson. We begin this chapter with a brief introduction of CAAE and the origins of *CF*, then turn attention to the specific vision and contributions of Isabel Wilson.

CANADIAN ASSOCIATION FOR ADULT EDUCATION

The CAAE was established in 1935 and was the key adult education national organization until it closed in the 1980s. Its two main purposes were stimulation and integration of adult education in Canada and public education. Annual conferences were held and several major public education initiatives were undertaken, including *National Farm Radio Forum*, (*NFRF*), which began in 1941. *NFRF* was focused on public education for rural life with weekly radio broadcasts, the topics of which were identified by the thousands of listening groups held in either farmers' homes or rural halls. Following the success of *National Farm Radio Forum*, *Citizen's Forum*, co-produced by the CBC and CAAE, was initiated in November 1942 (Faris, 1975). Wilson's history of this program (1980), written for the Ontario Institute for Studies in Education (OISE), gives a detailed treatment of the beginnings of the radio program all the way up through the challenges faced near the end of the program, when conflicts began to arise between the goals of the CBC and the CAAE as its primary sponsors.

As Sandwell notes, drawing on Wilson's 1980 report, postwar reconstruction of Canada was the focus of this program that served as a more "urban" counterpart to *NFRF* (Sandwell, 2012). The pilot broadcasts in early 1943, titled *Of Things to Come: An Enquiry into the Postwar World*, made explicit the program's reconstruction goals. As Wilson notes in her documentation of the beginnings of *CF*, there was much passion and concern evident in the early meetings, where it was argued that the CAAE take a lead role in public education: "The world must be rebuilt, old errors and injustices swept away, economic and political wrongs righted" (Wilson, 1980, p. 4).

The subtitle of *CF* eventually became, "Canada's National Platform," which signaled the program's purpose as being strongly aligned with a Canadian national identity, loosely defined. It hinged on the gathering together of Canadians from disparate sections of the country for some centralized forum-style discussion and debate. The pilot broadcasts were followed with a series entitled *Of Things to Come: A Citizens' Forum*, based on topics, which Jean Hunter Morrison, editor of the CAAE's journal *Food For Thought*, had been researching since the CAAE had adopted its plan for *CF* in late 1942 (Wilson, 1980, p.8).

The format of the program was ambitious, with weekly broadcasts between October and March across Canada. Like its rural precursor, *NFRF*, it was organized around weekly study pamphlets, and as of 1944, they were written by Isabel Wilson. As Wilson (1980) notes in her report on the history of *CF*, it was difficult to find readily available materials on all of the topics and thus we can argue that Isabel herself was not just an editor but also a researcher. In addition to seeking out individuals who were experts, she found additional information on topics that had not received serious treatment from journalists or academics. She also had to find a way to adapt statistics from the United States to the Canadian context. She was committed to writing a balanced view so that listeners could make up their own minds, and thus she worked hard to ensure the pamphlets included both the pros and cons. The forum engaged Canadian citizens across the country in dialogue on a sweeping scope of important issues facing postwar Canada, from health care to immigration, and from international trade to nuclear armament.

As the textual glue that held the program together, these pamphlets were distributed to participating groups and individuals who would discuss the week's broadcast and report back via "provincial secretaries." Summaries of reports from local discussion groups were broadcast at the end of the following week's program, allowing for an unprecedented level of participation in Canadian mass media (Selman, Cooke, Selman, & Dampier, 1998).

The radio program ultimately became so popular and successful that in 1955 production of a television broadcast of *CF* began (Wilson, 1980). The radio broadcasts persisted in the form of audio simulcasts of the television broadcasts, but changes in scheduling and continual disputes over funding and control of programming meant that *CF* had its final broadcast season in 1964–65.

ISABEL WILSON: TAKING ACTION
BEHIND THE SCENES OF *CITIZENS' FORUM*

It is clear that the story of *CF* is largely the story of Isabel Wilson's career. And likewise, much of the creativity and ambition which made *CF* such a powerfully influential and lasting Canadian mass media presence originated in Wilson's own motivation, her dedication to the cause of Canadian Adult Education, and to social justice causes like feminism. Furthermore, there is evidence that Wilson sometimes used her position as National Secretary of *CF* as a platform for activism on issues of particular importance to her, though she refers to the practices of the *CF* in this regard as "direct service" rather than as direct action (Wilson 1980, p.86). Wilson must have seen her role as National Secretary of *CF* as primarily a community organizer or consciousness-raiser, although she may never have used those exact words to describe herself.

Isabel Wilson was born Mary Isabel Creighton in Toronto in 1904, the youngest of three children and the only daughter of Laura Harvie Creighton and William Black Creighton, who was a Methodist minister. Given her family's involvement in her community—her father was, in addition to being a Methodist minister, an editor of two Christian newspapers in Toronto, and likewise, one of her older brothers, Donald Creighton, became a notable Canadian historian (Funeral Service Program, 1983)—it is not surprising that Isabel's career took the shape that it did. Wilson lived most of her life in Toronto, attending Howard Park Public (primary) School, and Humberside Collegiate (secondary) School before going on to attend the University of Toronto's Library School (Funeral Service Program, 1983). Graduating in 1926, Wilson went to work in the Toronto Public Library system. Her colleague there and lifelong friend Ruth McKenzie recalled in a letter to Wilson upon her retirement from the CAAE in 1970, the strong impression she had made. In 1932, Wilson, a young, single woman working in Canada's largest city, impressed McKenzie most of all with her "intelligence and generous spirit towards everyone" (McKenzie, 1970). And similar sentiments are echoed in all of the congratulatory letters that flooded in upon Wilson's retirement from the CAAE. E. A. Corbett himself devoted the last paragraph of the chapter on *CF* in his own memoir, *We Have with Us Tonight*, to praising Wilson's talent and dedication to her work at the CAAE (Corbett, 1957).

Corbett, in his role as the first director of CAAE, was responsible for hiring Wilson in 1944. And he, McKenzie, and Wilson traveled from Toronto to Amherst, Nova Scotia, by car together in 1951, as McKenzie recounted, to attend an adult education conference there, "with no reservations, just taking things as they come" (McKenzie, 1970). So it is clear that Wilson and Corbett became close friends. But Wilson was also a person Corbett trusted to be a public face of the CAAE. In 1954, Gordon Selman, who would go on to become one of the foremost historians of adult education in Canada and a Provincial Secretary of *CF* in British Columbia, had just gotten his first job in the Department of Extension at the University of British Columbia, when he decided to pay a visit to the CAAE offices in Toronto. Initially, Selman had intended to meet with Corbett himself, but when he arrived, Wilson was there to show him the ropes. Impressed, Selman left that meeting not disappointed at having missed Corbett, but rather energized and even more fully committed to adult education because of the introduction he had received to the field from Wilson (Selman, 1970).

Corbett's trust of Wilson is further evidenced by Wilson's complete editorial control over the content and oversight of the production of the *CF* study pamphlets. As has been noted, this involved considerable research as well as crafting of accessible materials on serious topics that included a balanced view.

PERSONAL COMMITMENTS: MAKING SPACE FOR ACTIVISM

In 1938, Isabel Creighton married her college sweetheart, Harold Godfrey Wilson. According to Wilson's niece, Cynthia Flood, Wilson and her husband were separated for a period of time when Wilson moved alone to Saskatoon. Here she took on a "radio job" (Flood, n.d., p. 11); it is possible that she was employed in some capacity with the *NFRF*, which began broadcasting in 1941. This previous experience in radio broadcasting gave her an advantage when she began working on *CF* in 1944. Wilson returned to Toronto in 1944, largely in order to care for her ailing parents, who both died in 1946. She also returned to her marriage with Harold and they would live out the rest of their lives together in Toronto, with Harold dying in 1971, less than a year after Wilson's retirement from her post at the CAAE. Isabel died in Toronto in 1983. Isabel and Harold Wilson never had any children, but Isabel did have a close relationship with her nephew Philip, son of Donald and Luella Creighton; with her sister-in-law Luella; and with her niece, with whom she would vacation on Mayne Island, British Columbia (Flood, n.d., p. 16).

It is easy to imagine Wilson as a woman who, in spite of, or perhaps, indeed because of the difficulties she faced in her private life, was all the more dedicated to her professional life. Similarly, in rereading the *CF* pamphlets that deal with issues, which Wilson likely had directly experienced, it is striking the even-handedness with which Wilson addressed each topic. Wilson's role as a researcher and educator—making information available to adults, encouraging free discussion and the autonomous formulation of individual points of view—is one which she clearly took very seriously. Wilson explains,

> Once speakers had agreed to take part in a broadcast, they voiced their own opinions, and produced what evidence they could muster in support of their own views. The pamphlets, however, were supposed to provide a sound basis for group discussion, a summary of fact, and a balance of opinion, in light of which the citizen could make up his own mind. (Wilson, 1980, p. 58)

Her commitment to the impartiality of the pamphlets is a major reason why no author, other than the CAAE, ever appeared on them. There were many volunteer contributors to the content of the study pamphlets over the years and Wilson (1980) lists many in her synopsis of *CF* (pp. 61–62). But Wilson's editorship was what held the process together.

One of the most exciting points of Wilson's career came in 1950 when the CAAE organized a campaign on "Equal Pay for Work of Equal Value: Are Women Getting a Fair Deal?" This ultimately led to the distribution of more study pamphlets than any other single program (CAAE, 1950). The CAAE was still receiving orders for this pamphlet the following spring (Wilson, 1980, p. 86). So, even though Wilson wrote in her characteristically even-handed tone, the zeal with which she organized the pamphlets' publicity illustrates not only how important this issue was to Wilson herself, but also her own implicit answer to the question posed in the title— "NO!" Thus Wilson and her other feminist colleagues within the CAAE, among them Clare Clark, who would become the head of CAAE's Joint Planning Commission that year, and others who organized this highly successful consciousness-raising campaign, were able to work to push the boundaries of Canadian societal norms, even as they trod the professional lines prescribed by their respective organizations (Selman, personal communication, March 22, 2013; Wilson, 1980). This successful activist effort of Wilson illustrates her attitude and approach to her job at *CF*. She was not simply an editor; rather, she was a researcher, one who gave *CF* a definite shape and direction, and she deserves recognition for that fact.

CONCLUSION

CF was a highly successful, widely popular, and technologically groundbreaking instance of Canadian Adult Education through mass media. While *CF* was a joint endeavor of the CAAE and CBC, the actual curriculum and adult education pedagogy were shaped by Isabel Wilson, who remained the uncredited editor of these pamphlets for much of *CF*'s 20-year broadcast run. The details of her private life and her commitment to the impartiality of the study pamphlets she produced, as well as the myriad forces in society that structure gender to the disadvantage of women, have all contributed to Wilson's status as an unsung heroine of the CAAE.

This handbook is part of efforts in the field of adult education to reexamine our histories and the histories of our organizations, seeking out moments when the louder voices may have drowned out those on the margins. Isabel Wilson's is only one example of a woman's voice that has yet to be fully heard, but it is not because she was silent. The more than 300 *CF* study pamphlets that Wilson edited are clear evidence of the power of her words and her commitment to her work.

NOTE

1. Our research into Isabel Wilson has relied heavily on the contributions of Cynthia Flood, Wilson's niece, a Vancouver author who has generously provided access to her aunt's papers and Flood's own unpublished memoir of her aunt's life, "A Life in Quotations." Earlier versions of this chapter were presented at Department of Educational Studies at the University of British Columbia's Research Day Conference in April 2014 and the 2013 Canadian Association for the Study of Adult Education's annual conference held at the University of Victoria, June 3–5, 2013.

REFERENCES

Canadian Association for Adult Education (CAAE). (1950, December 7). Equal pay for equal work: Are women getting a fair deal? *Citizens' Forum.*

Corbett, E. A. (1957). *We have with us tonight.* Toronto, Canada: Ryerson.

Faris, R. (1975). *The passionate educators: Voluntary associations and the struggle for control of adult educational broadcasting in Canada 1919–52.* Toronto, Canada: Peter Martin.

Flood, C. (n.d.). *A life in quotations* [Unpublished memoir]. Vancouver, Canada.

Funeral Service Program. (1983, October 27). Biographical note on Isabel Wilson. Private Collection of Cynthia Flood. Vancouver, Canada.

McKenzie, R. (1970, October 23). [Letter to Isabel Wilson]. Private Collection of Cynthia Flood. Vancouver, Canada.

Sandwell, R. W. (2012). Read, listen, discuss, act: Adult education, rural citizenship and the National Farm Radio Forum, 1941–1965. *Historical Studies in Education, 24*(1), 170–194.

Selman, G. (1970, October 22). [Letter to Isabel Wilson]. Private Collection of Cynthia Flood. Vancouver, Canada.

Selman, G., Cooke, M., Selman, M., & Dampier, P. (1998). *The foundations of adult education in Canada* (2nd ed.). Toronto, Canada: Thompson Educational.

Wilson, I. (1980). *Citizens' Forum: "Canada's national platform."* Ontario Institute for Studies in Education, Department of Adult Education, Toronto.

PART III

CONCLUSION

CHAPTER 29

WOMEN, GENDER POLITICS, AND ADULT EDUCATION IN THE CONTEMPORARY WORLD

Leaning in to "Progress"

Juanita Johnson-Bailey and Elizabeth J. Tisdell

What a legacy we have! As we reflect on the state of women and gender politics in the contemporary world of adult education, we recognize that we are standing on the shoulders of the heroines who are the subjects of the previous chapters in this book. What an honor to be their beneficiaries and to continue to shape this legacy! In this chapter, we begin by reflecting on the contemporary context on gender issues in North America, and then consider our own writing and analytic context around gender as professors of adult education for over 20 years. Finally, we briefly conclude with some thoughts for the future.

GENDER DISCUSSIONS IN 2013 NORTH AMERICA

We write this in the fall of 2013. There has been a fair amount of discussion about gender issues in the contemporary United States of late, in part

No Small Lives: Handbook of North American Early Women Adult Educators, 1925-1950,
pp. 263–272
Copyright © 2015 by Information Age Publishing
263

due to the publication of Sheryl Sandberg's (2013) new book *Lean In: Women, Work, and the Will to Lead.* Sandberg, the 44-year-old chief operating officer at Google, with two Harvard degrees, is listed by Forbes as the fifth most powerful woman in the world (Corrigan, 2013). In the early pages, she characterizes her text as "sort of a feminist manifesto, but one that I hope inspires men as much as women" (p. 9). We argue that Sandberg is an adult educator dealing with gender in the workplace since there are many adults reading her book and discussing gender issues. With her encouragement, women are learning to move beyond their socialization of being "nice," and needing to be liked, to take leadership, and to "lean in" to their ambitions. While Sandberg acknowledges institutionalized sexism and the way the system unfairly privileges men, she deals more with issues of women's internalized oppression, which is why feminist themselves have mixed views on whether or not *Lean In* is really a feminist book.

So why consider Sheryl Sandberg and her book in this final chapter on contemporary women adult educators in light of the history that's gone before us? After all, one could also argue that Sandberg is not an adult educator, given that she is primarily a businesswoman, and she does not embody the traditions of education and social justice that informed the women discussed in this book. Further, she is not the only voice discussing women's issues in the contemporary world. Hillary Clinton, bell hooks, and Rachel Maddow also discuss them as a form of critical public pedagogy (Sandlin, Wright, & Clark, 2013), and Manicom and Walters (2012) recently edited a book on the subject. But we begin with a brief consideration of Sandberg's (2013) work as a grounding place for three primary reasons. First, she is a contemporary woman's voice on the status of gendered leadership in the workplace (albeit from a privileged position) who is very much in the popular press, a position that affords her the benefit of a bigger voice in the public pedagogy of the media, undeniably a form of adult education. Second, she is younger than either of the chapter authors, and her voice might resonate with younger women in search of public pedagogues. Third, she is discussing some of the issues we have experienced in higher education.

Some of Sandberg's (2013) stories conjured up moments of déjà vu for us. One in particular stands out. She recounts the story of real-life venture capitalist Heidi Roizen, a case study that two professors from Harvard used to get students to explore their unconscious biases of seeing men and women differently, even when the men and women possess the same characteristics. In this exercise, one group received the actual case, the story of a Heidi, a very successful woman. The other group got the same account with one modification: the protagonist's name was changed from "Heidi" to "Howard." Both groups of students saw the two as equally competent, but Howard was seen as "more appealing." By contrast, Heidi was seen as "selfish" and "not the type of person you want to hire or work for" (p. 40), according to the students. Sandberg closes her discussion of the case by noting "The same data with a single difference—gender—creates a vastly different impression" (p. 40). Indeed, in the years that we have been in the field of adult education, we have each experienced many people seeing through their gendered lenses, though these lenses remain largely unconscious. We show in the pages that follow how this plays out in the field of academic adult education.

GENDER IN ACADEMIC ADULT EDUCATION: OUR OWN PAST AND THE CURRENT PRESENT

We met in 1990 as doctoral students. Back then, long before we ever knew that we would eventually co-author this chapter, we would discuss issues of gender and race in informal settings, and in some classes. So when Ron Cervero, our professor, was invited to write a chapter on the subject for a *New Directions for Adult and Continuing Education* sourcebook on the subject of gender and race (Hayes & Colin, 1994), he very graciously invited us to join him as co-authors. In "Sandberg-speak," Ron invited us to "lean in" to our passion, and our result was the chapter "Race, Gender, and the Politics of Professionalization" (Johnson-Bailey, Tisdell, & Cervero, 1994). Ron (and other White men) have been important allies for the struggle for gender and race equality, and it's very important to have good allies who represent more of the power culture. Frankly, we admit that the chapter likely had more credibility not only because he was a well-known name at the time and we were recent doctoral graduates, but also partly because he was a White man who thought that issues of gender and race were important; his voice gave more legitimacy and credibility to these issues. It is now some 20 years later, and the two of us as co-authors are delighted to be working together again to continue our discussion on gender in our field. We are both now full professors in the academy, and we are incredibly grateful to our mentors like Ron Cervero and Phyllis Cunningham and Sharan Merriam, who helped us figure out how to navigate the system. We know that our voices have more legitimacy now than they did some 20 years ago. Nevertheless, the issues of gender in the politics of knowledge production even in 2013 are alive and well, and as, we will illustrate, White men's voices still appear to carry more academic legitimacy.

Gender and the Changing Face of Adult Education Over 20 Years

A surface analysis of the field by sheer numbers indicates that things have changed for women in adult education. In 1993, just like most academic fields of study, men outnumbered women in the professoriate by more than 4 to 1. Based on a study of adult education graduate programs in North America conducted in fall of 2013 (Tisdell et al., 2013) of the 224 faculty that are easily identified online as professors of adult education in North America on websites, 136 are women, which is slightly more than 60%. Indeed, this is progress on the one hand. But sheer numbers do not always tell the whole story. Some 43% of the men are full professors while only 32% of the women are. Further, men are more likely to be administrators and in leadership roles in the field. For example, in examining our academic institutions, both have male deans of education, although women are the majority faculty. The Adult Education Program at University of Georgia (UGA), examined in our original book chapter, only recently appointed its first woman department head in 2009, following 30 years of male leadership. The point is that while there clearly have been changes, change is relative and the progress for women in the academy has been in part co-opted by existing societal power structures. This becomes much more apparent in considering scholarship and whose knowledge counts.

Scholarship: What Knowledge Counts, Whose Knowledge Counts?

When one reads adult education literature, certain names are consistently cited and thus emerge as the "thought leaders" of the field: Knowles, Houle, Mezirow, and Brookfield. To ascertain who students regarded as leading adult education figures, in one of the largest graduate programs in the United States, a group of graduate students in a dissertation completion class were asked the following questions regarding their use of literature in their research:

- Name the major authors that you read in your classes.
- Who are the major writers that you cite in your work?
- What percentage of the authors that you read are females/males?
- What percentage of your teachers are females/males?

Each class of students over three consecutive years, 2010, 2011, and 2012, totaling 33 students was queried in small group settings and through a content analysis of their work. In listing the most referenced and widely read authors in adult education, certain names repeatedly emerged: Knowles, Mezirow, Freire, and Brookfield. Yet, when students were asked to name the premier textbooks, the names of women adult educators surfaced: Merriam, Caffarella (both authors of numerous books in the field), and Kasworm, Rose, & Ross-Gordon (2010) (as editors of the recent *Handbook*). This very illuminating exercise reveals a secret whose pattern emerges repeatedly as we examine various areas of our discipline, suggesting that males lead as creators and purveyors of knowledge and that women perform the daily maintenance work in the field (Butler, 1997).

This same phenomenon was noted when graduate students, who presented their research at the African Diaspora Preconference of the Adult Education Research Conference in 2005–2011, were questioned by members of the preconference executive committee. They were asked why they used White male adult educators as secondary citations in their research, showing a preference for referencing authors who were basing their writings on the work of Black women adult education researchers, such as Colin, Sheared, Johnson-Bailey, and Alfred. In each circumstance, answers included the information that the students were citing the more significant researchers, and they were using the works that were better known or recommended by their professors. It is important to note that this preference for and use of the work of males over females took place despite the fact that the majority of the students' professors (85%) were women faculty. Upon asking the second group of graduate students probing questions, we discovered that even when students were exposed to research that was generated by women, they favored citing the male researchers who quoted or interpreted the women's work.

On the surface, this tendency seems to indicate that there are two factions: those who create knowledge and those who disseminate knowledge, with men occupying the more exclusive position of knowledge-makers and women inhabiting the less central role of the worker bees, who distribute and broadcast the product. To offer a more nuanced argument, we recognized that our own work in spirituality (Tisdell) and on the intersection of race and gender in the field (Johnson-Bailey) is widely cited when authors are discussing this work. And of course those writing about narrative learning cite Rossiter and Clark (2007). But such "fluffy" or marginalized work in the areas of spirituality, gender or race, or narrative learning is not seen as central to the field. Part of this is due to the fact that Knowles, Houle (both of whom are now deceased), Mezirow, and Brookfield have been around for a long time. But so have Phyllis Cunningham (now deceased), Sharan Merriam, and Rosemary Caffarella. While their work is cited to be sure, they are not seen as the knowledge leaders to the extent that men are, at least by students, and likely others as well. Therefore, we set forth in this chapter that what is occurring in 2013 in our classrooms is a replication of the gender bias for privileging male knowledge over that of female knowledge, an occurrence that is pervasive throughout our society. So men continue to be regarded as the titlehold-ers of the essential knowledge-production process even though an envi-ronmental scan of journals sponsored by the American Association of Adult Education (*Adult Education Quarterly*, *Adult Learning*, and the *Journal of Transformative Education*), reveal that well over one half of the articles are written or co-authored by women.

To be more specific and to use the example of the *Adult Education Quar-terly* (*AEQ*), a content analysis of the last 20 years of *AEQ* was conducted to obtain data for this chapter. The analysis revealed that the journal has seen a marked increase in articles about women and by women over a 20-year period. From 1993 to 2003, there were 172 articles published in *AEQ*. Of that total, there were 25 articles that focused on women's issues or used a gender frame. There were 59 articles written by women (includ-ing multiple women co-authors); 27 articles co-authored by men/women, and 86 by men. The next 9 years (data for 2013 is unavailable), there were 160 articles. Of that total, 19 articles centered on women as the topic of the research or employed a feminist methodology; 79 were authored by women (including women co-authors); 18 were co-authored by men/women; and 63 were authored by men. In comparing the two sets of data, the number of articles that focused on women has held steady considering the variation of the total articles and the difference of 10 years to 9 years. However, the number of articles written by women has increased from 59 to 79 and the numbers of women authors who co-authored with men has decreased from 27 to 18. Therefore, it can be suggested that women are generating more research, a point that is logical given that there are more women adult education graduate students and faculty. However, the expected pipeline from journal to research studies is leaking; the work of the women publishing in *AEQ*, which, given that it appears in the field's premier journal, is undoubtedly cutting edge and most current, is not being used by adult education students. We must ask ourselves why. The discernible and logical answer is the one supplied by two separate groups of students: there is a preference for male knowledge. Masculine knowl-edge is familiar; it has a long and elite tradition; it is considered better.

Curriculum and Administration

When we critically examined our own academic programs, two of the largest adult education programs in the United States based on the num-ber of students and faculty, we found at Penn State and the University of Georgia comparable courses that cover historical and contemporary adult education, as well as courses that address the philosophical and social context relative to the field. However, courses specific to women and gender issues are relegated to the level of electives. These courses were added to both institutions' curricula in the last 20 years to attempt to deal directly with gender, but it is of note that such courses are not core requirements. It is likely assumed that such issues are either addressed in the required "Social and Historical Issues" course, or that attention to gender is present in all courses throughout the curriculum. But if the issues were being directly dealt with, and we are in fact raising students' and faculty consciousness, why do students tend to consistently see men as the primary knowledge creators of the field? We think it is because most people assume that sexism no longer exists since there are now more women than men in the professoriate and therefore they do not attend to possible matters of gender inequity.

Finally, we move to a surprisingly revelatory assessment of the most recent *Handbook of Adult and Continuing Education* (Kasworm et al., 2010) and of one of the most widely incorporated textbooks, *Learning in Adult- hood* (Merriam, Caffarella, & Baumgartner, 2007). The most recent *Hand- book* does not have a chapter dedicated to gender or women's issues, but has maintained a chapter on race and added chapters on sexuality and spirituality, presumably because such issues are more marginalized than others and need to be considered. The text, *Learning in Adulthood,* also fol- lows this pattern of omission by neglecting to include gender as a solitary topic for consideration. The assumption appears to be that gender is not necessarily the pressing issue it once was because the sheer numbers of women professors in the field has surpassed that of men. While this is true in part, such omission might indicate that it is no longer needed for con- sideration in the curriculum. Yet, as we have indicated, the subtle effects of sexism are still quite real.

Furthermore, when we look at two significant measures in the field of adult education for an assessment of standing—book awards and the International Hall of Fame in Adult and Continuing Education (IACE- HOF)—the circumstance of place and importance is informative. Since the IACEHOF's inception in 1996, there have been 198 men inducted and only 67 women. Moreover, since 1994, the field's most prestigious of book awards, the Cyril O. Houle Award for Outstanding Literature in Adult Education, has been awarded to 12 males and to 6 women authors. The Okes award recipients for an article represent a similar gender break- down. Interestingly, at the 2012 AAACE Conference, there was a tie for the Okes award, and it was given to two co-authored articles (one by two men, the other by a man and woman). It is not that these authors are not deserving of such awards, but the point is that there is a pattern here: despite the increased presence of women in the field, men still tend to be seen as the knowledge bearers, especially the ones who carry the stan- dards of excellence.

Our Academic Environment: The Faculty
and Students Comprising Adult Education Programs

Our original 1994 chapter examined and focused on the curriculum and relationships in the adult education program at the University of Georgia (UGA) where we were students. At that time, the field was experiencing dramatic growth as the numbers of programs and students (especially women and people of color) were increasing. In 1993, the UGA graduate program had 107 students—76 women and 31 men; the faculty for this program included five men (three professors and two associate professors) and two women (one professor and one associate professor). But things have changed considerably. Now, in 2013, the UGA Adult Education Graduate Program has 229 students—163 women and 66 men. But the number of students of color at the University of Georgia has decreased among both domestic and international groups. In general, the numbers of faculty in the UGA Adult Education program have remained steady in the ratio of men to women faculty; but unlike the larger academic environment, the rank distribution of the 11 tenure-track faculty has changed for the better. Two of the five men are professors and three are associate professors; four of the six women are professors, with one associate and one assistant professor. In this regard, women have made tremendous gains in terms of numbers and rank as there are proportionately more women full professors. However, the faculty ratios at UGA are an anomaly when compared to other adult education programs. Nevertheless, what UGA does demonstrate is how the field of adult education has taken leadership on gender and adult education, a point that we will take up again in the conclusion.

A survey of the complete field, beyond UGA, shows that rather than growing in students and faculty, in 2013 the opposite is occurring, as adult education programs across the United States are disappearing, downsizing, or merging with human resource and organizational development and/or continuing and higher education programs. Correspondingly, as the numbers of women in graduate programs grew so too did the number of females entering the professoriate. And we reasoned that as women progressed through the ranks from assistant to full professors that they brought a change in all dimensions, especially in the areas of leadership and scholarship. Indeed, there have been some obvious gains in the way women have taken leadership. While the bulk of women in leadership positions tend to be only as high as the associate dean level and the majority of full professors are still men, we have seen considerable change. Part of it may be that women have not "leaned in" to their ambitions for leadership as administrators, but they have "leaned in" and taken leadership with their passion and their scholarship.

SOME GOOD NEWS AND SOME TENTATIVE CONCLUSIONS

During our 2 decades as adult education faculty, we have witnessed many changes. Foremost of the transformations has been an evolving gender consciousness that has been reflected in a modified curriculum that is infused with social justice around issues of gender, race, and sexuality. Additionally, being on the front lines has afforded us a vantage point from which to observe the field, witnessing the increased number of women who have flowed into the academy; our positions have given us the opportunity to assess their research and leadership, noting that their work indicates that they have embraced a social justice perspective in an attempt to "make space" (Sheared & Sissel, 2001) and to make a difference. They are—we are—actually "leaning in" to our ambitions in numerous ways. One of the things that Belenky, Clinchy, Goldberger, and Tarule wrote about back in 1986 is the importance of connection and relationship in women's knowing and learning. Indeed, it is this connection and relationship that caused us to come together to participate in this public discussion of gender and race with each other, with Ron Cervero, and with the field. It is this penchant for connection and relationship in learning and knowing that caused many women adult educators to come together to establish the African Diaspora and Pacific Rim preconferences at the Adult Education Research Conference, to form the Women's Special Interest Group at CPAE, and to meet numerous summers on Yukon Island in Alaska to support each other and to make change in the world. It is on that island, where we as women adult educators highlighted those women who have inspired us historically, and who have subsequently been written about so beautifully in this book, contributing to the knowledge base in the field. As women, we are pleased to join in contributing their stories to the knowledge base of our field. As women, we are grateful to our adult education foremothers, and of the legacy left to us by these women on whose shoulders we stand. We are also honored to share in the continued shaping of that legacy. Blessed be.

REFERENCES

Belenky, M., Clinchy, B., Goldberger, N., & Tarule, J. (1986). *Women's ways of knowing*. New York, NY: Basic.

Butler, J. (1997). *Excitable speech: A politics of the performative*. New York, NY: Routledge.

Corrigan, M. (2013, March 12). '*Lean in*': Not much of a manifesto, but still a win for women. NPR. Retrieved from www.npr.org/2013/03/12/174016175/

Hayes, E., & Colin, S. A. J., III. (Eds.). (1994). Confronting racism and sexism. *New Directions for Adult and Continuing Education, No 61*. San Francisco, CA: Jossey-Bass.

Johnson-Bailey, J., Tisdell, E., & Cervero, R. (1994). Race, gender, and the politics of professionalization. In E. Hayes & S. A. J. Colin III (Eds.), *Confronting racism and sexism* (pp. 63–76). *New Directions in Adult and Continuing Education, No 61*. San Francisco, CA: Jossey-Bass.

Kasworm, C., Rose, A., & Ross-Gordon, J. (Eds.). (2010). *The handbook of adult and continuing education*. Thousand Oaks, CA: Sage.

Manicom, L., & Walters, S. (2012). *Feminist popular education in transnational debates*. New York, NY: Palgrave MacMillan.

Merriam, S., Caffarella, R., & Baumgartner, L. M. (2007). *Learning in adulthood: A comprehensive guide*. San Francisco, CA: Jossey-Bass.

Rossiter, M., & Clark, M. C. (2007). *Narrative and the practice of adult education*. Malabar, FL: Krieger.

Sandberg, S. (2013). *Lean in: Women, work, and the will to lead*. New York, NY: Knopf.

Sandlin, J., Wright, R. R., & Clark, M. C. (2013). Reexamining theories of adult learning and adult development through the lenses of public pedagogy. *Adult Education Quarterly, 63*, 3–23.

Sheared, V., & Sissel P. A. (Eds.). (2001). *Making space: Merging theory and practice in adult education*. Westport, CT: Bergin & Garvey.

Tisdell, E., Redmon Wright, R., Taylor, E., Greenawalt, A., Boyd, G., & Bush, P. (2013). *A study of faculty perceptions of graduate programs in adult education: Current status and faculty satisfaction*. Presentation at the American Association of Adult and Continuing Education. Lexington, KY.

CHAPTER 30

THEMES ACROSS THE WOMEN'S LIVES

Susan Imel and Gretchen T. Bersch

The book's title, *No Small Lives,* was selected because it aptly describes the 26 women profiled. They were energetic and creative leaders who were innovative in their efforts, which touched directly or indirectly on the field of adult education, broadly defined. Many were involved in the development of the field and in shaping the knowledge base through their work as writers and editors. Others would not have considered themselves adult educators, although part of what they did involved teaching or training and/or advocating for adults. They worked in a period before women's rights were protected by law and they still made an impact. Also, "they were integral to the development of adult education in the twentieth century" (Rose, Chapter 1). This chapter looks across the women's stories to examine common themes. It begins with some general demographic information. Next, several themes are described, demonstrating commonalities across the diverse narratives. The chapter concludes with some observations about the need to continue the research into the lives of women who were instrumental in the development and shaping of the field of adult education.

DEMOGRAPHIC INFORMATION

Basic demographic information provides insights into the women included in the book. The women were born between 1868 and 1911. Nine, or nearly 35%, lived into their 90s and another five lived into their

No Small Lives: Handbook of North American Early Women Adult Educators, 1925-1950,
pp. 273–280
Copyright © 2015 by Information Age Publishing

eighth decade. As a group, they were remarkably long lived with a few exceptions. (See Table 30.1 for birth and death dates of all the women.)

Since most of the women whose names are identified with the field's early years were White, an effort was made to identify women of other races and cultures for inclusion in the book. Of the women profiled, 18 were White, 4 were African American, 2 were Hispanic, 1 was Native American, and 1 Native Alaskan.

For the era, the women were a remarkably well-educated group; all but 3 of the 25 for which information about education is available had at least some college. Four had a PhD, and several had advanced degrees. Five had degrees from Columbia University; three of these were a PhD, two of which were in adult education. Three had degrees in library science and beyond that the degree fields varied and included psychology, history, economics, ethics, home economics, French, and social work. (See Table 30.1 for information on education.)

In a time period when marriage and child bearing was an expectation for women, 10 were single, 1 was divorced, 3 were widowed, and none of the divorced and widowed women remarried. Only 7 of the 16 women who were (or had been married) had children. One can only speculate why more were not mothers. At least one, who was childless, lost two children in infancy; two others lost children as infants but went on to have other children who survived. Two—Jean Carter Ogden and Bonaro Wilkinson Overstreet—married men who had children from previous marriages and became partners in two-career marriages, factors that may have affected decisions about children. The narratives say nothing about possible struggles with infertility, which also may have been a reason more were not mothers.

CONNECTING THEMES

A number of common themes emerge from the narratives about the work of the women.

The Carnegie Corporation and Associations

All roads lead to Carnegie. Because Carnegie funded the American Association for Adult Education (AAAE), the connections between the two were almost seamless and this connection is evident in the work of a number of the women included in the book.

This connection was especially important during the Depression; Carnegie funding was the reason that the Association survived through

Table 30.1.   Demographic Information

Name	Birth Year	Death Year	Education (Terminal Degree)
Lucy Wilcox Adams	1898	1996	Stanford; left one semester before graduation
Nora Bateson	1896	1956	MA, McGill
Nannie Helen Burroughs	1879	1961	Secondary School graduate
Fabiola Cabeza de Baca Gilbert	1894	1991	BA, New Mexico State University
Olive Dame Campbell	1882	1954	BA, Tufts
Jessie Allen Charters	1880	1971	PhD, University of Chicago
Jean Carter Ogden	1897	1974	No information; taught school so assume at least a BA
Eve Chappell	1874	1949	No information
Mary L. Ely	1881	1950	MA, Columbia
Dorothy Canfield Fisher	1879	1958	PhD, Columbia
Mary Parker Follett	1868	1933	BA, Society for the Collegiate Instruction of Women (now Radcliffe); postgraduate study in Paris
Mae C. Hawes	1886	1979	MA, Columbia; postgraduate work
Maria Latigo Hernández	1896	1986	Secondary School graduate
Dorothy Hewitt	1897	1987	AB, Vassar
Virginia Estelle Randolph	1874	1958	2 years, Virginia State College
Ruth Kotinsky	1903	1955	PhD, Teachers College, Columbia
Roberta Campbell Lawson	1878	1940	BA, Hardin College
Florence O'Neill	1905	1990	PhD, Teachers College, Columbia
Bonaro Wilkinson Overstreet	1902	1985	MA, Columbia
Elizabeth Peratrovich	1911	1958	2 years, Bellingham Normal (now Western Washington College of Education)
Harriett Rouillard	1904	1987	BA, Smith
Amy Paddon Row	1884	1977	BA, Bella Vista College
Dorothy Rowden	1901	2000	BA, Simmons College
Hilda Worthington Smith	1888	1984	MA, Bryn Mawr; postgraduate work
Moranda Smith	1915	1950	Secondary School graduate
Isabel Wilson	1904	1983	BA, University of Toronto

that period. During the Depression, Carnegie funding of the Association supported the employment of a number of the women profiled as staff, researchers, and writers.

Between 1926 and 1941, eight of the women wrote books, published by the Association and funded by Carnegie, including Chappell, Ely, Fisher, Kotinsky, Rowden, Carter Ogden, and Overstreet; and the Association also co-published a book by Hilda W. Smith. The *Journal of Adult Educa-tion*, with Mary Ely as editor, was funded by Carnegie. Six of the women were on the AAAE staff as research or field representatives, directors of projects, or working in other roles including Eve Chappell, Mary Ely, Mae Hawes, Ruth Kotinsky, Dorothy Rowden, and Jean Carter Ogden. Four worked in projects or institutes outside of AAAE that were funded by Carnegie—Lucy Wilcox Adams, Nora Batson, Olive Campbell, and Jessie Charters. Lucy Adams and Dorothy Rowden worked with Carnegie-funded radio projects.

In Chapter 1, Rose describes the relationship between the Carnegie Corporation and Columbia University. Like AAAE, the university also played a role in the lives and work of several of the women. As shown in Table 30.1, several earned degrees from Columbia. Mary Ely also co-taught a summer course there. When Carnegie funding ended in 1941, Mary Ely and Dorothy Rowden carried on the adult education work as employees of the Institute of Adult Education at Columbia.

The Carnegie Corporation also provided some financial assistance that led to the formation of the Canadian Association for Adult Education (CAAE) in 1935 (Selman & Draper, 1991). Both Harriett Rouillard and Isabel Wilson were active in the publications program of CAAE, Harriett as the long-time editor of *Food for Thought* and Isabel as author of discussion guides for the *Citizens' Forum* radio program.

Discussion as a Delivery Method and Adult Education for Democracy

Discussion-based programming for adults as a delivery method was woven throughout several of the women's stories. Preparing adults to be more effective citizens in a democratic society was the goal of much of this discussion; this goal was consistent with the Carnegie Corporation's beliefs about adult education as described by Rose in Chapter 1. The Carnegie Corporation funded the California Association for Adult Education to develop discussion programs, and Lucy Wilcox Adams wrote about these efforts. Through AAAE, the Carnegie Corporation provided support for the book *Why Forums?* by Mary Ely. Ely traveled all over the country visiting Forums in order to assess their effectiveness as a means of preparing adults to address civic issues through discussion. At the Boston Center for Adult Education, Dorothy Hewitt also mounted an extensive program of discussion programs to fulfill her agenda of the "development of conscientious and responsible adults who would contribute to society" (Wolf, Chapter 16). Jessie Allen Charters was another proponent of discussion as a method of exposing group members to multiple perspectives on a topic. In collaboration with her spouse, Harry, Bonaro Wilkinson Overstreet wrote about the town hall, a form of discussion-based adult education. In Canada, Isabel Wilson authored pamphlets that were used by discussion groups following *Citizens' Forum* radio broadcasts.

Advocacy

The 19th amendment to the U.S. Constitution giving women the right to vote was ratified in 1920, just 6 years before the AAAE was organized, so it was a time of great change for women in North America as they continued to work for civil rights and social justice. Olive Dame Campbell was a social activist and community organizer in Appalachia; Isabel Wilson worked, especially through radio, for social justice and rights for women across Canada. While she might not be called an activist, Amy Padden Row was an advocate working with women in prisons.

Women of color worked for civil rights: Nannie Helen Burroughs was an activist who worked for African American civil rights; Mae C. Hawes taught and worked to give African American adults equal access to education and civic opportunities. Fabiola Cabeza de Baca Gilbert worked for Hispanic civil rights, and Maria Latigo Hernández worked for equal education and political involvement for Mexican Americans. Alaska Native Elizabeth Peratrovich gave moving testimony that prompted passage of civil rights legislation in Alaska; and Roberta Campbell, with her own American Indian heritage, supported Indian rights and promoted American Indian music and art.

Workers rights were an area of advocacy. Moranda Smith was a Black union activist in the South. Hilda Worthington Smith and Jean Carter, White women, were leaders in women's worker education especially for immigrant women. Virginia Estelle Randolph was a Black leader who focused on educational methods married with community development.

Leadership

Most of the women profiled demonstrated leadership, some of it in tandem with their advocacy work. Hilda Worthington Smith and Moranda Smith, for example, were leaders in labor education and, in Moranda's case, labor unions.

The women both founded and led existing organizations. Nannie Helen Burroughs, Olive Campbell, Sylvia Latigo Hernández, Dorothy Hewitt, Elizabeth Peratrovich, and Amy Paddon Row all started and led organizations. Both Dorothy Canfield Fisher and Roberta Campbell Lawson served as leaders of national organizations. Lucy Wilcox Adams became the director of the California Association for Adult Education. Roberta Campbell Lawson overcame racist slurs to become the General Federation of Women's Clubs national president. Several women, including Mary Ely, Harriett Rouillard, Dorothy Rowden, and Isabel Wilson provided leadership in the publications of AAAE and CAAE, and Mary worked closely with Morse Cartwright, Executive Director of AAAE.

Others exhibited leadership in education and government agencies. Jessie Allen Charters, who led the development of parenting skills in the United States, started the graduate program in adult education at Ohio State University. Florence O'Neill led a provincial government department of adult education. Nora Bateson provided leadership for the development of a regional public library system on Prince Edward Island, led library development work in the province of Nova Scotia and in Jamaica, and later became the director of the New Zealand Library School. As the first Spanish-speaking Cooperative Extension Agent in New Mexico, Fabiola Cabeza de Baca worked to improve the lives of New Mexico's rural population and, due to her success, later established programs in Mexico through UNESCO.

Building the Knowledge Base

Many of the women represented in this book were involved in editing books and journals, and writing books and articles that formed an important part of the literature base of the field during these years. In Chapter 1, Rose describes the significant role women played in the publication program of AAAE, pointing out that by 1941 women ran every aspect of program (but then lost their jobs when Carnegie ceased funding AAAE later that year). Mary Ely edited the *Journal of Adult Education*, Dorothy Rowden served as editor for the AAAE special publications program. One or the other of them edited the first three handbooks, a series that continues today. Likewise in Canada, Harriett Rouillard served as editor of CAAE's *Food for Thought* and Isabel Wilson was developing discussion guides for the *Citizens' Forum* radio broadcasts.

In addition to AAAE-sponsored publications, the women wrote books that were published by mainline presses. One of the best known of these works is Dorothy Canfield Fisher's *Why Stop Learning*, which was published by Harcourt Press. Ruth Kotinsky's *Adult Education and the Social Scene* was published by D. Appleton Century, and Dorothy Hewitt, co-authored *Adult Education: A Dynamic for Democracy*, published by Appleton-Century-Crofts. Olive Dame Campbell used her experiences from a visit to Denmark as the basis for *The Danish Folk School: Its Influence in the Life of Den-*

mark and the North, a book that was published by Macmillan. With her husband, Jess Ogden, Jean Carter Ogden wrote about their experiences in community development in the book, *Small Communities in Action: Stories of Citizen Programs at Work*, which was published by Harper. Bonaro Wilkinson Overstreet authored a number of books that were intended to help adults understand their lives. In conjunction with her husband, Harry, she also wrote *Town Meeting Comes to Town*, which was published by Harper.

The women also produced other types of materials for use by adult learners. Nannie Burroughs started and edited a magazine and wrote guides for the members of the Woman's Missionary Union of the Southern Baptist Convention. In Ohio, Jessie Allen Charters was busy producing materials on parent education. In New Mexico, Fabiola Cabeza de Baca Gilbert developed circulars on new methods of food preservation and also wrote *Historic Cookery*, a cookbook that was reprinted many times and sold more than 100,000 copies. Hilda Worthington Smith and Jean Carter Ogden produced material used in labor education. Mary Parker Follett's work was influential in shaping the ideas of the field's early leaders, including Eduard Lindeman. She wrote in diverse areas, including community organizing and organizational development, and her thinking was influential in Japan and Great Britain.

The contributions mentioned here are given much fuller treatment in the chapters on the individual women. Certainly the work of women in producing publications and contributing to the literature of the field was not insignificant, but much of it has been lost to the field because it is unavailable—even in most university collections.

CONCLUSION

Gender is the common denominator across the lives of the women featured in this book. In *Interpreting Women's Lives*, the Personal Narratives Group (1989) warns that using only gender as an organizing factor can mask "greater recognition and appreciation of differences among women" (p. 19). In describing some of the common themes, it was not our intent to diminish the diversity of the lives of the women. Rather it was an attempt to pull together some of the common factors across their stories and help the reader to make sense of a large number of narratives.

As told in the chapters in this book, the women's individual stories reveal little about their ideas regarding feminism and/or women's rights, although several worked for women's rights and some were involved in marriages in which they worked with their spouses and/or had strong support from a spouse. Since the profiles in this book reveal so little directly about their personal beliefs regarding women's rights, it can only be assumed that most would be considered feminists, that is, they probably believed that women and men should have equal rights.

The lives of the women bear out Rose's observations about women "being the work horses" and doing the "grunt work," but they also reveal other facets. They were leaders and advocates; they contributed to the field's literature base; they were feisty—at least three lost their jobs because they pushed back against organizational forces; they "leaned in" to their ambitions. They were central to building the enterprise of adult education (Hugo, Chapter 2). Why then have the contributions of most of these women been largely overlooked? In her chapter, Hugo cites three main reasons: (a) beginning in 1930, the focus on defining and establishing adult education as a profession; (b) the privileged position held by men—generally they held the power; and (c) the tendency of the field's historians "to draw on data sources that told of the story of the field becoming more clearly defined as 'purposeful' and 'systematic'" (Hugo, Chapter 2).

Have things really changed that much? According to Johnson-Bailey and Tisdell, even today, men are still considered the "thought leaders" in terms of whose work is cited, while women "perform the maintenance work in the field," that is, they still do the "grunt work." They also make the observation that many still view the field "through their gendered lenses, though these lenses remain largely unconscious" (Johnson-Bailey & Tisdell, Chapter 29). It is our hope that this book can play a role in changing some of the long-held perceptions about the role and contributions of women in the field of adult education.

REFERENCE

Personal Narratives Group. (1989). "Conditions not of her own making." In Personal Narrative Group (Eds.), *Interpreting women's lives: Feminist theory and personal narratives* (pp. 19–23). Bloomington: Indiana University Press.

Selman, G. R., & Draper, P. (1991). *Foundations of adult education in Canada.* Toronto, Ontario, Canada: Thompson Educational Publishing.

APPENDIX A

Other Notable Women From 1925 to 1950

Carole L. Lund

Jane Addams (1860–1935): Born in Cedarville, Illinois

Addams is known as a social reformer, feminist, and peace advocate. Although she was born into wealth and privilege, she was dedicated to helping the poor. She co-founded Chicago's Hull House in 1889, where services were provided to the poor and immigrants. Eventually the services included educational courses, kitchen, and social programs (Jane Addams, 2014). In 1931, Addams became the second woman to be awarded the Nobel Peace Prize. She was the co-winner of the award with Nicholas Murray Butler. Jane received the award for beginning the Women's International League for Peace and Freedom, where she served as president from 1919 to 1929 (Jane Addams, 2014, Other Roles, para. 4). She was known as a leading pacifist in the nation; she was dedicated to peace agreements internationally (Jane Addams, 2014).

Margaret E. Burton (1885–1969): Born in Newton, Massachusetts

When she was 23 years old, Burton accompanied her father to the Far East; during the trip she focused on the "state of women's education" (Stasson, n.d., para. 1). When she returned in 1909, she researched China's and Japan's history of education. She published *The Education of*

No Small Lives: Handbook of North American Early Women Adult Educators, 1925-1950,
pp. 281–293
Copyright © 2015 by Information Age Publishing
All rights of reproduction in any form reserved.

Women in China in 1911 and *The Education of Women in Japan* in 1914 as a result of her research. These books indicate her belief in "Christian missionaries" as key to women's education (Stasson, n.d., para. 2). She changed this view to one of the "world as a neighborhood ... problems of one country affect other countries" (Stasson, n.d., para. 3). She served on the executive board of the American Association for Adult Education and secretary for foreign students of the National YWCA and then the executive secretary of the Department of Education and Research of the National Board of the YWCA. After a return visit to China in 1921, she wrote *New Paths for Old Purposes: World Challenges to Christianity in our Generation* (1927) (Stasson, n.d., para. 3). Throughout her life, Burton was dedicated to women's education and believed there was a link between evangelism and education.

Mollie Ray Carroll (1890–1977): Born in Des Moines, Iowa

Carroll received her PhB in 1911, MA in 1915, and PhD in 1920 from the University of Chicago (Mollie Ray Carroll, 1926–1927, para. 2). She was the special agent and assistant inspector for the Child Labor Division of the U.S. Children's Bureau from 1917 to 1918; a staff lecturer at the Chicago School of Civics and Philanthropy from 1918 to 1920; assistant professor from 1920 to 1921; professor and chairman of the Department of Economics and Sociology beginning in 1924 at Goucher College. She was also an instructor at the University of Chicago the summer of 1926 (Mollie Ray Carroll, 1926–1927, para. 3). Later she was an industrial economist for the U. S. Department of Labor and training specialist in social security from 1942 to 1955 (Carroll, 1971, p. 1). Her publications include "Labor and Politics: The Attitude of the American Federation of Labor toward Legislation and Politics" (Hart, Schaffner & Marx Prize Essay) in 1923; Supplement to the Second Edition of R. F. Hoxie's "Trade Unionism in the United States" in 1923; and articles in *The Journal of Social Forces*, *American Federationist*, and the *Woman Citizen* (Mollie Ray Carroll, 1926–1927, para. 4). She also published "Bureaucratic Explosion" in 1971 (Carroll, 1971).

Eleanor Gwinnell Coit (1894–1976): Born in Newark, New Jersey

Coit received her AB from Smith College (1916) and AM from Columbia University (1919) (Eleanor Gwinnell Coit Papers, 1913–1974, para. 1). In 1910 through the 1920s, she worked in New Jersey and Buffalo, New York, with the YWCA. Coit was involved with the Bryn Mawr Summer School for Women Workers; she was one of the YWCA industrial secretaries who served the institution (Heller, 1989). This summer school became a model for others and by 1926 was admitting Black students for residential study (Heller, 1989, para.1). Coit became the education director of the Affiliated Schools for Workers in 1929 (Eleanor Gwinnell Coit Papers, 1913–1974, para. 11). From 1934 to 1962 Coit was the director of the American Labor Education Service. This organization was instrumental in establishing education programs for workers. She was also involved in the Committee of Correspondence (Eleanor Gwinnell Coit Papers, 1913–1974, para. 1). Coit published the chapter "Workers' Education" in the 1948 *Handbook of Adult Education in the United States* (Hugo, 1990). She was involved in the development of the Adult Education Association of the USA (AEA-USA) in 1950 as a member of the Joint Committee on Membership and the Sarah Lawrence College Working Conference. She was also on the AEA-USA's National Organizing Committee and in 1951 became a member of the AEA-USA's executive committee (Hiemstra, 2003).

Anna J. Cooper (1858–1964): Born in North Carolina

Cooper began life with her "enslaved mother … and her white slaveholder" (Harris-Perry & Stewart, 2012, para. 1). Cooper's career as an activist began at the age of 9 when she protested the "preferential treatment given to men" (Harris-Perry & Stewart, 2012, para. 2) so she could take classes only available to boys. She continued her academic career at Oberlin College where she obtained her BA in 1884 and went on to graduate with a master's in mathematics in 1887 (Harris-Perry & Stewart, 2012, para. 2). In 1924, she earned her PhD at the University of Paris, the fourth Black woman in the United States to achieve a doctorate. As a highly educated and articulate scholar, Cooper challenged the limitations and lack of opportunity for women of color throughout her lifetime (Harris-Perry & Stewart, 2012, para. 1). She began her academic career at M Street School, the "only all black school" (Harris-Perry & Stewart, 2012, para. 2) in Washington, DC, as a math and science teacher; she was promoted to principal in 1902. Her initiative to prepare her students for college instead of vocational trades was met with hostility, even though her students went to well-known universities; Harvard even gave M Street School accreditation (Harris-Perry & Stewart, 2012, para. 4). She was dismissed from M Street School in 1906 and was rehired in 1910. She retired from M Street School in 1930 and accepted the position of president at Frelinghuysen University, where she worked for 20 years (Harris-Perry & Stewart, 2012, para. 7). She left this school in 1954 at the age of 95. She was the founder of the Colored Women's League of Washington in 1892 and assisted opening the first YWCA chapter for Black women in 1899 (Harris-Perry & Stewart, 2012, para. 5). She challenged the women's movement for neglecting to advocate for Black women; the movement allowed racism to persist. She challenged the domination of White males and never relinquished her ideal, an equal society that was just (Harris-Perry & Stewart, 2012, para. 6). She was highly published, beginning with "A Voice from the South" in 1892; "Paper by Mrs. Anna J. Cooper" in 1894; "The American Negro Academy" in 1898; and "Colored Women as Wage Earners" in 1899 to name a few (Harris-Perry & Stewart, 2012).

Linda Eastman (1867–1963): Born in Oberlin, Ohio

Eastman was the first woman "to head a metropolitan library system [Cleveland Public Library from 1918 to 1938] in the U. S." (Eastman, n.d., Biography, para. 2). She was one of the women involved in the organization of the American Association for Adult Education (AAAE) and later served on the executive board of AAAE (Rose, Chapter 1, this volume). Eastman was instrumental in developing "adult education programs, the open shelf system, school and children's libraries, and a book distribution program for shut-ins" (Eastman, n.d., Biography, para. 2). Her innovations provided special services to children, the handicapped, blind, and hospitalized (Linda Ann Eastman, n.d., para. 1). She was at Western Reserve University's School of Library Science as an instructor (1904) and professor (1918–1937) and American Library Association leadership (1928–1929) (Eastman, n.d., Biography, para. 3). Eastman was the recipient of library awards and honorary degrees from Oberlin College in 1924, Western Reserve University in 1928, and Mount Holyoke College in 1933 (Eastman, n.d., Biography, para. 4). Some of her articles included: "A Library Pilgrimage" in *The Index* (1900); "Branch Libraries and Other Distributing Agencies" (1911) (Eastman, n.d., Inventory, #7).

Joan Erikson (1902–1997): Born in Toronto, Canada

Erikson was a "dancer, choreographer, jeweler, poet, teacher, writer, and researcher" (Benveniste, 1998, p. 1). She graduated from Barnard College and obtained a master's degree from Columbia Teachers College and "completed the course work for a doctorate and [went] to Vienna to do research for a dissertation on dance" (Thomas, 1997, para. 3). Erikson was a teacher at the Hietzing School in Vienna along with Erik Erikson in the 1920s and 1930s. In the 1940s, Erikson initiated the "creative arts program at the Austen Riggs Center, in Stockbridge Massachusetts, a residential psychiatric facility" (Benveniste, 1998, p. 1). She continued her work in the late 1970s as a "Senior Consultant on the Adolescent In-patient Unit at Mt. Zion Hospital in San Francisco" (Benveniste, 1998, p. 1). Erikson was a prolific writer, documenting her experiences at the Austen Riggs Center, *Activity, Recovery, and Growth: The Communal Role of Planned Activities* in 1976 (Benveniste, 1998, p. 2). Other publications included *Mata Ni Pachedi: A Book on the Temple Cloth of the Mother Goddess* in 1968; *The Universal Bead* in 1969, 1993; and *St. Francis and His Four Ladies* in 1970. Erikson was married to Erik Erikson, one of the foremost psychoanalysts in the world, for 64 years; she shared his passion for research on the Eight Ages of Psychosocial Development (Beneveniste, 1998, p. 1). After his death, she used his notes and her own experience to add the ninth stage of development; she covered this final stage of development by writing three chapters in the reissue of the book, *Life Cycle Completed* published in 1997 (Benveniste, 1998; Thomas,1997). She and her husband spent the 1960s at Harvard; they taught classes together in the 1980s at the Joan and Erik Erikson Center (Thomas, 1997, para. 17). She co-authored *Vital Involvement in Old Age* in 1986; and authored a number of publications up to 1996 (Benveniste, 1998, p. 2).

Winifred Fisher (1897–1967): Born in Delanson, New York

Fisher was valedictorian of her Schenectady High School class in 1911 (Miss Fisher dies, 1967, p. 10). In 1914, she attended the student government convention at Radcliffe College as a representative of Syracuse University (Syracuse University Annals, 1914, p. 209). Fisher was the executive director of the New York Adult Education Council, Inc. (NYAEC) from 1942 to 1948; she served with Harry J. Carman, president, and Eduard C. Lindeman, vice president. In 1953, she was a member of NYAEC. She was awarded the George Arents Pioneer Medal in 1946 for excellence in her field of study as alumnae of Syracuse University (Syracuse University Archives, 2010). Fisher (1943) authored the book, *The People are Ready to Discuss the Post-War World: A Report of an Experiment in Adult Education.* She was the co-editor of the book, *The Story of a Discussion Program: Veterans and their Neighbors Get Together on Public Issues / by Joseph Cahn and Others* (Ballaine & Fisher, 1946). Fisher (1953) also published "Eduard C. Lindeman, 1885–1953."

Jennie Maas Flexner (1882–1944): Born in Louisville, Kentucky

Although Jennie Flexner never finished higher education, she joined the Free Public Library of Louisville as a staff member in 1903. After 2 years she moved to the Louisville Public Library as a secretary, her first paying job (Halpert, 2009). In 1908 she did attend the School of Library Service at the Western Reserve University of Cleveland (Halpert, 2009). From 1912 to 1928 she returned to the Louisville Public Library and was in charge of the circulation department. She advocated for a "reader-centered" library instead of book-centered. She also advocated for "service to the black community and the training of black and white librarians" (Brody, 1996, para. 5). In 1926 she was on the curriculum staff of the American Library Association to work on the selection and resources for professional education of librarians. In 1927 she wrote "Circulation Work in Public Libraries;" it was used as a text in library schools (Brody, 1996). Flexner was dedicated to building a library collection for all ages and various "racial, social and ethnic backgrounds" (Brody, 1996, para. 8). In the 1930s she continued her involvement in training and education by working with refugees coming to America. She was hired by the New York Public Library in 1928 as a readers' adviser and held this position until she died. She published "Readers and Books" in the *Library Journal* in 1938 (Halpert, 2009, para. 4) and "Making Books Work: A Guide to the Use of the Libraries" in 1943 (Halpert, 2009, para. 5).

Mary John, Sr. (1913–2004):
Born in Lheidll, Prince George, British Columbia

Although Mary John's childhood was marked with struggle, she remained optimistic about the future. She and her husband raised 12 children, all born outside of a hospital between 1930 and 1949. During this same time she worked at St. John's Hospital in Vanderhoof where she later taught terminology to the staff. She was also a local midwife in the community (Twigg, 2005). In 1942 she "was the first President of the Saik'uz chapter" of the BC Homemakers Association (Erickson, 2004, Obituary). In the 1950s Mary John began a welfare committee to help place children in indigenous foster care. In the 1970s she "taught language and culture in St. Joseph's School." She also taught Carrier for adults; Carrier is an Eyak-Athabaskan language of Canada (Lewis, Simons, & Fennig, 2013, p. 1). She became involved in the Yinka Dene Language Institute and was involved in the *Saik'uz Children's Dictionary* and other resources for teaching (Erickson, 2004, Obituary). She continued to use her language and worked to preserve it by contributing to the Saik'us Dictionary; the dictionary now has "over eight thousand entries" (Erickson, 2004, Obituary). Mary John Sr. became the Citizen of the Year in Vanderhoof; she was the first Native recipient of this award (Erickson, 2004, Obituary). Her popular book, *Stoney Creek Woman: The Story of Mary John* (14th ed.) (Moran, 2007) received the Lieutenant Governor's Medal for Historical Writing from the B. C. Historical Federation in 1990 (Twigg, 2005). In the 1980s she and her family began the Stoney Creek Elders Society; this organization was concerned with the "economic, social and political process" (Erickson, 2004, Obituary). John never forgot to teach others about culture.

Louise Leonard McLaren (1885–1968):
Born in Wellsboro, Pennsylvania

McLaren was the originator of the Southern Summer School for Women Workers and known for being a labor leader. McLaren attended the School for Girls in Harrisburg in 1904 and entered Vassar College; she graduated with an AB in 1907 (Frederickson, 1980). In 1927 she attended Columbia University to study economics and graduated with an AM degree (Frederickson, 1980). In the early years she taught history in high school and then in college. By 1914 she decided to leave teaching and began her career as the YWCA Industrial Secretary; in 1920 she became the Industrial Secretary for the South (Frederickson, 1980). This position held her interest for "the next 25 years" (Frederickson, 1980, p. 452). In 1921 McLaren organized the Southern Summer School for Women Workers in Industry. The school was modeled after the Bryn Mawr Summer School for Women Workers (Frederickson, 1980). "More than 300 working-class women came to summer residence sessions" (Frederickson, 1980, p. 453). McLaren resigned as the director in 1944. In New York she served as the CIO Political Action Committee along with a number of other jobs. She finally returned to workers' education in a teaching and research position with the American Labor Education Service (Frederickson, 1980).

Nina Otero-Warren (1881–1965): Born in Las Lunas, New Mexico

Otero-Warren attended Maryville College of the Sacred Heart in St. Louis, Missouri (1892–1894) (Adelina "Nina" Otero-Warren, n.d., para. 1). Throughout her life she was dedicated to being a suffragist, educator, politician, entrepreneur, and writer (Massmann, 2000). Part of her legacy was her initiative to preserve historic buildings in Santa Fe and Taos; she renewed "interest in and respect for Hispanic and Indian culture" (Adelina "Nina" Otero-Warren, n.d., para. 4). She fought the "Americanization" required in the schools that conflicted with Spanish values. Otero-Warren was one of the first women to serve as a government official as the Santa Fe Superintendent of Instruction and chair of the State Board of Health (1917–1929) (Adelina "Nina" Otero-Warren, n.d., para. 3). She was also noted for securing the right for women to vote in 1920 by convincing the New Mexico congress to pass the 19th Amendment (Adelina "Nina" Otero-Warren, n.d., para. 1). She was chair of the Board of Public Health (1910–1920) and superintendant of schools (1931) for 12 years in Santa Fe County (Massmann, 2000, p. 877). Although she was defeated, she ran for congress in 1922; "she was the first woman in New Mexico's history to run for this office" (Massman, 2000, p. 892). In 1936 she wrote the book *Old Spain in Our Southwest* (Massmann, 2000, p. 877). A chapter from her book, "Count La Cerda's Treasure" was included in *An Anthology of Mexican America Literature* by Phillip Ortego (Massman, 2000, p. 893).

Lillie M. Peck (1888–1957): Born in Gloversville, New York

In 1922 Lillian M. Peck began her work in the settlement movement (Williams, 2012) while attending Simmons College in Boston. She began work in the National Federation of Settlements as a volunteer and then became a staff member, serving as assistant secretary and executive secretary from 1930 to 1947 (Chicago Journals, 1957, p. 217). A great deal of her time was dedicated to working internationally; she was instrumental in establishing the International Federation of Settlements in 1922 (Williams, 2012). From 1924 to 1926 she traveled to Europe to work with settlements in "England, France, Austria, Germany, and the Scandinavian countries" (Chicago Journals, 1957, p. 217). She continued her work in Europe after World War II in postwar reconstruction; she helped rebuild communication and programs. From 1949 to 1951 she was president of the International Federation of Settlements (Williams, 2012). She was awarded the Barnett fellowship and used it to study "the community center movements in England" (Chicago Journals, 1957, p. 217). Lillie M. Peck published chapters in the 1934 and 1936 *Handbook of Adult Education in the United States* publications (Rowden, 1934, 1936) and an article, "Social Workers in One World" in 1946 (Peck, 1934). At the time of her death she was a delegate to the United Nations Economic and Social Council as well as honorary president of the International Federation of Settlements (Chicago Journals, 1957).

Esther F. Peterson (1906–1997): Born in Provo, Utah

Peterson graduated from Brigham Young University in 1927 with a degree in physical education and a master's from Columbia University Teachers' College in 1930 (Molotsky, 1997, para. 9). "From 1930 to 1937, Peterson taught at the Winsor School for Girls in Boston. At night she volunteered to teach classes at the Boston YWCA for domestic workers and those in the garment trades" (Ford, 2008, p. 360). She also worked at the Bryn Mawr Summer School for Women (Ford, 2008). It was during this time that she published the articles "The Medium of Movement" in the *Journal of Adult Education*; "Dramatics and Recreation"; and "Bryn Mawr Summer School, 1937: Dramatics" (Hollis, 2004). Peterson was devoted to working women's rights as assistant secretary of labor and director of the Women's Bureau under President Kennedy in 1961 (Lyles, 2013, para. 2). She worked for both Presidents Johnson and Carter as their special adviser for consumer affairs (Molotsky, 1997). She was instrumental in getting the Equal Pay Act passed in 1963 (Lyles, 2013, para. 2). She addressed women's issues of "job discrimination, equal pay for equal work, and the need for daycare for working parents" (Lyles, 2013, para. 2) in a report titled, "American Women." Peterson served with three U.S. presidents: Kennedy, Johnson, and Carter as special assistant for consumer affairs. She changed the food industry by labeling foods with nutritional information and price per unit (Molotsky, 1997). She was inducted into the U.S. Department of Labor Hall of Honor (Esther Peterson, n.d.) and the National Women's Hall of Fame in 1993 (Esther Peterson, 1993). "Peterson was an educator, a labor organizer, a public official and an advocate of women's rights" (Molotsky, 1997, para. 5).

Cora Wilson Stewart (1875–1958): Born in Farmers, Kentucky

Cora Wilson Stewart attended Morehead Normal School and the University of Kentucky and began to teach school in Rowan County in 1895 (Crawford, 1993, para. 4). She was the first woman president of the Kentucky Education Association (Cora Wilson Stewart, 2009). In 1911 she began the Moonlight School movement in Rowan County; she wanted to "raise the standard of living of the poor people" (Cora Wilson Stewart, 2009, para. 2). She was instrumental in putting together simple textbooks for her adult learners, "The Country Life Readers;" she even recruited volunteer teachers to help with her schools (Crawford, 1993, para. 4). More than 1,200 adults learned to read and write as a result of her efforts the first year and more enrolled the second year (Crawford, 1993, para. 8). By 1914–1915 about "40,000 Kentucky adults had learned to read and write in the schools" (Crawford, 1993, para. 9). By the following year, 18 other states had adopted her concept of educating adults. It is estimated that millions of adults were impacted by her schools; "within the first 20 years of the program, 700,000 Kentuckians attended the adult literacy schools" (Cora Wilson Stewart, 2009, para. 4). She was also the director of the National Illiteracy Crusade. President Hoover appointed her chairperson of the Commission on Illiteracy from 1929 to 1933. In addition to her accomplishments in education, through photography, she documented Rowan County during the late 1800s and early 1900s. Cora Wilson Stewart was inducted into the Class of 2009 of the International Adult and Continuing Education Hall of Fame (Cora Wilson Stewart, 2009).

Eva vom Bauer Hansl (1889–1978): Born in New York City

Vom Bauer Hansl was a journalist in print and radio; she concerned herself with the multiple roles for educated women (Bowen, 1988). She graduated from Barnard College in 1909 and joined the Intercollegiate Bureau of Occupations, a founding organization dedicated to employment for women. She not only wrote for the *New York Evening Sun*, but was the editor of the women's page from 1912 to 1916 (Hansl, 1927–1967, p. 3). She was also an associate editor of *Parents Magazine* and coordinated parent study groups. In 1936 she began a women's interest service, Trend-File. She was instrumental in bringing three radio series: "Women in the Making of America" and "Gallant American Women" for NBC (1939–1940) and "Womanpower" for CBS (1942–1943) (Hansl, 1927–1967, p. 3). She wrote several books: *Minute Sketches of Great Composers* (1931), *Artists in Music Today* (1933), *Trends in Part Time Employment of College Trained Women* (1949), and many articles (Hansl, 1927–1967, p. 3).

Betty Ward (1917–2012): Raised in Clarinda, Iowa

Ward graduated from high school and the University of Iowa in the 1930s and went to graduate school at Cornell where she "learned my first real application of adult education" by working with union and worker education (Bersch, 2005). She went on to work for the U.S. Department of Agriculture and the U.S. Department of the Army in the 1940s (Bersch, 2005). Ward is noted for receiving the 1996 U.S. Department of Education Award for 49 years of Dedicated Public Service and the International Adult and Continuing Education Hall of Fame award (Betty Ward, 2012). She traveled throughout the world as the International Education Policy Specialist (Betty Ward, 2012). During those years she was also an adjunct educator at Howard University (1956–1986) and served as president of the American Association of University Women's DC Branch. She was president of the Adult Education Association of the USA (1975–1976) (Betty Ward, 2012). She published "Education on the Aging: A Selected Bibliography" in 1958 (Jarvis, 2003, p. 399).

REFERENCES

Adelina "Nina" Otero-Warren. (n.d.) *Women of the West Museum*. Retrieved from http://theautry.org/explore/exhibits/suffrage/oterowarren_full.html

Ballaine, A., & Fisher, W. (Eds.). (1946). *The story of a discussion program: Veterans and their neighbors get together on public issues/ by Joseph Cahn and others*. New York, NY: New York Adult Education Council.

Benveniste, D. (1998). The importance of play in adulthood: A dialogue with Joan Erikson. *The Psychoanalytic Study of the Child, 53*, 1–15. Retrieved from http://internationalpsychoanalysis.net/wp-content/uploads/2011/06/9.-Joan-Erikson-Importance-of-Play.pdf

Bersch, G. (Producer). (2005). *Conversations on lifelong learning: Betty Ward* [DVD]. Anchorage, AK: Larry Moore.

Betty Ward (2012). International Adult and Continuing Education Hall of Fame. *The University of Oklahoma Outreach—College of Continuing Education.* Retrieved from http://www.halloffame.outreach.ou.edu/1996/ward.html

Bowen, B. A. (1988, April). *Eva vom Baur Hansl: Brain-ideas vs life-ideas. Kellogg Project, Syracuse University.* Retrieved from http://www-distance.syr.edu/evahansl.html

Brody, S. (1996) *Jewish heroes and heroines of America: 150 true stories of American Jewish Heroism.* Hollywood, FL: Lifetime. Retrieved from Jewish Virtual Libraryhttp://www.jewishvirtuallibrary.org/jsource/biography/flexner.html

Carroll, M. R. (1971, March). Bureaucratic explosion. *Task Force, 17*(11), 1, 3. Retrieved from http://cdm15942.contentdm.oclc.org/cdm/compoundobject/collection/p15942coll11/id/1014/rec/8

Chicago Journals. (1957, June). Lillie M. Peck, 1889–1957. *Social Service Review, 31*(2), 217–218. Retrieved from http://www.jstor.org/stable/30017394

Crawford, B. (1993, April 23). 'Moonlight Schools'; A teacher's crusade helped illiterate adults. *The Alexander Stewart Family of Kentucky: The Courier-Journal Louisville, KY.* Retrieved from http://www.kentuckystewarts.com/WilliamG/CoraWilsonStewartArticle.htm

Cora Wilson Stewart. (2009). Class of 2009. *International Adult and Continuing Education Hall of Fame.* Retrieved from http://www.halloffame.outreach.ou.edu/2009/stewart.html

Eastman, L. A. (1925–1958). Eastman, Linda Ann, 1867–1963 [Biography]. Papers, 1925-1958: A finding aid (A-73/M-74). Schlesinger Library, Radcliffe Institute. *Harvard University Library Oasis.* Retrieved from http://oasis.lib.harvard.edu/oasis/deliver/~sch00186

Eleanor Gwinnell Coit Papers. (1913–1974). Sophia Smith Collection (Collection Number: MS 35). Smith College, Northampton, MA. Retrieved from http://asteria.fivecolleges.edu/findaids/sophiasmith/mnsss229.html

Erickson, C. (2004). Eulogy for Mary John, Stoney Creek woman. *ABC Bookworld.* Retrieved from http://www.abcbookworld.com/view_author.php?id=4048

Esther Peterson (n.d.). Hall of Honor Inductee. *United States Department of Labor.* Retrieved from http://www.dol.gov/dol/aboutdol/hallofhonor/2013_peterson.htm

Esther Peterson (1993). *National Women's Hall of Fame.* Retrieved from http://www.greatwomen.org/women-of-the-hall/search-the-hall-results/details/2/119

Fisher, W. (1943). *The people are ready to discuss the post-war world: A report of an experiment in adult education.* New York, NY: New York Adult Education Council.

Fisher, W. (1953, May 1). Eduard C. Lindeman, 1885–1953. *Adult Education Quarterly, 3*(5), 133. doi:10.1177/074171365300300501

Ford, L. E. (2008). *Encyclopedia of women and American politics.* New York, NY: Infobase.

Frederickson, M. (1980). Mc Laren, Louise Leonard, Aug. 10, 1885–Dec. 16, 1968. In C. H. Green & B. Sicherman (Eds.), *Notable American women: The modern period.* Cambridge, MA: Belknap Press of Harvard University Press.

Halpert, S. (2009, March 1). Jennie Maas Flexner. *Jewish Women: A comprehensive historical encyclopedia.* Retrieved from http://jwa.org/encyclopedia/article/flexner-jennie-maas

Hansl, E. vB. (1927-1967). Eva vom Bauer Hansl collection of women's vocational materials. *Syracuse University Libraries, Special Collections Research Center.* Retrieved from http://library.syr.edu/digital/guides/h/hansl_coll.htm

Harris-Perry, M., & Stewart, A. (2012). Anna Julia Cooper's biography. *Anna Julia Cooper: Project on Gender, Race, and Politics in the South.* Retrieved from http://cooperproject.org/about-anna-julia-cooper/

Heller, R. (1989, March). The women of summer: The Bryn Mawr Summer School for Women Workers, 1921-1938. In R. W. Rohfeld (Ed.), Breaking new ground: The development of adult and workers' education in North America (pp. 214-223). *Proceedings from the Syracuse University Kellogg Project's First Visiting Scholar Conference in the History of Adult Education.* Syracuse, New York: Syracuse University Kellogg Project. Retrieved from http://www-distance.syr.edu/breaking.html

Hiemstra, R. (2003, March 7). *Founding of the AEA of the USA—1949–1955: Crucial roles played by Howard McClusky, Malcolm Knowles, and Cyril Houle.* Presentation at the 2003 Hall of Fame Conference, Fayetteville, New York.

Hollis, K. L. (2004). *Liberating voices: Writing at the Bryn Mawr summer school for women workers.* Carbondale: Southern Illinois University.

Hugo, J. M. (1990, Fall). Adult education history and the issue of gender: Toward a different history of adult education in America. *Adult Education Quarterly, 41*(1), 1–16. doi:10.1177/0001848190041001001

Jane Addams. (2014). *The Biography Channel.* Retrieved from http://www.biography.com/people/jane-addams-9176298

Jarvis, P. with Griffin, C. (Eds.). (2003). *Adult and continuing education.* New York, NY: Routledge.

Lewis, L. M., Simons, G. F., & Fennig, C. D. (Eds.). (2013). *Ethnologue: Languages of the world* (17th ed.). Dallas, TX: SIL International. Retrieved from http://www.ethnologue.com

Linda Ann Eastman 1867–1963. (n.d.). *History and prominent residents. Riverside Cemetery.* Retrieved from http://www.riversidecemeterycleveland.org/rs_hs_a.htm

Lyles, L. (2013, August 26). *Champions of women's work. United States Department of Labor* [Blog]. Retrieved from http://social.dol.gov/blog/champions-of-womens-work/

Massmann, A. M. (2000, Winter). Adelina "Nina" "Otero-Warren: A Spanish-American cultural broker. *Journal of the Southwest, 42*(4), 877–896. Retrieved from http://www.jstor.org/stable/40170156

Miss Fisher dies; Sch'dy HS graduate. (1967, October 27). *Schenectady Gazette,* p. 10. Retrieved from http://fultonhistory.com/newspaper%208/Schenectady%20NY%20Gazette/Schenectady%20NY%20Gazette%201967%20Grayscale/Schenectady%20NY%20Gazette%201967%20%20a%20Grayscale%20-%201150.pdf

Mollie Ray Carroll (1926–1927). *John Simon Guggenheim Memorial Foundation: Foundation's Report*. Retrieved from http://www.gf.org/fellows/2328-mollie-ray-carroll

Molotsky, I. (1997, December 22). Esther Peterson dies at 91; worked to help consumers. *The New York Times*. Retrieved from http://www.nytimes.com/1997/12/22/us/esther-peterson-dies-at-91-worked-to-help-consumers.html?pagewanted=all&src=pm

Moran, B. (2007). *Stoney Creek woman: The story of Mary John*. Vancouver, Canada: Arsenal Pulp.

Peck, L. M. (1934). Adult education in settlements. In D. Rowden (Ed.), *Handbook of adult education in the United States*. New York, NY: American Association for Adult Education.

Peck, L. M. (1946, October). Social workers in one world. *The Survey*, 249–251.

Rowden, D. (1934). *Handbook of adult education in the United States*. New York, NY: American Association for Adult Education.

Rowden, D. (1936). *Handbook of adult education in the United States*. New York, NY: American Association for Adult Education.

Stasson, A. H. (n.d.) Burton, Margaret Ernestine. *Boston University School of Theology: History of missiology*. Retrieved from http://www.bu.edu/missiology/missionary-biography/a-c/burton-margaret-ernestine-1885-1969/

Syracuse University annals. (1914). *Syracuse University*. Retrieved from http://www.google.com/url?sa=t&rct=j&q=&esrc=s&source=web&cd=3&ved=0CC8QFjAC&url=http%3A%2F%2Fsurface.syr.edu%2Fcgi%2Fviewcontent.cgi%3Ffilename%3D2%26article%3D1003%26context%3Dannals%26type%3Dadditional&ei=QTNhU4-6KIKgyATi_oCoAQ&usg=AFQjCNGoqLlNQRB28n0_7mt9XMbMLKPzhA&bvm=bv.65636070,d.aWc&cad=rja

Syracuse University Archives. (2010). *Awards and honors: The George Arents Pioneer Medal: 1946*. Retrieved from http://archives.syr.edu/awards/arents.html#1946

Thomas, R. (1997, August 8). Joan Erikson is dead at 95; shaped thought on life cycle. *New York Times*. Retrieved from http://www.nytimes.com/1997/08/08/us/joan-erikson-is-dead-at-95-shaped-thought-on-life-cycles.html

Twigg, A. (2005). John, Mary: Aboriginal authors. *ABC Bookworld*. Retrieved from http://www.abcbookworld.com/view_author.php?id=4048

Williams, J. S. (2012, September 7). Lillie M. Peck: Overview. *Washington Nuclear Museum and Educational Center (WANMEC)*. Retrieved from http://www.toxipedia.org/display/wanmec/Lillie+M.+Peck

ABOUT THE EDITORS

Susan Imel is retired from Ohio State University (OSU), where for many years, she directed the ERIC Clearinghouse on Adult, Career, and Vocational Education. Dr. Imel also served as principal investigator and project director for a number of other projects, including the Ohio ABLE Evaluation Design Project, Building Linkages for At-Risk Youth and Adults in Ohio/For the Common Good, and the Kyrgyzstan Training Project.

Since 1996, she has been editor or co-editor-in-chief of the Jossey-Bass New Directions for Adult and Continuing Education series. She has contributed chapters to many books, including two *Handbooks of Adult and Continuing Education*. While with the ERIC Clearinghouse, she wrote many brief synthesis products that provided an introduction to many topics in the field of adult and continuing education.

After retiring from OSU, she served as an adjunct instructor at a number of institutions including University of Alaska Anchorage and North Carolina State University. In 2009, she was inducted into the International Adult and Continuing Education Hall of Fame. Since 2007, she has been engaged in research to uncover the stories of early women contributors to the field of adult education and has made presentations at five recent Adult Education Research Conferences. Dr. Imel holds a PhD in adult and continuing education and a master's in library science, both from the University of Michigan. Her undergraduate degree is in social studies education from Indiana University.

For 35 years, **Gretchen T. Bersch** was a professor of graduate adult education, taught mathematics, and wrote curriculum for rural Alaskan adults through the University of Alaska Anchorage system, retiring in 2006 as professor emerita. In the summers, she hosts groups, courses, and retreats at her Yukon Island Center on her family homestead. Since 1989, she has been involved in Magadan in the Russian Far East, sister city to Anchorage, where she is an honorary professor.

Since retirement, she has focused on programs for older adults, including OLÉ! (Opportunities for Lifelong Education, learning for folks over 50) chairing the board, and both teaching and learning. She has had time to continue editing and producing programs for the *Conversations on Lifelong Learning* series of interviews with adult and continuing education scholars. By the time of this book, she had filmed over 80 scholars and produced 50 programs.

Gretchen has continued to be involved in adult education nationally and internationally, doing adult education research and writing/publications. Among her honors, she was inducted into the Alaska Women's Hall of Fame and into the International Adult and Continuing Education Hall of Fame. She also devotes time to her family history passion and her grandchildren and great-grandchild.

ABOUT THE CONTRIBUTORS

Sue Adams is a cheerfully retired academic librarian and adult educator, having enjoyed a long career at St Francis Xavier University and its Coady International Institute in Antigonish, Nova Scotia, Canada. Her research interests focus on the often-overlooked practice of adult education in librarianship, especially as embodied by activist librarians. She enjoys sharing her research through academic publication, storytelling, and popular theater.

Geleana Alston is an assistant professor in the North Carolina Agricultural & Technical State University Adult Education program and an alumnus of the PhD in Adult, Professional, and Community Education program at Texas State University in San Marcos. Her research interests include history of African Americans in adult education, mentoring relationships within graduate programs in higher education, feminist grounded theory, women and minorities as adult learners, and adult and continuing education for healthcare professionals.

Susan (Bracken) Barcinas is an adult education faculty member at North Carolina State University. She has more than 25 years of higher education experience and has worked as an administrator and faculty member. Her research and teaching interests include adult learners in postsecondary institutions, community college research, university/community partnerships, and women's or gender issues in adult and higher education.

Lisa M. Baumgartner is associate professor in the Educational Administration and Human Resource Development Department at Texas A&M University. Her research interests include adult learning and development, chronic illness, identity development, and issues of diversity. She received a Cyril O. Houle Scholars W. K. Kellogg grant to investigate civil rights leader Septima Clark's contributions to adult education. In 2007 Lisa received the Cyril O. Houle Award for Outstanding Literature in

Adult Education for *Learning in Adulthood: A Comprehensive Guide* (3rd ed.) co-authored with Sharan B. Merriam and Rosemary S. Caffarella.

Diane Benson is professor of Alaskan literature and women/native studies in Alaska. She is a published writer and a playwright and actor, and has presented her play about Elizabeth Peratrovich throughout Alaska, the nation, and in London, England. She also performs the role of Elizabeth in the PBS documentary she helped to produce, *For the Rights of All: Ending Jim Crow in Alaska*. Diane is a speaker on violence against Alaska Native women, posttraumatic stress and recovery, and is an active associate of veterans organizations. She has received several state and national awards in recognition of her public service.

Marcie Boucouvalas is professor and program director of Adult Learning and Human Resource Development at Virginia Tech/National Capital Region. Director of AAACE's Commission for International Adult Education and immediate past president of the Coalition of Lifelong Learning Organizations, she serves on the editorial boards of *AEQ* and *Adult Learning*. Her research interests continue to focus on international dimensions of adult development/learning, with emphasis on individual and societal transformational issues and consciousness studies, particularly transpersonal development. She serves as editor for the *Journal of Transpersonal Psychology* and has worked in a variety of national and international contexts with an array of populations.

Shauna Butterwick is associate professor in the Department of Educational Studies at UBC. She teaches different courses, but her primary academic home is in the area of adult learning and education. Community-engaged scholarship informed by feminist, critical, and decolonizing frameworks and the power of creative and expressive arts to educated and politicize are at the heart of her inquiries. In her research, she has focused on women's learning in institutional, workplace, and community contexts, including social movements, and has also conducted studies of welfare reform. She is a research associate of the Canadian Centre for Policy Alternatives.

Bernadine S. Chapman recently retired from North Carolina Agricultural & Technical State University as an associate professor and coordinator of the Adult Education program after 20 years of service. She continues to teach at the institution as an adjunct. Chapman's research interests include leadership, women adult educators, as well as international adult literacy. She has presented nationally and internationally on a variety of topics reflective of community and adult education, northern philanthropy and African American adult education, factors that influence leadership development of adult learners, and aging well within the African American community. Chapman's individual and co-authored publications are also representative of these areas.

Dominique T. Chlup is associate professor in the Adult Education and Human Resource Development (HRD) program and an affiliate faculty member of the Women's and Gender Studies program at Texas A&M University. Additionally, she is the associate director of the Promoting Outstanding Writing for Excellence in Research (POWER) initiative. Her research interests focus on the sociohistorical dynamics of women's learning in early 20th century prison reformatories, the politics and practice of contemporary prison and jail education, college access related to parental involvement, and the development of reading, writing, and creative/artistic abilities in adult learners.

Opal Easter-Smith is adjunct professor in the Department of Spirituality and Pastoral Ministry at Catholic Theological Union (CTU), a graduate school of theology and ministry in Chicago. Prior to this she was the director of Continuing Education and Ministerial Formation at CTU. She is active in adult faith formation at Holy Name of Mary Catholic Church. Her published dissertation was on Nannie Helen Burroughs' leadership training of Black women and girls.

Leona M. English has a research interest in varied aspects of adult education including gender and learning, history of women's contributions, and health and learning. She is presently studying the women writers and editors of the Canadian Association of Adult Education. She is professor of adult education at St. Francis Xavier University, Antigonish, Nova Scotia, Canada.

Jonathan B. Fisher currently lives with his partner, Yuco, and their young son, Oliver Kiyotake, near Hiroshima, Japan. When he is not looking after Oliver, preparing meals, or cleaning the apartment, he teaches English as a foreign language to adults and children.

Sylvia Fuentes recently retired from the Division of Student Affairs as the director of Planning and Research Development at Northern Illinois University. She has written extensively about the plight of Latinos in the United States and is nationally recognized as an expert on this topic. Dr. Fuentes' research of interest includes diversity issues and the discrimination of Latinos/as in higher education.

Jane M. Hugo recently retired as a national staff member with ProLiteracy, Syracuse, New York. She is adjunct in education at LeMoyne College, Syracuse. She completed her PhD in adult education (1996) at Syracuse University. Hugo's interests are the education of women and educational access in general, both from a contemporary standpoint and from a historical perspective. Her professional life has focused on assisting undereducated women and men trying to improve their basic education skills or to succeed in higher education. She has published articles on adult education history, the value of feminist theory to adult education, and learning in communities.

Juanita Johnson-Bailey, who holds the Josiah Meigs Distinguished Teaching Professorship, is the director of the Institute for Women's Studies and a professor of adult education in the Department of Lifelong Education, Administration and Policy at the University of Georgia. She is the author of *Sistahs in College: Making a Way Out of No Way* (2001), which received the Phillip E. Frandson Award for Literature in Continuing Higher Education and the Sadie T. Mossell Alexander Award for Outstanding Scholarship in Black Women's Studies. Dr. Johnson-Bailey is a member of the International Adult and Continuing Education Hall of Fame, a Houle Scholar, and a Lilly Teaching Fellow. She has lectured nationally and internationally and her most recent book is a co-edited text, the *Handbook on Race and Racism in Adult and Higher Education: A Dialogue* (Sheared, Johnson-Bailey, Colin, Peterson, & Brookfield, 2010).

Carol Kasworm is the W. Dallas Herring Emerita Professor of Adult and Community College Education, North Carolina State University, Raleigh. Her interest in this chapter was energized by her prior participation in the rich nonformal learning experiences at John D. Campbell Folk School with opportunities to sing during family meals, participate in community exhibits of its new arts and crafts, and the impact of new personal learning in this unique setting. Her historical scholarship has focused upon adult learners in higher education and the varied structures, policies, and settings which support adults to succeed.

Carole L. Lund is currently associate professor of business at Alaska Pacific University (APU) in Anchorage. She is also the director of Business Administration and Management. After teaching in the adult education program at a larger state university, she decided to teach adults at a smaller, more intimate university. Her teaching interests include leadership, values and ethics, and research. Lund's teaching background and passion for teaching adults began almost 20 years ago when she taught in a graduate adult education program. Her tenure at APU began in 2005 where she currently teaches qualitative research methods, values and ethics, and research methods for undergraduate and graduate students. Her research interests include racism, White privilege, and White racial identity development.

Katherine McManus, PhD, is the director of the Writing and Communications Program at Simon Fraser University, British Columbia. Her academic background is in rhetoric and composition and adult education. Dr. McManus has national and international experience in instructional design for online learning and in the promotion of best practices for teaching and learning.

Lisa R. Merriweather is assistant professor at the University of North Carolina, Charlotte. She received her PhD in adult education with a graduate certificate in qualitative inquiry from the University of Georgia in 2004. Her research focuses on issues of equity and social justice within the historical discourse of adult education, informal education, and doctoral education. She explores the philosophy and sociology of race and employs Africentric Philosophical theory, critical race theory, and qualitative and historical methodology to investigate topics found at the nexus of race and adult education. She presents at international and national conferences and publishes in a variety of adult education, qualitative inquiry, and interdisciplinary outlets.

Vivian W. Mott is professor and interim associate dean in the College of Education at East Carolina University in Greenville, North Carolina. She joined East Carolina University in 1996. Mott earned her PhD from the University of Georgia and her BS and MS in education from the University of Tennessee. She also holds graduate certificates in gerontology, women's studies, and ethnic studies. She is a Cyril O. Houle/Kellogg Research Scholar, Salzburg Fellow, recipient of the ACHE Exemplary Professional Contributions Award, the NCAEA Gruman Award for Lifelong Service to Adult and Continuing Education, East Carolina University's Women of Distinction Award, as well as other teaching and research awards. Dr. Mott's research interests focus on the development of professional expertise, multicultural issues, and ethics in education and business.

Norma Nerstrom, EdD, has a diverse background in business and academia that spans the fields of health care, libraries, and higher education. She currently serves as the manager of Continuing Education Career Training at Harper College in the Chicago area and specializes in program development for programs regulated by Illinois licensing requirements, as well as other job training initiatives. Her dissertation, *Truths about Transformative Learning: The Narrative Inquiry of Adult Educators' Experiences in Graduate Education* (National Louis University) was completed in 201. Norma has presented at conferences including AAACE, AERC, International Transformative Learning Conference, and International Congress on Qualitative Inquiry.

Rosalie C. Otero is a University of New Mexico Honors College professor emerita. She served as the director and associate dean of the Honors Program/College until her retirement in 2013. She is the author of several articles on honors education and short fiction. She co-edited her most recent book, *Santa Fe Nativa: A Collection of Nuevomexican Writing* with Gabriel Meléndez and Enrique Lamadrid; the book also featured photography by Miguel Gandert (University of New Mexico Press, 2009).

Marilyn McKinley Parrish is special collections librarian and university archivist at Millersville University, where she engages students in learning with primary source materials and in oral history projects. Her dissertation research focused on women learning in the Catholic Worker movement. Additional research interests include learning in social movements, learning in cultural institutions, teaching and learning with primary sources and oral history projects, women's narratives, and the history of education.

Yvonne K. Rappaport, retired director of the University of the Virginia (UVA) Northern Virginia Center, also spearheaded and led the UVA Continuing Education for Women Program. Previously she worked as a management systems analyst (and personnel officer) for the US Air Force, consultant, trainer, and script writer for a variety of organizations and served in key leadership roles in state, national, and international adult and continuing education associations as well as the League of Women Voters. Her doctoral dissertation, earned from Virginia Tech, focused on Bonaro and Harry Overstreet's contributions to the field of adult education.

Amy D. Rose is professor emeritus at Northern Illinois University. She has written broadly on the history of adult education, focusing on the period between the World Wars, the development of the GED, and literacy policy. She has also written on a variety of policy issues related to the intersection of adult education, the workplace, and higher education. She is a past president of the American Association for Adult Continuing Education. In addition, she was a co-editor of the *Handbook of Adult and Continuing Education: 2010 Edition* and has served as an editor of *Adult Education Quarterly*.

Jovita Ross-Gordon is professor in the Counseling, Leadership, Adult Education, and School Psychology (CLAS) Department at Texas State University. Dr. Ross-Gordon's research centers on teaching and learning of adults, with foci on diversity and equity in adult education and on adult learners in higher education. She is the author or co-author of numerous books, articles and book chapters. She is co-editor-in-chief of the *New Directions for Adult and Continuing Education* series, and a co-editor for *Adult Education Quarterly*. Dr. Ross-Gordon was recently awarded the Career Achievement Award by the Commission of Professors of Adult Education.

Charlene Sexton's interest in adult education history and Dorothy Canfield Fisher began in the University of Wisconsin-Madison Adult Education doctoral program, where she studied under Dr. Robert D. Boyd. She read avidly about Fisher's life and work in literature, languages, and education, which paralleled her own interests. Dr. Sexton applies adult learning, psychology, and bibliotherapy to medical student training in palliative medicine and interdisciplinary teams, and clinically, with patients and families. Her publications include a bereavement study, *Smith College Studies in Social Work* (2013) and "Words and the Chemistry of the Soul at End of Life," *Journal of Pastoral Care and Counseling* (2009).

Elizabeth J. Tisdell is professor of adult education at Penn State University-Harrisburg and is the chair of the Commission of Professors of Adult Education (2012–2014), and the former co-editor of the *Adult Education Quarterly*. Her research interests include spirituality and culture in adult development; spiritual pilgrimage, the role of wisdom in adult learning; teaching and learning in the health and medical professions; feminist and cultural issues in adult education.

Constance Wanstreet received her PhD in workforce development and education from Ohio State University. She is adjunct assistant professor in the College of Education and Human Ecology and adjunct faculty at Franklin University. Dr. Wanstreet has developed and implemented training programs for adult learners in workplace settings and has served as a consultant to the Ohio Board of Regents and the Judicial College of the Supreme Court of Ohio. She has presented at national and regional conferences, primarily on teaching and learning in online environments.

Mary Alice Wolf is professor emerita of gerontology at the University of Saint Joseph, West Hartford, Connecticut. Before retiring in 2011, she was the director of the Institute of Gerontology at Saint Joseph. Currently she is book review editor of *Educational Gerontology*, an international journal, and frequent contributor to the literature of learning and aging. A fellow of the Gerontological Society of America, the Association of Gerontology in Higher Education and the recipient of several awards, including the Distinguished Service Award of AGHE and Connecticut Department of Elderly Services. She is a member of the International Adult and Continuing Education Hall of Fame.

CPSIA information can be obtained at www.ICGtesting.com
Printed in the USA
LVOW04s1959121214

418605LV00003B/33/P

9 781623 968830